Furta Sacra

❖

Furta Sacra

THEFTS OF RELICS IN THE CENTRAL MIDDLE AGES

❖

Patrick J. Geary

PRINCETON UNIVERSITY PRESS

PRINCETON, NEW JERSEY

Library of Congress Cataloging-in-Publication Data
Geary, Patrick J., 1948–
Furta sacra:
Thefts of relics in the Central Middle Ages.
Bibliography: p.
Includes index.
1. Relics and reliquaries—Thefts. 2. Relics and
reliquaries—Europe. 3. Social history—Medieval,
500–1500. I. Title.
ISBN 0-691-00862-0, pbk. (alk. paper)
BX2333.G42   364.1′62   77-85538

Publication of this book has been aided by a grant from
The Andrew W. Mellon Foundation

First Princeton Paperback printing, with revised text, 1990

Princeton University Press books are
printed on acid-free paper, and meet the guidelines
for permanence and durability of the Committee
on Production Guidelines for Book Longevity
of the Council on Library Resources

Printed in the United States of America

5   7   9   10   8   6

TO MARY

✤

❖ Contents ❖

❖ *Preface to the 1990 Edition* ❖

I FIRST CAME to write *Furta Sacra* because I wanted to examine how people of the ninth through eleventh centuries integrated essential aspects of the sacred sphere into the mundane. I found that exploring narratives of furtive relic translations allowed me to interpret the meanings of generalized practices and attitudes within the matrices of specific, ongoing historical processes. The narratives themselves were often linked formally and echoed each other, both textually and through oral reports of other translations. At the same time, each was constructed around specific circumstances and within particular social, political, and economic contexts. As a result, the book dealt with two subjects, thefts or purported thefts and the accounts of these thefts, neither of which is wholly subsumed by the other and neither of which is comprehensible without reference to the other.

The opportunity to republish the book in paperback has made it possible to correct the many errors of detail which marred the first edition, and to update and expand the text somewhat, largely by taking into account more recent literature. However, books have a life of their own and I have resisted the temptation to use the republication as an opportunity to write a new book or to discuss the many additional cases of furtive translations I have since found. The *Furta Sacra* of 1990 remains in its essential focus, documentation, and argument faithful to the *Furta Sacra* of 1978.

Were I writing the book today, I would explore in greater depth a number of issues raised by recent historical and critical scholarship, some of which I have discussed elsewhere. First, anyone now writing on relics can benefit from the increasingly sophisticated literature which has brought this once neglected aspect of the cult of the saints from the periphery to the center of medieval religious and social history.[1] Second, I would further investigate the central place of relics, these neutral depositories of constructed meaning, with reference to medieval symbiotics, only hints of which appear in the book. Third, I would place the theft of relics within the continuum of means of establishing social bonds and exchanging goods in medieval society. In such a perspective, theft appears as an appropriate alternative to the neutrality of purchase or the positive bond of gift exchange—an alternative that says as much about social and political relations as it does about the desire for relics themselves.[2] Finally, I would explore the process of restructuring sacred geography in the Carolingian and post-Carolingian periods, a process which gave birth to the *translationes* that are the primary sources exploited in this study.[3] Thus *Furta Sacra* is not the last word on the theft of relics. I hope rather that it will encourage other scholars to go beyond it in their investigation of the rich complexities and contradictions of medieval societies.

Patrick J. Geary
Gainesville, Florida
February 1990

ARLY IN THE twelfth century Teodaudus, a cleric of Bèze, wrote an account of how the body of Saint Prudentius had arrived several centuries earlier in Burgundy. In 881, Teodaudus explained, Bishop Geylo of Langres went on pilgrimage to Compostela. On his return he passed through Aquitaine, which had been ravaged and depopulated both by the fratricidal wars of Louis the Pious's sons, and by the invasions of the Normans, Danes, and Britons. He spent a night in a nearly deserted village where the church of Saint Prudentius was located. His host told him of the saint's virtues and martyrdom, and so that night Geylo rose and went with his chaplain to chant Laudes in the church. There he found that the saint was receiving little of the attention and honor due him. Not only was the church itself in poor repair, but even the reliquary was falling apart. Overcome with sadness at this sight Geylo sighed, "In truth we would be so happy if you would wish to come with us, O holy martyr!"

Hearing this exclamation, the bishop's chaplain suggested that since the chapel was in ruins and mass was celebrated there only once each year, the bishop should indeed take the saint home with him to Langres. Geylo agreed and secretly removed the relics which he then brought back with him to Burgundy. There he deposited them in Bèze where they were received with great joy. In response to this reception Prudentius worked numerous miracles for the faithful of the region.[1]

The *Translatio Sancti Prudentii* is by no means unique in medieval hagiographic literature. It was written at the end of a centuries' old tradition of *furta sacra* accounts, many of which resemble closely Teodaudus's story. A monk or other cleric goes on pilgrimage; he stops in a town or village where rests the body of a saint. Impressed with what he has heard of the saint's life, virtue, and miracles, he determines to steal the body for his own community. The thief waits until the

dead of night, then enters the church and exhorts the saint
to come with him. He then breaks open the tomb, takes the
relics, and hurries home where the new saint is greeted by a
joyful throng of the faithful.

From the reign of Charles the Great until the age of the
crusades, we have nearly one hundred relic theft accounts,
many quite similar to that of Teodaudus, others describing
thefts by various other sorts of thieves. These stories are, at
first reading, bizarre: monks creeping into a neighboring
church to force open a tomb and flee with the body of a long
dead saint; merchants landing on distant shores fully armed
to capture a church and force its guardians to divulge the
resting place of its patron; professional relic-mongers systematically despoiling the Roman catacombs for the benefit of
Frankish ecclesiastics. But even more bizarre for modern
readers is the almost universal approval of contemporaries
who heard of these thefts. Far from condemning them as ab-
errations or as sins against the fellow Christians from whom
the saints were stolen, most people apparently praised them
as true works of Christian virtue, and communities such as
Bèze boasted of their successful thefts.

In order to elucidate this peculiar and apparently contradictory phenomenon, the present study undertakes a twofold
task: first, it attempts to analyze the social and cultural contexts within which these thefts, genuine or alleged, acquired
their significance; second, it examines the particular perception of relics and relic thefts that underlay this social and cultural significance. The first part of this investigation consists
primarily of traditional historical analysis of the social, political, and economic circumstances that gave rise to specific
theft accounts. These accounts themselves had certain obvious advantages over other methods of recording acquisitions—accounts of gifts, inventions, and purchases. If a relic
were willingly given away, one might conclude that the
donor had not prized it highly. But if a relic had to be stolen,
then it must have been worth having. Further, as we shall
see, the narrative itself made a good story and the story increased the value of the relic.

Thefts were, however, more than random acts or good stories appearing from time to time across Europe. They were perpetrated (or, more frequently, alleged) at particular moments of crisis by members of religious or secular communities as calculated means of crisis intervention. Further, not only were thefts similar to each other in the types of crises that gave them birth, but in many cases contemporary descriptions of them betray their authors' awareness that in describing thefts they were writing in a particular hagiographic tradition, that of *furta sacra*, which had its own limitations, *topoi*, and forms.

The recognition of this hagiographic tradition, and, more particularly, of an underlying structural similarity within widely disparate accounts of thefts, raises certain questions that cannot be entirely resolved by traditional historical investigation. Thus Chapter 6 attempts to examine in a tentative manner the moral hesitations, perceptions, and meanings which these sacred thefts acquired within their communities, by appeal to similar phenomena encountered by anthropologists. When the theft of relics is placed within the entire spectrum of practices, devotions, and uses of relics described in the first five chapters, it becomes evident that relics were perceived as the living saint, and that the translation account is really that of a ritual kidnapping by which the saint passed from one community to another. Of course, the richness of documentation necessary to elucidate fully these perceptions and values is lacking for the central Middle Ages, and thus such observations and parallels are presented as suggestions for thought as historians continue to investigate the place of the sacred in the medieval world.

❖

I have been extremely fortunate in the course of my research to have had the advice and support of a great number of outstanding scholars, only a few of whom I can mention here. To the late Robert S. Lopez, and Jaroslav Pelikan who directed the Yale University dissertation from which this study has evolved, I owe a great debt of gratitude for their counsel, support, criticism, and friendship. I wish also to acknowledge a number of other scholars who have been generous with their advice: John Freccero of Stanford and Jeremy Adams of Southern Methodist University; Giles Constable of the Institute for Advanced Study and Ihor Sevčenko of Harvard; the late Rev. Baudouin de Gaiffier, S.J., President of the Société des Bollandistes; Martin Heinzelmann of the Deutsches historisches Institut of Paris; the late Victor Turner; the late Joseph Strayer, Edward Champlin and Lawrence Stone; Richard Bosley and Stuart Frentz. In preparing the revisions, I have benefited greatly from suggestions and criticisms made in the many reviews of the first edition and particularly from the careful editorial assistance of Carol Lanham and Pegeen Connolly. The errors and omissions which remain are entirely my own responsibility. Finally I am most of all grateful to my wife Mary for her support, advice, and understanding through the years that have seen me occupied with the first and second versions of *Furta Sacra*.

❖ Abbreviations ❖

AASS	*Acta Sanctorum.* 3rd ed. 62 vols. Brussels-Paris, 1863–1925.
AASS OSB	*Acta Sanctorum Ordinis S. Benedicti,* ed. J. Mabillon. 9 vols. Paris, 1668–1701.
Anal. Boll.	*Analecta Bollandiana*
Annales	*Annales: Economies, Sociétés, Civilisations*
BHL	*Bibliotheca Hagiographica Latina.* 2 vols. and supplement. Brussels, 1898–1911.
CCSL	*Corpus Christianorum series latina.* Turnhout, 1953–
CSEL	*Corpus scriptorum ecclesiasticorum latinorum.* Vienna, 1866–
DACL	*Dictionnaire d'archéologie chrétienne et de liturgie,* ed. F. Cabrol, H. Leclercq, and H.-I. Marrou. 15 vols. in 30. Paris, 1907–1951.
DEJ	*Das Erste Jahrtausend. Kultur und Kunst im werdenden Abendland an Rhein und Ruhr,* ed. V. H. Elbern. 3 vols. Düsseldorf, 1962.
HGL	C. de Vic and J. Vaissete. *Histoire générale de Languedoc,* rev. E. Dulaurier, E. Mabille, and E. Barry. Vols. I–VI. Toulouse, 1872–1892.
JGLGA	*Jahrbuch der Gesellschaft für lothringische Geschichte und Altertumskunde*
Mabillon, *Annales*	J. Mabillon. *Annales Ordinis S. Benedicti. . . .* 6 vols. Lucca, 1739–1745.
Mansi	G. Mansi et al. *Sacrorum conciliorum nova et amplissima collectio.* 57 vols. Venice, Florence, 1759–1927.
MGH	*Monumenta Germaniae Historica*
Capit.	*Capitularia*
Concil.	*Concilia*
Epist.	*Epistolae*
Poet. Lat.	*Poetae latinae*
SSRG	*Scriptores rerum germanicarum in usum scholarum*

SSRL	*Scriptores rerum Langobardicarum et Italicarum*
SSRM	*Scriptores rerum Merovingicarum*
SS	*Scriptores*
MIÖG	*Mitteilungen des Institutes für österreichische Geschichtsforschung*
PG	*Patrologia graeca*, ed. J. P. Migne. 166 vols. Paris, 1857–1866.
PL	*Patrologia latina*, ed. J. P. Migne. 221 vols. Paris, 1844–1864.
RHC	*Recueil des historiens des Croisades. Historiens occidentaux.* 5 vols. Paris, 1844–1895.
Settimane	*Settimane di studio del centro italiano di studi sull'alto medioevo*

Furta Sacra

❖

CHAPTER ONE

Relics and Saints in the
Central Middle Ages

THE SUBJECT of this study is not, as one might expect from
the title, relics, but rather people. As such, it will not attempt
to discriminate between genuine and false relics, to provide a
criticism of this peculiar manifestation of religious devotion,
or even to trace the developing forms of reliquaries. The relics themselves, physical remains of saints, are essentially passive and neutral, and hence not of primary importance to historians. It is the individuals who came into contact with
these objects, giving them value and assimilating them into
their history, who are the proper subject of historical in-
quiry. As long as a scholar concentrates on the things rather
than on the persons, he can do little more than add to the already considerable number of treatises, first appearing in the
Middle Ages, which condemn the cult of relics to a greater
or lesser extent as a barbarous superstition. Such studies, represented most recently by the work of Patrice Boussel, are at
once valuable and entertaining, particularly since tracing the
origins of such relics as the milk of the virgin, or counting
the number of extant relics of the sacred foreskin lends itself
today to humorous rather than polemical treatment.[1] But because of these authors' focus, their works do not begin to explain the significance of saints' relics as a human phenomenon, an integral part of medieval civilization. Faced with
these seemingly absurd and embarrassing vestiges of early
Christian and medieval piety, historians until recently have
tended to minimize their importance, to describe devotion to
them as primarily typical of the less educated, and to rele-
gate the entire subject to the level of antiquarian curiosities.
When, however, the subject of investigation is not the relic itself but the people who honor it, invent it, buy or steal it,

the fact emerges that contrary to the wishes of a more "en-
lightened" generation of historians, relics hold a fundamental place in the fabric of medieval life. While their
significance differed from place to place and from person to
person there was no class of individuals, be they theo-
logians, kings, or peasants, for whom relics were not of
great importance. From the church where they were a required equipment of altars, to the court of law where they
were necessary for oath taking, to the battlefield where they
helped bring victory in the hilt of Roland's sword, relics
were an indispensable part of daily life, accepted as unques-
tioningly, in fact, as life itself.

In order to understand rather than to judge the relationship between people and relics, certain important conces-
sions must be made to medieval ways of seeing the world.
Historians, like anthropologists, must accept their subjects'
system of viewing reality. Thus, for the purpose of this
study, certain phenomena will be accepted without question:
the relics discussed herein are all genuine until proven otherwise by contemporaries; these relics are miraculous, giving
off pleasant odors when touched, healing the sick, and otherwise expressing the wills of the saints whose remains they
are. Without the acceptance of these postulates, the entire
phenomenon becomes incomprehensible and scholarly investigation remains at the level of antiquarian triviality or
anachronistic skepticism.

On the other hand, sympathy for the contemporary view
of these sacred objects must not be equated with accepting
relic cults as pure manifestations of religious devotion devoid of all extraneous considerations. This view would be as
naive as, say, considering the contemporary interest in collecting art objects as the spontaneous expression of aesthetic
appreciation, completely divorced from any interest in sound
financial investments. Unraveling the complexity of motivations which lead to investment in art today or resulted in
relic thefts in the Middle Ages is always difficult. The medieval problem is perhaps the more problematic since people's
attitudes towards relics were seldom clearly articulated or dif-

ferentiated in categories of human perception immediately recognizable today. As a result, the successful completion of this investigation demands careful exploitation of available sources, keeping in mind their peculiar nature and employing a methodology that will allow them to yield satisfactory results.

Relics as Symbol

While the subject of this study is not relics themselves, we cannot get very far in our examination of the people who gave them such an honored place in their lives if we do not take into consideration the peculiar nature of these objects. Although symbolic objects, they are of the most arbitrary kind, passively reflecting only exactly so much meaning as they were given by a particular community.

It is tempting to approach the theft of relics from the comparative perspective of the stealing of other objects of cultural or religious significance, as for example the theft of manuscripts or sacred art. But in reality, the nature of relics is quite different from these other things, and the difference makes any examination of their function in medieval life extremely problematic. As a physical object, divorced from a specific milieu, a relic is entirely without significance. Unlike other objects, the bare relic—a bone or a bit of dust—carries no fixed code or sign of its meaning as it moves from one community to another or from one period to a subsequent one. By contrast, a manuscript will always have some potential significance to anyone capable of reading it, although the associations the reader may make when confronted with the text may vary depending on his cultural horizons. In an illiterate society a codex may mean nothing at all, or may be little more than a strange or even quasi-magical artifact from another world. But anyone who knows the language of the manuscript and can read the hand can appreciate the symbolic value of the text in a much more satisfactory way. This is not to say that the manuscript will have exactly the same

symbolic function in the society in which it was written and
in a much different society. Ovid's *Ars amatoria*, hardly a devotional work, could be interpreted in the Middle Ages as an
allegorical prefiguration of Christ's love for his Church.
Even so, there was some continuity of symbolic function,
and later scholars could reinterpret it in a way that more
closely approximated its original purpose.

Similarly, a representational work of visual art can carry
an intrinsic code comprehensible within a relatively wide cultural tradition. A picture of a man or a woman, or even
more specifically of a monk, priest, warrior, or bishop will
be recognizable to anyone within a broad Christian tradition. This sort of code is completely lacking in relics. Bones
may be the "pigges bones" of Chaucer's pardoner, those of
an ordinary mortal, or the relics of a saint, according to the
culturally induced perception of an individual. Moreover, unlike a book or illustration, a relic cannot itself transmit this
perception from one community to another, even if these
communities share identical cultural and religious values. In
order to effect this transmission, something essentially extraneous to the relic itself must be provided: a reliquary with an
inscription or iconographic representation of the saint, a document attesting to its authenticity, or a tradition, oral or
written, which identified this particular object with a specific
individual or at least with a specific type of individual (a
saint).

In times of disaster or other temporary discontinuity, the
extraneous signs identifying relics could be destroyed or become dissociated from their relics, thus erasing their symbolic meanings. Even without such crises, long neglect or
changing cultural values could result in the loss or attenua-
tion of the oral tradition which assigned a specific identity to
a specific relic. In either case, in order for an object to be venerated as a relic, a new symbolic function had to be assigned—a function that had its origin in the fabric of the society in which it was to be venerated. Thus the symbolic
value of a new or rediscovered relic was only a reflection of
the values assigned by the society that honored it. Any

change in the nature, force, or direction of its cult had to come entirely from the society itself and not from some dialectic between old signs contained in the relic and the new significance given to these signs.

The implications of the above discussion of relics as signs are most important for any examination of their place in medieval societies, but particularly in an investigation of their theft. Obviously the very act of theft often broke the cultural context that gave the relic its meaning. When a relic was stolen or sold, it was impossible to steal or sell its old function in its original location. Thus the theft could not result in the transferral of ideas or of religious or cultural values. In its new location it became an important symbol only if the society made it one, and this symbolism was necessarily a product of that society. Concretely, this means that translations from Spain, Egypt, or the Near East did not and could not in themselves result in the introduction of cultural or religious values from these places into the communities which received the relics. Venetians were able to bring the body of Saint Mark from Alexandria to the Rialto, but this translation did not result in the introduction of Greek or Coptic devotion to the saint in Venice. Nor could the translation of the remains of the martyrs of Córdoba to St. Denis result in the introduction of Mozarabic traditions in the Isle de France. In both cases, the translations could be effected only because of previously shared cultural values concerning saints in general and evangelists and martyrs in particular. Any new appreciation of these saints had to come from extraneous symbols introduced along with the relics. For Saint Mark, this was said to have been accomplished by the relocation in Venice of two monks from Alexandria who had been custodians of his body. The precise virtues of the Córdoban martyrs were told in the north in Aimoin's account of their translation.

Thefts of relics introduced a further difficulty since most were said to have taken place during some period of invasion, destruction, or other sort of cultural discontinuity. Hence the cultural symbolism of the relic, its identity, was usually lost or at least placed in doubt. This difficulty was recognized by contemporaries, and the very literature from which we learn of these thefts is largely an effort to overcome this loss of continuity. In these texts, a variety of means was used to preserve the identity and context of the relics. Since relics' authenticity rested ultimately on human testimony, characters who identify the remains of the saints regularly appear in accounts of thefts. Frequently, of course, the only person who could serve as link between the society from which the relic was stolen and its new society was the thief himself, obviously a biased source. Hence the texts often attempt to improve his credibility by extolling his virtues, sanctity, and devotion to the particular saint. Often, too, hagiographers introduced individuals outside both communities who could appear as knowledgeable but unbiased observers able to inform the thief of the relic's location and identity. In the *Translatio Beati Vincentii*, this individual was a Moor. In Einhard's *Translatio SS Marcellini et Petri* it is a Greek living in Rome. In any case, the *translatio* and the other hagiographic texts written about the saint are the means by which his identity is standardized and stabilized during this perilous move from an old to a new symbolic context.

The final implication of the symbolic nature of relics is that we must be quite clear that we understand just what we are examining when we say that we are studying relic thefts. We are not primarily trying to determine whether or not the theft actually took place in the way described in contemporary sources. Nor, with few exceptions, are we studying the motivations or justifications of the thieves. What we are really examining is the cultural and social context that gave the relic its symbolic function after the theft, and in particular we are examining the mentality within that context which accorded importance to the theft narrative as a "history" of the transition from old community to new.

By studying the perceptions and uses of stolen relics in various communities as they reconstructed new symbolic functions for them, we can approach differences in mentalities, religious values, and social needs within these relatively similar communities. The mentalities thus examined will necessarily be primarily those of hagiographers, a limitation to be sure, but not so great as one might expect. As we examine the nature of these hagiographic sources, particularly *translationes*, we realize that the propagandistic function of these texts and their public liturgical nature demanded that they reflect values and attitudes espoused by their audiences, if they were to be effective. As a result, the values of hagiography mirrored, as a reality or as an ideal, the consensus of the community in which and for which the text was written.

BETWEEN HAGIOGRAPHY AND HISTORY

The sources for a study of relic thefts are not limited to any single type of document but include every possible shred of evidence, both written and monumental, that can be used to determine the role assigned to these thefts in medieval life. The most important body of documents is, of course, the vast literature of medieval hagiography edited for the most part in the *Acta Sanctorum* and in the *Monumenta Germaniae Historica*. The difficulties involved in using hagiographical materials for the reconstruction of history are notorious. This is particularly true of *vitae* which are fundamentally literary rather than historical or biographical in purpose; only rarely does their content approach what is today considered historical fact.[2] A medieval hagiographer wrote the life of a saint, not to tell his readers anything about the subject's personality or individuality, but rather to demonstrate how the saint exhibited those universal characteristics of sanctity common to all saints of all times. Because this demonstration was much more important than a mere account of the particulars of the saint's life and death, examples and anecdotes demonstrating these characteristics need not necessarily come from the particular saint's own life. Instead of a view of the saint and his world, the *vita* provides a vision of the stereotypic world in which truth takes precedence over fact, a world which is composed of the *topoi* gleaned from other *vitae*. Hence, to the extent that the hagiographer was successful in his purpose, the historian is thwarted. When he did incorporate particular details and accurate descriptions, one might almost say that the author failed in his craft, because such details turn the reader's mind from the eternal ideal to the fleeting moment of this world. And as if this situation were not bad enough for the historian, it is usually impossible without independent checks to tell where the hagiographer has nodded and allowed something of the *saeculum* to enter his account. Such clues as vividness and freshness of narrative, detailed description, and accurate topography are no guarantees of the authenticity of the *vita*'s historicity; the Bollandist Hippolyte Delehaye was able to draw up a list of popular "heresies" committed by unwary historians bent upon wrenching "historical data" from these literary creations.[3]

But in spite of the obvious difficulties and dangers presented by hagiographic materials, an historian must still recognize them as precious documents for the investigation of medieval religion and culture. Composed of *topoi* as they are, they are nonetheless differentiated in the choice and arrangement of *topoi*; and while little can be learned from *vitae* in the way of specific factual data, changes in religious devotion and attitudes towards a great variety of activities can be inferred from differences in subject matter, types of miracles, and structure of *vitae* of different periods.

Translationes, the most important sources for this study, are in many ways hybrids, spanning the hiatus between the purely literary *vitae* and the more "historical" forms of medieval writing, chronicles and annals. Possibly because they are neither entirely hagiography nor entirely history, they have been too long neglected and misunderstood by hagiographers and historians alike. This lacuna has been recently and expertly filled by Dr. Martin Heinzelmann in his study of *Translationes* and other related texts.[4] As he points out, the form of *translationes*, like that of *elevationes* and other similar hagiographical genres, evolved from late classical forms, in particular sermons, panegyrics delivered on the occasion of the *adventus* of an emperor or other dignitary, and from early Christian letters such as that from the priest Lucianus concerning the discovery of the remains of the protomartyr Stephen. During the Merovingian period accounts of translations were often found in *vitae* and *passiones* and served as a bridge between *miracula ante mortem* and *miracula post mortem*. Although originally these accounts were quite short, one can see a gradual tendency towards a fuller treatment of the translation which resulted, during our period (ninth through eleventh centuries) in greatly elaborated, independent compositions often forming independent *libelli*. Both in new texts composed during this period and in the reworking of previous hagiographical dossiers one finds in general a *vita* or *passio*, a *translatio*, and a *liber miraculorum*.

This development of the *translatio* as a substantial hagiographic subgenre was the result of the growing circulation of fragments of saints' remains, of the proliferation of translations from Rome and elsewhere during this period, and of the growing importance of the liturgical celebration of the anniversaries of translations—celebrations which required new liturgical readings. Whatever their form, *translationes* were more intimately connected with the physical remains of the saints than with their lives or virtues. *Vitae* and *passiones* were concerned with the *exempla* of the saints' virtues; *translationes* were connected with the *testimonia* of relics' powers. *Translationes* were closely connected with the memory of particular church dedications and other forms of liturgical and secular processions. Thus at best, because of this focus on a particular, historical event of great importance in the life of a specific church or monastery *translationes* can provide a valuable insight into the activities of a religious community at an important moment of its existence.

Unfortunately for the historian, *translationes* are by no means uniform in their accuracy or veracity. Like other forms of hagiography, they belong to a literary tradition which molded them both in content and in form.

Because of the importance attached to the date of the arrival of a new saint in a church and the liturgical celebration associated with this anniversary, translations have been noted since the earliest days of historical calendars. Often, too, early historians such as Gregory of Tours included brief descriptions of relic transfers in their historical works.[5] One of the earliest and most influential accounts of a translation of relics, which provides some detail on the search for relics, their discovery, and translation is the account of the invention of the holy cross by Empress Helen.[6] This text, which was widely known in the West in the eighth century, provided many of the details that would become common in other accounts of translations: the search for the relic, miracles upon its discovery, difficulties of moving it, and its joyful and honored reception. This account, along with the version of the acquisition of Saint Benedict by Fleury told by Paul the Deacon, which we will examine below, helped to standardize the form many *translationes* would take from the ninth century forward. First the bishop, abbot, prince, or the entire community decide to move the body. Frequently, they seek permission from ecclesiastical or secular authorities. At a public ceremony they open the tomb with reverence and remove the body. Often initial efforts to carry off the saint fail, and success comes only after fasting, prayer, and repeated invocations addressed to the saint. On the route back the saint is accompanied by the religious of the community and a joyous multitude who witness numerous miracles. Finally the saint reaches his new home and after the abbot or bishop has examined the relics to confirm their authenticity, they are deposited in their new shrine amid general rejoicing.

This brief sketch does not begin to do justice to the variety of forms the *translatio* can take. Its length can be anywhere from one line to a considerable treatise, and its style may vary from the terse Latin of a legal report to a florid rhetorical exercise. Nor does the plot always follow that described above. Many *translationes* from the ninth through the twelfth centuries are extremely individualistic and, partic-

ularly when they are reported by persons who actually participated in the translation, rank among some of the most vivid
and fascinating glimpses of medieval society. But again one
must be careful not to be deceived by colorful narration.
Even if most *translationes* were written to tell how a particular relic was acquired, there is no reason to accept these accounts at face value. Often they were written years or even
centuries after the acquisition of the relics, and the origin
may have been a mystery even to the author. Or, as will become clear in the following chapters, the *translatio* may have
been written to establish a claim on a particular relic or to
make acceptable the presence of a saint's body in a remote
monastery with which he never had any connection. Hence
the account may be entirely fictitious, and the author may
have made use of the same sort of *topoi* found in the *vitae* to
explain the acquisition of the relics.

A further obstacle to the proper exploitation of *translationes* as historical sources results from a consideration of
their original function in the communities where they were
written. Although set down to commemorate a specific
event, most frequently this commemoration was public, communal, and ritualistic—the liturgical celebration of the anniversary of the translation. Historians and hagiologers often
forget that the actual *translationes* were frequently part of
the liturgy of the feast, and were divided into lessons to be
read through the hours of the day. As part of the public
prayer of the community, it is not surprising that they
tended toward schematization and stylization, just like other
portions of the liturgy.

As a result, an accurate account is often impossible to dis-
tinguish from one containing a kernel of truth or one that is
complete fabrication. This is particularly true when dealing
with accounts of relic thefts. The account may be at variance
with the truth in one of two opposite ways. On the one
hand, the official tradition may try to mitigate the dishonest
elements of the deed and claim that the relic was acquired by
gift rather than by theft. When, for example, one reads that
Jumièges acquired the relics of Saint Valentine when a priest

from that famous Norman monastery on pilgrimage to Rome was given them by a total stranger eager for the ultramontane provinces to benefit from Valentine's patronage, one suspects the veracity of the tale.[7] On the other hand, the object of falsifying the story of a translation is not always to disguise the theft. Quite the opposite. As H. Silvestre has pointed out, monasteries often claimed that their patron's relics had been obtained by theft, when the account of the theft masked a perfectly regular acquisition, a purchase, or simply an invention in the medieval and modern senses of the term.[8] Exactly why one would wish to claim that a relic was stolen will be dealt with later, but it is true that often the theft never took place. This is the case of the supposed stealing of the body of Mary Magdalene from Provence and its translation to Vézelay.[9]

The establishment of the historical circumstances reported in a *translatio* is important, but by no means all that a *translatio* can tell. This is only the beginning. Fact or fiction, an account of a theft gives historians much more to work with than a simple *vita*. In either case, there is a story to be told concerning the purpose of writing the account, and the story behind a fictitious theft is often more interesting than that behind a real one. In both cases, the intention of the author is fundamentally different from that of the hagiographer; his intention is to describe the immediate world of human events in order to inform or to deceive, but in neither case does he limit himself to the ideal world of the legends of the saints.

These general remarks about *vitae* and *translationes* are not limited in application to these two genres. As every medievalist is aware, chronicles, annals, and other medieval "histories" move freely between hagiographical and historical worlds depending on the subject being treated. One cannot treat the account of the theft of the relics of Saints Chrysogonus and Anastasia by monks of Benedictbeuren, found in the chronicle of that monastery, any differently from a *translatio* in the strict sense of the term simply because it was inserted in a chronicle.[10] The characteristics of the *translatio* depend on subject, not form, and when a chronicler writes of the posthumous glory of a saint, he is not bound by the feeble confines of the historian's rules.

Because the purpose of this study is to investigate the role of relics in the communities in which they were found, the sources are not limited to those discussed above. The account serves as a clue that there is something important going on at a moment in history, and it may suggest where to start looking to discover the larger context in which the activity took place. From the *translatio*, one must go to cartularies, books of liturgy, itineraries of pilgrimages, everything that will help recreate the world where the theft was alleged to have taken place.

THE EVOLUTION OF SAINTS' CULTS IN THE CENTRAL MIDDLE AGES

The choice of the term "central Middle Ages" to designate the period from the ninth through the eleventh centuries is largely an arbitrary one; the choice of the period itself is anything but arbitrary. The name can be justified only by the lack of a more appropriate one. It might just as well be called the "later Carolingian and post-Carolingian period," but the appellation is cumbersome. Other historians have staked a claim to the term central Middle Ages to designate the period 962–1154.[11] Perhaps their prior claim should be respected, although I think that the period of 800–1100 is more deserving of the term, not only because it more closely approximates the middle of what historians have unfortunately chosen to label the "Middle Ages," but also because this period of transformation, disintegration, and restructuring gave birth to the cultural, economic, and political structures of the later Middle Ages.

Because this period was so significant in the cultural formation of Europe, it is particularly appropriate for an examination of the role of relics in general and of thefts in particular. In spite of the largely uniform functions of relics throughout the entire Middle Ages, during this period they assumed

their broadest and most essential roles. Before the ninth century most of Europe was insufficiently Christianized (or perhaps hagiosized) for relics to assume the immense importance we will be encountering throughout this study. After
this period, they faced increasingly stiff competition from
other sources of mundane and celestial power.

History is a study of change over time, and at a crucial
level it can be argued that the function of relics has changed
very little from the early Middle Ages to the present. For the
believers, relics work miracles, and the miraculous cures of
the eighth century vary but little from the cures of the
fifteenth or even the twentieth. Are we then faced with an ex-
trahistorical subject? Is the history of relic cults another
form of "histoire immobile"? I think not. Even if miracles
do not vary within western society to any great extent (and
even this is not altogether the case) the societal functions of
relics varied widely across the Middle Ages, as they filled
functions necessary in the communities in which they were
venerated. This evolution through medieval society becomes
obvious when one isolates those functions which, at various
times, relics were deemed capable of fulfilling. Their roles
cannot be examined in isolation, however. They must be examined in comparison with other instruments or agents that
may fulfill similar requirements.

Such an examination is fraught with difficulties. The evolution of relics' roles in medieval society is neither linear nor
continuous. Not all sectors of society used relics in the same
way at a given time, nor did similar sectors of society change
in a uniform way. Thus one is faced both with the possibility of regional and societal variations, and the occurrence of practices that may seem archaic or remarkably
advanced depending on local circumstances and individual
temperaments. For example, Bishop Claudius of Turin, a
ninth-century ecclesiastic, and John Calvin share quite similar opinions of relics and the vanity and idolatry of devotion
to them. Moreover, it must be remembered that Christianity
evolved from beginnings as a centralized urban religion in a
well-organized political and social structure; through a pe-

riod of essentially rural, agrarian society devoid of any effective central institutions, lay or ecclesiastic; and then, starting in the twelfth century, into a new world of towns, commerce, and centralized institutions. At any given moment, therefore, the continuing Christian tradition contained elements of belief, practice, and custom which were, in effect, fossils of an earlier age. The practices surrounding the cult of saints are not exceptions, and throughout the Middle Ages Christian society had at its disposal a multitude of symbolic rites, practices, and formulae, both "official" and "popular," that could be reemployed and rearranged to meet new circumstances in which relics might be used. Thus there is little that is entirely new in the roles of relics in the Middle Ages; almost every custom, even the most bizarre, can be traced to early Christian or pre-Christian precedents. But lack of originality does not indicate lack of innovation or evolution. Rather, uses of relics must be "read" as, in the tradition of Ernst Curtius, one reads medieval literature. Each isolated practice—oaths on relics, pilgrimages to relics, humiliation and theft of relics—should be seen as a *topos*, a commonplace, which is part of the entire Christian tradition. The individual *topos* acquires specific meaning only when it is read in conjunction with the other *topoi* with which it is associated. Like medieval literature, medieval religious culture is a mosaic and can be understood not by simply examining each particle of stone or glass, but by observing the whole system in which these pieces are used.

When so examined, the role of relics in medieval society is clearly a changing one, and when compared with other competing means of satisfying basic social and personal needs, the place of relics in the central Middle Ages emerges as quite different from that of previous and subsequent periods. The prominence of relics throughout society during this period was to a large extent the result of conscious Carolingian policy. But gradually, under the influence of a variety of factors, they were replaced by other persons and things in many of their roles even while they grew in importance in others. Moreover, as people at various levels of society turned from relics to other objects for identity, security, protection, and devotion, they themselves underwent change.

The brief period of the so-called Carolingian renaissance solidified the forms in which relics and society were for centuries to interact.[12] As in almost every other sector, the Carolingians added little that was original in the cult of relics, but as we shall see in Chapter 2, their ecclesiastical reforms did manage to set the tone for the use of relics in the following centuries.

The first phase of Carolingian concern for relics was the active support of their use in secular and ecclesiastical life. The canon *Item placuit* of the Fifth Council of Carthage (401) was reinvoked, requiring that all altars contain relics. Official encouragement was given to the practice of swearing oaths on relics, and the centrality of saints and their relics was increased through the encouragement of pilgrimages to the tombs of saints.

The second and more lasting contribution of the Carolingians was the augmentation of the relic supply north of the Alps. In the mid-eighth century and again a century later Carolingian ecclesiastics procured numerous bodies of saints from Italy and even Spain to glorify and protect the Frankish Church. These translations were made with a specific purpose. Through the latter part of the ninth century as the over-extended, centralized system of Carolingian government receded before the rising power of local and regional aristocracies, ecclesiastical institutions were forced to look elsewhere for support and protection. Far-thinking churchmen looked beyond mortal efforts to supernatural defenders, and in importing saints hoped to find a solution to their society's ills. And in this hope they were not altogether disappointed. As Paschasius Radbertus said, "Nor would I say that it is without reason that miracles of saints long asleep in Christ have recently begun to flash forth. Never before have so many and so great things been done at one time by the relics of saints since the beginning of the world, for everywhere saints in this kingdom and those brought here excite each other to song even as cocks at cockcrow."[13] Across Europe, saints were responding to the crisis and assuming those tasks so eagerly pressed upon them by a disintegrating social and political system.

In fact, saints did preserve what could be preserved of western civilization in the difficult centuries that followed. Many of the other Carolingian achievements would ultimately be rediscovered and contribute to the development of the high Middle Ages: educational reforms would reemerge in the schools of the twelfth century; legal reforms would influence the English writ and the Capetian *enquêteurs*; the monastic reforms would influence Cluny; the concept of empire, the course of German history. But these Carolingian programs had little role in immediate post-Carolingian history. Saints, however, succeeded where other efforts failed or faltered. They alone provided not only a focus for religious devotion (something they had done all along) but just as importantly they gave whatever sense of identity, means of protection, and economic vitality religious institutions of Europe would know for centuries.

A world that looked to saints for identity, protection, and economic sustenance was far different from one that depended on national identity, central government, and fiscal planning to provide the necessary secure framework within which monastic communities could devote themselves to the work of God. We should therefore consider the unique ways saints fulfilled these needs.

The profoundly fragmented world of post-Carolingian Europe provided little in the way of identification and organization. The fundamental unit of organization in the secular society was the family. As Georges Duby has demonstrated, the feudal elite of the first feudal age, far from being composed of new men lacking family or tradition, was in fact organized by family structures.[14] These horizontal and vertical structures provided unity and order to human relations. Religious communities, too, were families—families of the patrons of the monastery. This provided the means by which religious communities could find their place among other families in the area. Usually, the noble families of any specific geographical region were related by ties to each other through some distant ancestor, thus forming a few larger clans to which virtually all the local nobility belonged. Similarly, in the tenth and eleventh centuries religious communities often formed the family of a scion of a local noble family who had acquired the status of saint, as with Saint Gudule of Brussels and Saint Géraud d'Aurillac.[15] The monastic family was thus frequently one more branch of the local noble family, sharing with other branches a common lineage and thus integrated into feudal society by the only acceptable means, that of blood ties.

As both ancestor and living head of the monastic family, saints were obligated to defend the members of their families in their bodies and possessions. To whom else could the communities have turned? Central authorities had ceased to exercise any real power of *defensio* over religious institutions; *advocati* originally intended to protect religious houses were in fact often the source of their greatest danger. Relatively rich and unable to offer physical resistance, monasteries were always a tempting source of plunder. Thus the only sources of protection were supernatural. By praying for the nobility monasteries made themselves useful and thus worthy of support and protection; when attacked or victimized they could curse those who dared to infringe upon their rights; and they could appeal to patrons for protection.

One must ask how effective such defenses were. The subject of curses has only recently begun to be examined and the results cannot be anticipated.[16] The effectiveness of saints is more readily ascertainable. In general they seem to have worked quite well, or at least better than anything else available. This does not mean that the nobility, quaking in fear before the supernatural power of the saint, spontaneously ceased their depredations at the invocation of the saint's name. This may have happened at times, but as we shall see below, the saint more often provided a focus of public opinion directed at the noble that might, in time, force him to reach an understanding with the monks. Alienation of the *honores* of the monastery was alienation of the *honores* of the saint—a connection emphasized by the offended monks. The saint might strike down the noble, but more likely he would retaliate indirectly by ceasing to work miracles, ceasing his assurance of successful harvests, etc. These results were graphically implied in the practice of humiliating relics. A saint who had been dishonored would be physically dishonored by his monastic family. He (that is, his relics) would be placed on the ground, covered with thorns, and the candles in his church would be extinguished. There he would remain humiliated and abandoned until his wrong had been righted. The psychological effect of this action must have been enormous on the inhabitants of the area, and the passive pressure brought to bear on the offender in this way frequently forced him to some compromise.[17]

In the tenth and eleventh centuries, saints further extended their power of protection as they formed the foci of peace movements. The regional councils at which nobles swore to limit the extension and duration of their violence were usually convened around a particular saint, and it was before the saint that the oath to preserve the peace was extracted.

Saints were also fund-raisers. The translation of Saint Foy to Conques was justified as necessary for the health and salvation of the area. The second aim is impossible to judge, but the saint was certainly successful in supporting the economic health of Conques for centuries. Everywhere, saints were counted upon as the vital means of inspiring the generosity of the faithful. Donations were made for the redemption of one's soul and the souls of one's ancestors, but these donations had not yet taken on the narrow contractual arrangement of offerings for masses for the dead, which would characterize donations of the later Middle Ages and the modern period. They were made to the saint himself, and intended to obtain the saint's favor as much in this life as in the next. These offerings, made at the great pilgrimage sites, whether by the local faithful or by pilgrims from across Europe, were vital for the communities that received them in the saint's name. Economic productivity was abysmally low during the central Middle Ages, even on monastic estates. Incomes necessary to support a prosperous community were frequently uncertain and monasteries, like their secular neighbors, were often in debt. Thus extra income from offerings to saints was hardly extra, and formed rather a vital source of revenue. This was particularly true at a time when large amounts of capital were needed for improvements such as renovation or reconstruction. Hence the practice arose, late in the tenth century, of traveling with relics to raise money for construction.

Obviously the political, economic, and social functions of relics in post-Carolingian Europe are conceivable only if seen in relation to their fundamental religious functions. They provided the point of contact between mundane existence and the divine world. They were part of the sacred, the numinous; but incarnated in this world, as had been Christ, without losing their place in the other. Moreover, they provided the only recourse against the myriad ills, physical, material, and psychic, of a population defenseless before an incomprehensible and terrifying universe. The miraculous power of the saint was the basis on which his other power rested, and from this ability and willingness to perform miracles developed his following, his *famuli*, his devoted slaves. This following was the basis of his propagandistic value, his economic strength, and his political leverage.

❖

Already in the tenth century, however, the seeds of change were evident which would greatly alter the role of relics in medieval society. Saints had worked well to provide social integration, political protection, and economic stability in an intensely local, fragmented Europe. And in some locations, they continued to so function, even to this day. But the demands for integration into a wider world that affected monastic communities from the tenth century onward were increasingly to be met by other means. Under the influence of

Cluny, identity and integration into society came more and more to be found through identification with another family, that of the monastic order. This tendency was accentuated by the monastic reforms of the twelfth century, for which identity as a Cistercian house was stronger than identity as the family of some local saint. In fact, immunity from local interference meant freedom from the interference of local saints; the patron of Cluny was Saint Peter, and Cistercian churches were uniformly dedicated to the Virgin. Of course not every monastery abandoned its attachments to its local patron. It is particularly significant that such pilgrimage centers as Conques, which had been successful in universalizing their local patron, did not feel the need to join a reform order. But the attraction of Cluny and Cîteaux was too strong for many hundreds of other monasteries.

Protection and peace, too, were increasingly provided more thoroughly and effectively by the reemerging political institutions that would in time develop into the modern state. As protectors, central authorities were more effective than local saints; and as antagonists, counts, kings, and emperors had to be met by more powerful defensive weapons than humiliation of relics or curses. By the thirteenth century such practices had therefore almost entirely disappeared.

The economic revival of the eleventh and twelfth centuries brought new possibilities of economic planning and growth that reduced but did not eliminate the importance of saints' financial contributions. The first phase of this development was the regularization of monastic incomes and the reorganization of the budget, a process which began at Cluny under the abbacy of Peter the Venerable.[18] Increasingly, economic matters were subject to human control, at least in the planning stage, and human intervention could make a difference in economic success. Also significant were the effects of agricultural improvements, particularly evident in Cistercian houses which gave monasteries a degree of fiscal independence never before seen. Thus by the thirteenth century, although saints would still be called upon for financial help, particularly at times of great capital outlay, they would be for most monasteries but one of the sources to be tapped to meet financial obligations.

There remained the religious and miraculous functions of relics in society. But even in these areas, the twelfth through fourteenth centuries witnessed fundamental changes. Just as the broadening of the political and social horizons weakened the political and social importance of relics, so too did the broader cultural horizons weaken the religious. First, increased communication and mobility resulted in the widespread diffusion of the universal saints throughout Christendom. Not that the Virgin, the Apostles, and others had been previously unhonored. But in the course of the eleventh and twelfth centuries the cult of the Virgin expanded enormously across Europe. The reasons for this diffusion are still incompletely understood. The agents of the diffusion, Cistercian and, later, mendicant spirituality are hardly explanations since they in turn must be explained. But the growing popularity of the Virgin undeniably detracted from the relative importance of other, local saints.

Other pan-European phenomena fostered the development of cults of other universal saints. Papal insistence on the dignity of the successor of Peter enhanced the apostle's reputation throughout Europe. The far-flung commercial activities of the twelfth and thirteenth centuries introduced Saint Nicolas, patron of merchants, from Bari to Scandinavia. And of course the crusades, particularly the fourth, introduced such a flood of relics of all sorts throughout Europe that the Apostles and early martyrs could be almost omnipresent through their relics duplicated and scattered all over the West. The physical presence of saints throughout Europe and the particular devotion to the Virgin whose corporeal relics were almost nonexistent, could not but reduce the relative importance of any particular saint's body. Now, saints might be honored as much as ever, or even more, but they could be honored anywhere and not only at their tombs.

Not only did the importance of relics diminish in the face of competition from universal saints, but they were particularly affected by the growing importance of the cult of Christ. Obviously Christ was always at the summit of Christian devotion, but the summit was for most of the early Middle Ages often obscured by clouds. Even in monasteries the cult of Christ entered popular devotion by stages; and only gradually, in the course of the twelfth century, did it become rooted in lay devotion. The process moved from the cult of a physical relic of Christ, the host, which was to be treated rather like other relics, through a stage of competition between this relic and other lesser relics, to the final popular recognition that the eucharist enjoyed a unique position in Christian worship.

An informative way of tracing this evolution is to examine the progressive relationships between the eucharist, relics, and altars through the thirteenth century. In the ninth century, as we shall see in Chapter 2, the eucharist was one relic among others. True, it was the most worthy because it was the body of Christ, but it functioned just as did many other relics. In church dedications, it could be placed in altar stones either along with other relics or alone since it was the body of Christ. Moreover, relics, like the eucharist, might be placed on the altar.[19]

This practice continued through the central Middle Ages, although in the tenth century some tension between the eucharistic devotion and that accorded other relics was evident in the Cluniac tradition. Odo of Cluny tells of the relics of a saint which ceased working when exposed on the altar of a church. It was of course proper and even necessary for relics to be found *inside* the altar, but the saint explained in a vision that she could not work miracles when placed on the altar where only the majesty of the divine mystery should be celebrated.[20] The practice of exposing relics on altars did not disappear, but this text indicates that doubts about its propriety were expressed in Cluny at this date.

The next three centuries saw vastly increased devotion to the eucharist. Raoul Glaber reports eucharists working miracles usually performed by saints.[21] The popular desire to view the host at the consecration became an eagerly sought

visual communion that resulted in the practice of the elevation and that continued to affect the liturgy of the canon of
the mass throughout the Middle Ages. By the thirteenth century, the eucharist was universally accorded an extraordi-
nary, unique reverence. The practice of placing particles of
the eucharist in altars disappeared and was finally condemned as a deformation of its purpose; since it was the
food of the soul, it should not be used for other purposes.[22]

This evolution of the role of the eucharist from one
among many other relics to sacred object quite distinct from
relics, parallels the evolution of medieval religious devotion
from an essentially hagiocentric practice to a christocentric
one. But this does not mean that saints were unimportant in
later medieval religion. Clearly nothing could be further
from the truth. Although not the center of the Christian
world, they were still essential. Their traditional role as intercessors, for a time lost, was reemphasized. They remained
thaumaturges and as such continued to draw thousands of
pilgrims seeking physical and psychic health. However, their
relative place in this world had changed. First, as we have
seen, they were increasingly subordinated to Christ and the
universal saints. Second, and possibly as significant, was the
increasing subjectivization of the relationship between the
faithful and the saints, which began toward the end of the
eleventh century. In the long period from the fourth through
eleventh centuries, individual saints, through the presence of
their relics in churches which carried their names (*pa-
trocinia*), had held something of a monopoly on the devotion of the local populace. From the later eleventh century
these "official" patrons lost ground in the piety of the faithful as the latter increasingly reserved the right to select their
own personal, subjectively chosen patron.[23]

Increasingly, the broad social and religious functions that
had made saints so crucial to every segment of society in the
central Middle Ages had been assumed by other powers,
human or divine. The myriad religious and magical functions of saints so well delineated by Keith Thomas in his description of the Middle Ages were characteristic of those seg-

ments of society little touched by the dramatic changes of the twelfth and thirteenth centuries.[24]

Obviously then, the role of relics was quite different in the ninth through eleventh centuries. It was at this period that their importance was at its zenith, not only for the "people," but in every segment of Christian society. They were more vital, more active, more alive than later. And it is therefore to this formative period of medieval history that we shall turn to examine people interacting with relics in the particular modality of theft.

CHAPTER TWO

The Cult of Relics in Carolingian Europe

AROUND THE middle of the ninth century, Bishop Amolo of Lyons, the successor of the famous Agobard, received a request for advice from his fellow bishop Theodboldus of Langres. Theodboldus was perplexed by a new popular devotion that had taken root in the church of Saint Benignus in Dijon and from there had spread throughout his diocese. The forms of devotion that characterized the phenomenon did not appear altogether healthy to the bishop: in the church, women fell and writhed as though buffeted by some outside force although no visible signs of injuries appeared. But what was most irregular about the devotion was its origin. Amolo, in his reply to Theodboldus, summarized the beginnings of the cult, saying, "[Your coadjutor Ingelrannus] told us that last year two individuals claiming to be monks brought to the basilica [of Saint Benignus] what they said were the bones of a saint which they claimed to have carried off from Rome or from some other part of Italy. The name of this saint they claimed, with amazing impudence, to have forgotten."[1]

Since that time, one of the individuals had died and the other, who had been sent back to Italy to ascertain the forgotten name, had not been seen or heard from since. The story sounded as spurious to Amolo as it does to us, and he recommended that the bones be quietly buried outside the church.

Similar spontaneous unauthorized popular devotions have frequently appeared through the history of Christianity and this particular incident would hardly be remarkable were it not such an excellent illustration of the characteristics typical of the cult of relics in the ninth century. The wandering monks, the Roman or Italian origin of the relics, the more than questionable means of their acquisition, the instant excitement they caused not only in Dijon but throughout the diocese of Langres: all are markedly similar to occurrences elsewhere in the Carolingian Empire. Carolingian ecclesiastics of the generation preceding Amolo's had encouraged the development of saints' cults in the empire to strengthen both the faith and the cohesiveness of Frankish society. They had strengthened the role of saints within and without the Church, and they had begun the practice of translating saints, particularly from Italy, into the heart of the empire. Now their successors faced the task of continuing to nurture this devotion while dealing with the inevitable abuses and scandals that accompanied it.

The Carolingians had given a great emphasis to the cult of saints' relics, but the practice of revering the physical souvenirs of great men was not invented in the Middle Ages; it was at least as old as Christianity and in many respects older. Nor was it limited to western Europe. The cult of the heroes of classical antiquity[2] and the veneration of relics of Mohammed and the Buddha indicate that relic cults are a common means of religious expression shared by many societies.[3] Moreover, the veneration of Lenin's body in its Red Square mausoleum proves that the attraction of relics is by no means limited to traditional religions. But in the European Middle Ages men were most attracted to those physical objects which in some way put their possessor in direct contact with the person whose remains they were.

RELIC CULTS TO THE NINTH CENTURY

Devotion to the remains of saints can be traced to two fundamental antecedents: the pagan cult of heroes, and the Christian belief in the resurrection of the body. Fortunately, it is not the task of this study to determine the exact connection between the cult of heroes in pagan antiquity and the cult of saints in Christianity.[4] The Bollandist Hippolyte Delehaye is most probably correct in his conclusion that the two devotions, although arising from the same human predisposition, are not directly related. However, the cult of heroes undoubtedly prepared the inhabitants of the Graeco-Roman world for the veneration of the bodies of outstanding men, and it is not surprising that the veneration of Christian martyrs very early centered on their tombs. But almost as soon as it began, the cult of martyrs exceeded the veneration of heroes which, for all its popularity, had remained a form of veneration of the eternally dead. The bodies of the martyrs, unlike those of heroes, would not remain dead forever. Early Christians took literally Christ's promise of the resurrection and thus expected that on the last day the martyrs' physical bodies would be taken up again by their owners. The earthly presence of such a sacred body was thus a pledge or deposit left as physical reminder of salvation to the faithful. Christians believed that physical proximity to these bodies was beneficial, and that those buried near a saint's tomb would be raised up with the saint on the day of judgment. Whenever possible, bodies of martyrs were recovered and given proper burial, just as Joseph of Arimathea had obtained and buried the body of Christ.[5] But primitive practices went beyond simple burial, and bits of the martyrs remains, such as a blood-soaked handkerchief, were carefully preserved as memorabilia.

The cult of relics spread with the cult of martyrs, and as the demand for the bodies of these martyrs increased, it was natural that they should be moved from place to place.[6] As the period of the great persecutions came to an end and competition increased for the remains of certain martyrs, Christians divided up these bodies and went to great lengths to obtain them, including buying and stealing them from other Christians.

Of course, in the early Church and in official dogma throughout the Middle Ages, Christ and not the saints was at the center of Christian devotion. Martyrs (and later other saints) might be honored, or even called upon as intercessors before Christ, but he alone was adored. Despite the increasingly large place given saints in the official worship of the

Church, they remained mere channels through which God's grace was distributed. However, if Christ was always at the center of official Christian worship, this centrality was not fully appreciated by the masses of incompletely Christianized laity and ecclesiastical "proletariat." It appears that the religion of the majority of the semibarbarian inheritors of the empire in the West was hagiocentric. Certainly the official cult of the Church was that of Christ, and certain individuals or communities developed and maintained a devotion to the second person of the trinity. Kings and emperors found it advantageous to identify themselves with this cult; identification with Christ the King was politically useful.[7] But judging from church dedications, liturgies, and popular devotions such as the one which introduced this chapter, at the close of the eighth century Frankish religion was and had long been essentially one of mediation through the saints.

For whatever reasons, whether the transformation of pagan deities, a projection into the spiritual sphere of a profoundly fragmented system of social and political control, or, as Heinrich Fichtenau suggests, a natural inclination to think of power and influence in personal terms, the religious and devotional practices were directed toward beseeching, placating, and otherwise dealing with various local saints. Franks tended to ascribe events, both good and evil, to persons rather than to fate, fortune, or impersonal magic.[8] In dealing with supernatural powers, they naturally focused their attention on those objects which afforded immediate contact with the source of these powers; the most convenient objects were relics. The sources of relics did not even have to be dead. The famous incident in the late eighth century involving Aldebertus, the peripatetic Gaul who attracted a great following and even gave away bits of his hair and nails for the veneration of his followers, is proof that people were eager to focus their attention on some physical reminder of the persons whose power they sought.[9]

Usually, however, as in the case of the anonymous relics in Dijon, the focus of popular religion was on the remains of saints. Such devotions often sprang up without warning or apparent reason following an epidemic or natural disaster. This seems to have been the case of the brief but intense and, in some ecclesiastics' view, excessive devotion to the remains of Saint Firminius described by Agobard of Lyons. Around 829 a severe infection of unknown origin, symptomized by seizures similar to epilepsy and sores like sulphur burns, spread throughout the countryside around Uzès. In terror, people flocked to the shrine of Firminius, a mid-sixth-century bishop of Uzès, bringing offerings in return for hoped-for cures. Evidently encouraged by certain unscrupulous clerics who exploited this crisis for their own profit, pilgrims continued to come to the shrine even though no cures were effected.[10]

Agobard spoke our against these pilgrimages, but, in spite of his generally critical view of popular superstitions, he did not object to such pious devotional practices in themselves. His objections were entirely directed at unscrupulous exploitation of pilgrims by the clergy. That one of the most clear-headed churchmen of his day condoned such devotions indicates the almost universal acceptance of relic cults and their importance in the Church. With the single exception of the radical bishop Claudius of Turin, the cult of relics was accepted as a natural, integral part of Christian tradition, and even Claudius himself admitted that in his opposition he stood alone.[11]

THE NATURE OF RELICS

What were these objects so avidly sought after by peasants and bishops alike? Richard Southern accurately describes the position of relics in the medieval universe:

> Relics were the main channel through which supernatural power was available for the needs of ordinary life. Ordinary men could see and handle them, yet they belonged not to this transitory world but to eternity. On the Last Day they would be claimed by the saints and become an integral part of the

kingdom of Heaven. Among all the objects of the visible, ma-
lign, unintelligible world, relics alone were both visible and
full of beneficent intelligence.[12]

This general description can be improved by examining how different groups of individuals reacted to the presence of these powerful objects. For the masses of pilgrims to
Dijon, they were probably magical. Although the saint's identity was unknown, the pilgrims believed that the proper ma-
nipulation of the relics would bring about certain desired effects. One can only speculate about how the pilgrims to Uzès
saw the remains of Firminius. Perhaps he was a close
confidant of God who would obtain divine help in their time
of need, or was himself a god who would dispense aid to
those of his choosing. More likely, the victims of the epidemic didn't even bother to think about the nature of the person to whom they made their offerings. It was enough for
them to know that Firminius was powerful, and that he
could help if he would. But even in this ambiguous case, the
power of the relics was quite different from that of magic.
The difference lies in the identification of the relics with the
saint. Unlike the anonymous relics, most Dijon relics
identified with particular saints were extremely personal and
even capricious sources of power effective only for those
they chose to aid. If Firminius refused to come to the pilgrims' assistance, he did so not because the necessary
prayers or incantations had been pronounced incorrectly, or
because the saint was powerless; he simply chose not to
help. Moreover, not only could the saint choose whom he
would help, but he could change his mind and decide to
move elsewhere in order to favor another community with
his power.

The most obvious was the external power shown to those
who invoked him for cures or other miracles. Clearly this
power was sought by the thousands of pilgrims who flocked
to the tombs of saints. But this thaumaturgic power was
only a small part of their enormous potential. Much more
important to the communities which possessed the relics was

their ability to bring the continual action of divine provi-
dence to a local level. The relics ensured special protection to
the community, shielding its members from enemies both
spiritual and temporal and assuring their community's prosperity. One means by which a saint could assure this prosperity was of course the continuing performance of miracles,
which inspired rich and poor to give alms in honor of the
saint. At the same time, these miracles reminded the unscrupulous that this same power for aid could be used to chastise
those seeking to harm the saint's chosen community.

This protection and favor could extend beyond the
confines of the particular church or monastery in which
dwelled the saint's remains, and benefit the larger community of the Frankish kingdom. Many persons of both high
and low estate saw the veneration of relics as the best hope
for deliverance from the troubles which multiplied as the
ninth century progressed. We saw above how the theologian
and abbot Paschasius Radbertus used the image of cocks
awakening each other at dawn to convey his impression of
how saints buried in the empire or recently brought into it
were responding to the crisis of the later ninth century.[13]

Finally, as physical remains of saints, relics were more easily understood and appreciated by ninth-century laymen and
ecclesiastics than the more abstract elements of their Christian heritage. The relics *were* the saint; they had more than a
mere mystical or spiritual connection with the eternality of
God and his heavenly court. Symbols of divine favor continuing to operate on behalf of men, they were also the reality
symbolized since they referred not beyond themselves but to
themselves, as the saint residing among his followers. Hence
they were most important in helping men understand more
difficult and central aspects of Christianity such as the eucharist. The primary illustration of this fact comes from England, but it is representative of a way of thinking about relics and the eucharist evidenced on the continent as well. In
fact the eucharist was itself a relic differing only in its being
"the body and blood of our Lord Jesus Christ," rather than
the body and blood of one of his saints. This was the judg-

ment of the Council of Chelsea in 816, and the passage in which the identification appears, not intended to make any theological or speculative statement on the nature of the eucharist or of relics, is most eloquent on both:

> When a church is built, let it be consecrated by the bishop of its diocese. Let it be blessed and sprinkled with water by him and let him complete it according to the ritual as it is found in the service book. Afterward let the eucharist which is consecrated by the bishop through the same office be inserted by him along with other relics in a container and let it be preserved in that same church. And if he is unable to place in it other relics, nonetheless this alone is surely sufficient because it is the body and blood of our Lord Jesus Christ.[14]

Obviously the relics of saints and the relics of Christ differ only in importance. And the offhand way in which the eucharist is spoken of along with "other relics" indicates that the participants at the council accepted this equation without question. This same identity is found over the next centuries on the continent, where sacramentaries call for the deposition of bits of the eucharist in altar stones at the time of church dedications.[15]

CAROLINGIAN REFORM AND THE CULT OF RELICS

The centralizing and reforming efforts of Charles the Great and his son Louis did nothing to weaken the importance of the cult of saints and their relics in the West. In fact, the Carolingians' efforts were directed toward strengthening and expanding the place of relics in Frankish life. This tendency is evident in the use they and their councilors made of them in their propaganda directed against the East, but even more significantly in their ecclesiastical legislation, judicial reforms, and political programs.

In the later years of the eighth century, western Europe was defining itself in relation to the eastern Roman Empire both in terms of politics and of religion. The role of saints in every area of life was of key importance in the religious systems of East and West, but there existed a profound distinction between the place of relics in the West and icons in the East. Exactly why this difference existed has never been clear to historians. André Grabar pointed out in 1946 that in the East the cult of relics developed prior to the cult of images. He theorized that a transition from cult of physical object to cult of visual representation took place in Byzantium while in the West this development never progressed beyond the level of the image-reliquary.[16] More recently Ernst Kitzinger has suggested that the cult of images did not develop from the cult of relics as Grabar had supposed, but rather that it was the result of a conscious policy of emperors who expanded the official cult of the emperor's image to include a cult of the images of Christ and the saints.[17] Whatever the origins of this uniquely Byzantine devotion, it was not appreciated by the Latins. This much is clear in the *Libri Carolini*, that polemical treatise composed around 792, probably by Theodulf of Orleans, as the official Frankish response to the "heresy of the Greeks."

The real objection to the honor the Greeks paid images, translated *adoratio* in the *Libri Carolini*, centered not in the opposition between *proskunesis* and *latreia*, as has been frequently alleged, but rather in the object of this *veneratio* or *adoratio*.[18] As Gert Haendler points out, in ninth-century Latin the terms were interchangeable, as in the *Annales regni Francorum* describing the "adoration" of Charles following his imperial acclamation in 800: "Et post laudes ab apostolico more antiquorum principum adoratus est."[19] Clearly *adoratio* did not necessarily refer to the adoration reserved for God; it also meant the traditional honor afforded the emperor. The real objection of the Franks, as presented in the *Libri Carolini*, was that the proper objects of this devotion, whatever it might be called, were not images but rather relics: "They [the Greeks] place almost all the hope of their credulity in images, but it remains firm that we venerate the saints in their bodies or better in their relics, or even in their clothing, in the ancient tradition of the Fathers."[20]

The author of the *Libri* insisted that there could be no equality between relics and images, since relics alone would share in the resurrection at the end of the world.[21] Images might be more or less faithful representations and more or less beautiful, but they could not have any more than a didactic function. Any greater honor or veneration was reserved for relics alone.[22]

This precedence is even more striking in the efforts at reform of the cult of relics carried on under Charles the Great. As in other areas such as liturgy, education, and monastic reform, he did not attempt to reduce the importance of relics but rather to bring their veneration under central control and to use them to bolster his general program of political, social, and religious consolidation.

In 801 and again in 813, the canon *Item placuit* of the Fifth Council of Carthage requiring that all altars lacking relics be destroyed was reenacted in the Frankish empire.[23] The most obvious effect of this legislation was to focus attention on the remains of saints in every altar and to increase the demand for more relics for new churches and chapels or for those lacking relics. The solemnity of the rituals used during the transfer of relics to altars, rituals such as those found in the formulary entitled the *Liber Diurnus* and liturgical books, indicates that importance was attached to these translations and depositions.[24] Faced with the problem of cementing the conversion of the recently and only superficially Christianized Saxons and Avars, Charles used these splendid rituals to focus the faith of nominal Christians. In so doing, he was acting in the tradition of Gregory the Great, who had ordered relics placed in pagan temples newly converted to Christian churches.[25]

Charles also encouraged expansion of relics' legal and social significance by making the ecclesiastical practice of using them for oath taking normative for all oaths. In Germanic law, an oath could be taken on any object: one's own beard, a ring, or the chair of a leader.[26] The ecclesiastical practice of swearing on a relic had been long established, and in 794 it was considered remarkable when Bishop Peter of Verdun took an oath "without relics and without the holy evangels, only in the presence of God," because he could not find any at hand when he was ready to swear.[27] Merovingian kings had also been in the habit of swearing oaths on the *cappa* of Saint Martin or on some other relic.[28] In 803 Charles made this practice normative, ordering that "all oaths be sworn either in a church or on relics."[29] The emperor's throne, still in position in his Aachen chapel, with its compartments for the insertion of relics, symbolized the perfect combination of these Germanic and Christian traditions: one could swear on the throne, containing relics, in a church. The formula prescribed for use in these oaths was, "May God and the saint whose relics these are judge me,"[30] a formula that became the standard oath of Charles's successors, being used by Charles the Bald in 853[31] and Louis the Second in 860.[32]

At the same time that Carolingian reforms were increasing relics' importance in society, reformers were beginning to require that only respectable saints be the object of veneration by the faithful. In the last decade of the eighth century, an effort was begun to regulate and control the numerous local cults of saints that had flourished since the earliest days of Christianity in the Frankish kingdom, where saints had replaced the local divinities of wood, river, and grove. One of the first actions in this direction was to prevent the establishment of any new cults. The Synod of Frankfurt in 794 ordered "that no new saints might be venerated or invoked . . . but only those who were chosen by the authority of their passion or by the merit of their life are to be venerated in church."[33] This attempt at the closing of the frontier, so to speak, coincided with the expansion of the role of relics in society, producing a crisis for churches and monasteries short on supplies of popular relics. With the foundation of new monasteries, the beginnings of the establishment of a system of parishes, and the reform of places of worship that had fallen into disuse, the demand for acceptable relics must have greatly exceeded the supply. The reasons for this are not difficult to find.

Although even in the Merovingian period the absolute identity between martyrs and saints had ceased to be officially recognized, and confessors were honored in local cults throughout the West, in the ninth century the most admired holy men were still the martyrs.[34] But real martyrs were in very short supply during this period. With the exception of Boniface and his companions, who were more the victims of political assassination than true martyrs, the expansion and consolidation of the Carolingian Empire and its religion had taken place with little persecution of Christians or loss of missionary life. In fact, the only true martyrs had been those pagans slaughtered by Charles because of their refusal to convert. True, Isidore had said, "They also are martyrs who, had they lived in the time of persecution, would have been martyrs."[35] But even these were scarce among the ecclesiastics and courtiers of the eighth and ninth centuries. As Heinrich Fichtenau has pointed out, Einhard, Hrabanus Maurus, and even Benedict of Aniane were not men whose lives were the sort to inspire pious devotion.[36] Hence a church or monastery had to look elsewhere for other means of providing saints if it was to participate in the mainstream of religious fervor.

Since no new martyrs were being produced in the empire and it was becoming increasingly difficult simply to introduce the cult of a hitherto unknown saint, three possibilities were open to a church hoping to begin or increase its collection. First, the church might profit from a redistribution or rediscovery of those relics already *in situ*—the remains of the semi-legendary Gallic martyrs of the last Roman persecutions or the remains of Merovingian bishops, confessors, and hermits. In an ancient Gallo-Roman city, a martyr might appear to a pious monk or priest in a vision and reveal his burial place, lost for centuries, in a corner of the crypt. But this method was generally an unacceptable alternative, particularly in the case of recent foundations, and ecclesiastics tended to look elsewhere for relics. They might visit a neighboring town fortunate enough to possess them in abundance or, if no local saints were available, they might go beyond the Pyrenees to Moslem Spain—the only area where martyrs were still being produced. Finally and most commonly, they could search for remains of martyrs in Rome, that inexhaustible treasure house of relics.

Since redistribution of local or foreign saints was the most practical alternative, lay and ecclesiastical reformers recognized that these translations would require regulation. This need was particularly evident, since even in the opening years of the ninth century motives behind these translations were often recognized as greed rather than piety. In 811 Charles ordered that these translations be investigated since " . . . people who as if acting out of love of God and of the saints, whether martyrs or confessors, transfer the bones and remains of holy bodies from place to place and there construct new basilicas and vehemently exhort whomever they can that they should donate their goods to it."[37]

In order to prevent this and other types of exploitation of popular piety, the Synod of Mainz in 813 ordered that all translations be approved: "Bodies of saints shall not be transferred from place to place. Hence, let no one take it upon himself to transfer bodies of saints from place to place without the consultation of the prince and/or [vel] of the bishops and the permission of the holy synod."[38]

For important imperial officials like Abbot Hilduin of St. Médard of Soissons, obtaining this permission was no problem. Following the execution of the papal notary Theodore and the nomenclator Leo in 823, the Franks seized the opportunity to intervene in papal affairs. Lothar, co-emperor since 817, was able to obtain oaths from Pope Eugenius II which effectively placed the papacy under the emperor's tutelage.[39] Frankish churchmen like Hilduin took advantage of this new state of affairs to extract from the pope some of Rome's most valuable assets—its vast store of bodies of the early martyrs. Thus Hilduin received the body of Saint Sebastian and placed it in his monastery in Soissons.

Not that this Frankish fascination with Roman relics was entirely new; since 397, when Victor of Rouen brought the relics of twenty-three martyrs to that city from Rome, pilgrims from Germany and Gaul had occasionally brought home relics from the eternal city.[40] But with Hilduin's coup in 826, a new and particularly intense desire to possess Roman relics swept the empire. Soissons rapidly became an important place of pilgrimage and the abbot's success sparked envy among his fellow churchmen as they watched the crowds of pilgrims leaving their dioceses to visit Saint Médard's. They were no doubt concerned about their own loss of prestige, to say nothing of their loss of revenue. When Odilo of Saint Médard wrote a highly fictitious account of this translation of Saint Sebastian a century later, he placed a sermon in the mouth of Ostroldus, the mid-ninth-century bishop of Laon. Although a literary set speech, it probably reflects accurately the feelings of many of Ostroldus's contemporaries. Odilo has Ostroldus say, addressing his congregation, "What do you seek in journeying to Soissons, as though you would find the martyr Sebastian? You know that after his martyrdom he was buried in Rome and there he lies, moved by no one. You have here the church of the venerable Mother of God; frequent it, in it swear your vows and make your contributions. You should not wander to other places to seek external help. All that you ask faithfully through her will be given by the Lord."[41]

Such exhortations generally fell on deaf ears. During the next decades at least thirty such translations were recorded, and rivalry among ecclesiastics was intense.[42] The Roman martyrs were immensely popular and regardless of which other saints and martyrs reposed in one's own crypt, abbots considered the acquiring of some famous body from Rome a necessity.

The Frankish interest in Roman saints was paralleled by a similar, long established interest in Spanish martyrs. Ever since 527 when Childebert brought the stole of Saint Vincent to Saint Germain des Près,[43] the Spanish deacon had been venerated in the north. In the second half of the ninth century, Frankish interest again focused on Spain as a source of relics, since the despair of the Christian community of

Córdoba had produced a number of men who actively sought martyrdom at the hands of reluctant but ultimately cooperative Moslem officials.[44] These martyrs first came to the Franks' attention following the expedition of Usuard in 858.[45]

Not every monastery enjoyed the political connections of a Hilduin or a Usuard through which they could acquire new relics. Nevertheless, they too needed relics to meet the new demands placed on these objects by both the Carolingian elite and the Frankish masses. Every monastery needed relics for altars, for oath objects, and for foci of religious devotion. Relics alone could attract pilgrims and secure the laity's devotion to a particular religious foundation. Moreover, as Carolingian Europe faced a progressively worsening political and social climate, people everywhere, like Radbertus, looked to saints to help them restore stability and order. The need for relics was thus too great to be denied, even if normal channels for their acquisition were lacking. As a result, monasteries were forced to deal with middlemen such as the "monks" encountered in Dijon. Often these persons were travelers who claimed to have acquired relics from Rome or some other pilgrimage site. To control these wanderers, efforts were made to place them under supervision of the bishops in whose dioceses they appeared.[46] But these ordinances were not carefully enforced, and wandering clerics were one of the banes of every ecclesiastical administrator's existence. For example, Benedict of Aniane, taking his cue from Benedict of Nursia and Augustine, condemned these "eternally wandering monks . . . some of whom sell part of martyrs' bodies (if indeed they are martyrs)."[47]

These condemnations were largely ineffectual because the itinerant clerics were too important to the very ecclesiastical administrators who were to limit their activities. Some of them were professional relic merchants who lessened the gap between relic supply and demand by operating what Jean Guiraud accurately described as a "commerce in contraband."[48] They were usually merchants and thieves, stealing relics whenever possible and then selling them to eager ecclesiastics or other members of the ruling elite. We will examine their operations and the reactions of their customers, who both needed them and mistrusted them, in the following chapter.

CHAPTER THREE

The Professionals

Professional relic thieves were by no means unique to the Carolingian period. They appear in hagiography and literature throughout the Middle Ages. The relic-mongers of the ninth and tenth centuries resemble nothing so much as the suppliers of objects of art in the twentieth. At best the thieves were high-class fences, at worst grave robbers. In either case, they emerge from contemporary hagiography as marginal characters, often attached in some capacity to the Church, and looking for the opportunity to make a profit in stealing and smuggling relics.

Perhaps because of the limitations of extant historical sources, relic thieves of the ninth through eleventh centuries seem to have dealt exclusively with elite customers—important abbots, bishops, and kings. Georges Duby has suggested that it is only in the later Middle Ages that the aristocratic practice of having personal relic collections spread through the lower levels of European society.[1] Whether or not this suggestion is correct, it is clear that elite customers were particularly desirous of relics. This demand created a special breed of merchant, as thieves sought to accommodate those customers most in a position to reward them. In the ninth century, their best customers were Carolingian bishops and abbots; in the tenth century Anglo-Saxon kings dealt most readily with relic-mongers. The Ottonians were no less avid collectors of relics, but unlike the two above-mentioned groups of connoisseurs, they enjoyed sufficient power in Italy to procure a steady supply of relics without having to contact professional thieves.[2]

Relic thieves operated much like other types of merchants. Deusdona, the most famous of the Carolingian suppliers, organized periodic caravans which crossed the Alps in spring and made the rounds of monastic fairs. In the tenth century thieves working for Anglo-Saxon kings traveled back and forth from Normandy and Brittany like other traders of the same period. Although documents make no mention of other trades in which these men engaged, the frequent mention of relic thieves in the company of other merchants suggests that many of them dealt in a wide variety of merchandise and simply added relics to their wares whenever the opportunity arose.

Shifting tastes in relics were accurately reflected in the varieties offered by these thieves. In the ninth century, Carolingians wanted Roman and Italian martyrs. Thus Deusdona provided Roman saints, while other Frankish thieves operating in Italy dealt in saints not only from Rome but from as far away as Ravenna. Anglo-Saxon kings were interested in continental saints from Brittany and Normandy. In order to supply them, relic-mongers acted as agents, buying them from desperate and unscrupulous clerics or simply stealing them from poorly guarded churches.

THE ITALIAN TRADE

The best known of the ninth-century relic merchants was Deusdona, a deacon of the Roman Church who provided Einhard with the bodies of Saints Peter and Marcellinus. Deusdona was no occasional thief but rather the head of a large and highly organized group of relic merchants.[3] Envious of his friend Hilduin's acquisition of the body of Saint Sebastian and needing important relics to endow his newly founded monastery at Mulinheim, Einhard engaged Deusdona's services for the first time in 827.[4] The deacon had just arrived in Aachen and although he pretended to be there in order to plead the help of the emperor, it is most likely that he was actually looking for business.[5] A contract was drawn up and Deusdona agreed to take Einhard's notary Ratlecus to Rome with him in order to procure the relics. On their way south, they stopped at Soissons where

Hilduin contracted for the procurement of the remains of Saint Tiburtius. Deusdona seems to have kept his part of the bargain, but Hilduin's agent attempted to cheat Einhard out of his relics by secretly stealing them from Ratlecus and returning with them to Soissons. It was only later, when by chance Einhard learned from Hilduin that Soissons had the relics of Peter and Marcellinus, that he was able to force their surrender. This attempted deceit and the subsequent pretensions of the monastery of St. Médard to possess the relics led Einhard to write his version of the translation.[6] In spite of the general acceptance of this account, the monastery continued over the subsequent centuries to claim possession of the two martyrs.[7]

The picture of this operation that emerges from the accounts of Einhard and other ninth-century writers is a fascinating one. Deusdona is described as living near the basilica of St. Peter in Chains.[8] While it is highly improbable that he was charged with the ecclesiastical jurisdiction of the third cemetery district of Rome as Jean Guiraud has suggested, he was certainly well acquainted with the catacombs.[9] Evidently he managed to get free access to them, aided by the fact that for centuries they had been in ruins and for the most part deserted; and he was able to capitalize on his familiarity with them. He was helped by his two brothers: Lunisus, at whose house the relics were secured after being removed from the catacombs and who operated in southern Italy, and Theodorus, who traveled with Deusdona on a second German expedition in 830.[10]

In this year the merchants went directly to Mulinheim with a large number of relics, arriving in early June. Deusdona did not remain there long, however, because he soon heard that a monk of Fulda, Theotmar, was in Mainz on monastery business (possibly looking for relics for Fulda). The Roman hurried to meet him and soon negotiated an agreement to provide Fulda with relics. Thus the monastery received the remains of Saints Alexander, Sebastian, Fabian, Urban, Felicissimus, Felicity, and Emmerentina among others.[11]

On a third visit to Mulinheim in 834, Deusdona brought Einhard the relics of Saint Hermes.[12] After this trip nothing is known about his activities, but two years later one of his partners, Sabbatino, crossed the Alps to deliver still more relics to Fulda.[13]

Apparently Deusdona and his associates did not limit their operations to the north. Einhard records that the deacon could not immediately lay his hands on the remains of Peter and Marcellinus because his brother Lunisus was in Benevento on business and possibly had the relics with him.[14] This business in Benevento was in all likelihood the family one.

Supplying relics to the Franks was apparently a lucrative occupation. Einhard does not say how much he actually paid for his relics, but the gift of a mule which he does mention is clearly only a small part of the price.[15] When the monk Theotmar struck his bargain with the deacon in 830, he promised that "he would be well paid for it by him."[16] The outfitting of a caravan to cross the Alps with one's wares was no small enterprise in 836, and the operation was quite similar to later medieval merchant expeditions. During the winter months, Deusdona and his associates systematically collected relics from one or another of the Roman cemeteries. Apparently they concentrated on a different area of the city each year, possibly to avoid the wrath of ecclesiastical officials. Thus in 826 Deusdona's relics came primarily from the via Labicana.[17] In 835 nine of the thirteen relics came from the area of the via Pinciana-Salaria.[18] The following year the associates concentrated on the via Appia,[19] as they did again two years later when ten of the thirteen relics Sabbatino brought north came from that area.[20] In spring the merchants arranged the timing of their crossing to coincide with important feast days celebrated at the monasteries of their customers. June 2, 835, the feast of Saints Marcellinus and Peter, found Deusdona at Mulinheim with his stock.[21] Two days later he arrived at Fulda in time for the feast of Saint Boniface celebrated June 5.[22] Just as merchants of the later Middle Ages discovered, pilgrims to these celebrations made ideal customers, particularly for the type of merchandise Deusdona had to offer. Seeing the glory that the remains of Marcellinus and Peter had brought to Einhard, for example, customers were probably eager to acquire relics which would bring them and their communities similar benefits.

Deusdona's considerable organization operated on the largest scale. But there were lesser figures engaged in similar activities. Among these was a certain Felix, who dealt in relics of all sorts from various places rather than specialize in Roman relics like his competitor Deusdona. Felix shared some of Deusdona's customers and, indeed, even sold some of the same saints.

Liutolfus, a monk of Fulda, described Felix as a Frankish cleric who traveled about the empire selling relics. He sold Archbishop Otgarius of Mainz what he claimed was the body of Saint Severus, bishop of Ravenna. According to the story he told at the time of the sale, as recounted in Liutolfus's life of Saint Severus, Felix had been visiting the monastery of Saint Apollinaris in Ravenna when he saw an opportunity to steal the body. Upon so doing, he was pursued by monks from the monastery and in the course of his flight he happened to meet Otgarius. The archbishop agreed to purchase the relics and Felix escaped on a horse provided by the Frankish ecclesiastic.[23] It is likely that Otgarius had been involved in similar acquisitions for some time, and when Theotmar of Fulda visited him in 830, it may have been with the intention of meeting Felix in order to purchase relics for his monastery. At any rate, on April 5, 838, this same Felix appeared at Fulda with the remains of Saints Cornelius, Callistus, Agapitus, Georgius, Vincentius, Maximus, Cecilia, Eugenia, Digna, Emerita, and Columbana.[24] Around this same time, Felix visited Freising, where he sold the body of Saint Bartholomew to Bishop Erchambert.[25]

Because of the fragmentary and partisan nature of our sources, it is difficult to determine the spirit in which these and other merchants were received by Frankish ecclesiastics. Not only was there some recognition of the illegality and questionable morality of such acquisitions but, as we shall see, there were quite practical concerns about the authenticity of the relics thus obtained. Nevertheless, the multiplicity of sources which speak of Deusdona and Felix allow some certainty in outlining their operations and describing their techniques of collection, transport, and sales. The operations of the next group of professional thieves, however, are difficult to visualize as clearly, owing to the extreme paucity of sources.

ENGLAND

While the Carolingian monarchy disintegrated as a result of squabbling dynasties and ineffectual defense against external invaders, the Franks ceded to the English their reputation as the most avid relic collectors. England also faced a shortage of relics, as the canon of the Synod of Chelsea suggested. When, in the the tenth century, King Athelstan emerged as a great collector whose passion for saints' relics far surpassed that of other rulers of his century,[26] he had to look outside his kingdom to satisfy this passion. Athelstan was intimately involved in continental affairs through numerous marriage alliances and through his diplomatic negotiations on behalf of Louis d'Outremer.[27] By means of these relationships with continental rulers he garnered a vast array of relics, presents from those who courted his favor. He augmented this collection by purchases from Brittany and Normandy.[28]

Athelstan and his Anglo-Saxon successors well into the eleventh century were eager and able to pay for relics without too much concern for the means by which their suppliers came by them. It was only natural that merchants would soon appear to cater to this sort of clientele. Although sources on these agents are unsatisfactory, it is possible to discover something about their efforts.

The first thief to appear in tenth-century sources is Electus, an Englishman, who attempted to steal the remains of Saint Bertulfus in order to sell them to the king. The *Vita*

Sancti Bertulfi[29] and the closely related *Sermo in translatione Sancti Gudwali et Sancti Bertulfi*[30] tell how Bertulfus's body had been removed from its resting place in Renty near St. Omer to Boulogne during the Norman invasions. Sometime between 935 and 939, Electus managed to steal the body from Boulogne and hide it near Audinghem along with a collection of other relics he was amassing to sell in England. However, before he could dispose of his merchandise, Count Arnulf of Flanders and Bishop Wigfred of Thérouanne discovered the crime and forced Electus to surrender Bertulfus's remains, as well as those of Saint Gudwaldus which he had also stolen.

The second recorded English theft is that of Saints Maximus and Venerandus from Acquigny (cant. Louviers, Eure) in 964.[31] An anonymous hagiographer described the thief as a man "from across the sea" who had been led by a vision to the tomb of the saints. The visionary had no difficulty opening the tomb and carrying off the remains, but as he approached a ship to book passage for England, he was miraculously moved to act in such a drunken way that the sailor collecting the fare grew suspicious. The sailor forced the thief to accompany him to the monastery of Fontenelle where he confessed the theft and the identities of the stolen relics. The duke of the Normans, who was then consulted on the disposition of the remains, decided that they should remain at Fontenelle.

Neither of these accounts presents an historical picture of the efforts of English thieves in the tenth century. The *Vita Bertulfi* was written over a century after the events it describes were said to have taken place. Little verifiable information in the *vita* is accurate, and the unverifiable information concerning Electus must be treated with caution. Moreover, Oppermann has shown that the author of the text had a specific polemical purpose in writing the *vita*—he intended to bolster the claims of the monastery of Saint-Bertin to possess the bodies of Bertulfus and Gudwaldus in opposition to the stronger claims of the church of Harelbeke.[32] While the author of the *vita* claimed to have learned the details of the theft from a now lost document in the monastery's archives, this claim is so frequently a ploy in medieval forgery cases that it ceases to carry much weight. The text is a most unreliable source for the activities of Electus.

The same must be said of the *Inventio Sancti Wolframi*. The monastery of Fontenelle, in which the *inventio* was written, had been restored in 960, only a few years before the date of the alleged translation.[33] A newly restored monastery needed new powerful patrons to attract pilgrims whose offerings would pay for the restorations. If it did acquire the remains of Venerandus and Maximus, this acquisition came at too appropriate a moment to be the result of a chance encounter between a drunken thief and a suspicious sailor. One might rather suspect that the miraculous event was choreographed, manipulated by solicitous monks or by the duke.

Whether or not these particular thefts took place in the ways reported by eleventh-century texts, or even at all, the accounts are surely valuable indications of what was in fact a fairly common event. Most significant, as J. Laporte pointed out, is that such acts were so readily attributed to Englishmen.[34] Enough Anglo-Saxons must have been combing northern Europe for relics that hagiographers could introduce them into their accounts to explain how relics had been acquired or to demonstrate the power of their saints to resist the efforts of thieves. As far away as Cologne, for example, hagiographers told of attempted relic thefts by English.[35] In the eleventh century, the monk Rainier, reworking an older book of miracles of Saint Gislenus, could add the rumor that men from "across the sea" had in the previous century attempted to steal his monastery's patron although the original text made no reference to this tradition.[36]

This readily accepted *topos* must have had a basis in fact. Although the specific accounts may not be verifiable, as long as Anglo-Saxon kings and their families were in the market, thieves materialized to sell them relics. Some thieves might have been driven to the extremity of selling relics by pressing financial circumstances. Such was the case of a monk of

Rouen reported by William of Malmesbury who sold the remains of Saint Ouen to Queen Emma in order to ransom his
nephew.[37] Others probably resembled Electus, systematically
collecting relics to sell to his royal customer. Widespread
knowledge that such people existed made it possible to at-
tribute to Anglo-Saxons the theft of relics from any area of
Europe that saw a fair number of English merchants.

CONCLUSIONS

Commerce was an important source of relics for individuals
and religious communities throughout the Middle Ages.
Since the merchants could hardly come by their wares le-
gally, they were necessarily also thieves or, in some cases, em-
bezzlers, selling the relics entrusted to their care by their religious communities. Although irregular and surreptitious,
these transactions benefited everyone involved. From the merchants' point of view, relics were excellent articles of trade.
They were small and easily transported, since entire bodies
of saints centuries dead were nothing more than dust and a
few bones that could be carried in a small bag. As highly desirable luxury items, they brought excellent prices in return
for little capital investment. The risks were minimal, other
than falling into the hands of the local populace irate at having their patron stolen (if the merchant bothered to steal genuine relics) and the possibility of having the relics stolen in
turn if the trader-thief were not careful. Perhaps the best aspect of all, owing to the difficulties of communication between communities involved, was that the body of a popular
saint already sold might be sold again to another customer.
This could be done in either of two ways: parts of the body
could be offered for sale, as in the case of the body of Saint
Alexander which Deusdona divided and sold, part in Switzer-
land and part in Fulda;[38] or the merchant could appear with
yet another relic of a saint although the body had been
bought *in toto* by a previous customer. The tooth of Saint Sebastian was sold in 835 although the entire body had been

translated to St. Médard ten years earlier. The multiplicity of bodies or identical relics of saints was a constant phenomenon that only occasionally caused serious disputes or disagreements.

The relic trade was not only beneficial to merchants and customers, but even to the authorities who might have been expected to raise the strongest objections to it. Obviously Anglo-Saxon kings, as the principal recipients of stolen relics, were in no position to object to the means by which their suppliers acquired them. But even the pope, who might have wished to protect the catacombs from violation, indirectly enjoyed considerable benefits from allowing the commerce to flourish. It was certainly in his political interest to keep the Frankish ecclesiastics well disposed toward him by refraining from interfering in the trade, even if he could have done anything to stop it. Furthermore, the popularity of Roman relics in the north could only enhance the Roman pontiff's prestige. Every martyr's body that found its way into a Frankish church served to impress upon the Franks the dignity and importance of Rome as a center of Christianity. In a period when Rome was less important as the see of the pope than as the tomb of Peter, Paul, and the other Roman martyrs, the best possible means of reminding the rest of Europe of this importance was the selective dissemination of Roman relics.[39]

Finally, owing again to the peculiar nature of relics, Rome and the pope gave up very little in allowing some to be removed, stolen, sold, or carried away. The fact that Eugenius II had given the body of Saint Sebastian to Hilduin in 825 did not prevent Gregory IV from solemnly translating the body of that same martyr from the catacomb in which it lay to an altar in the chapel of Gregory the Great in Saint Peter's.[40]

The customers themselves were also for the most part satisfied with their purchases. True, they were often justly concerned with the authenticity of the relics purchased from traveling relic-mongers. Such concern is evident in Amolo's letter to Bishop Theodboldus of Langres. But in reality there

was little that they could do to establish the authenticity of
their purchases. The most direct means was Einhard's
method; he sent an agent to Rome to supervise the acquisition of relics. But this method was not possible when a merchant appeared with relics he had already acquired; and
even if an agent could be sent to Rome with the merchant,
he would not know enough about Rome and its catacombs
to expose any but the grossest kind of fraud. Occasionally a
suspicious ecclesiastic might send one or more investigators
to Rome to check the story told by the merchant. This is
what was done to authenticate relics of the Empress Helen
brought to Hautvilliers.[41] But once in Rome, northern investigators were seriously handicapped by the clandestine nature
of this commerce. It would hardly do to make too many in-
quiries; the Roman populace, always volatile, took a dim
view of efforts to carry off their saintly patrons and defenders. Moreover, judging from the results of the Hautvilliers in-
quest, the investigators themselves could easily fall prey to
more unscrupulous merchants in Rome itself. These monks,
for example, returned not only with what they considered to
be assurances that the remains were actually those of Helen,
but also with the relics of Saints Polycarp, Sebastian, Urban,
and Quirinus.

The most effective means available from the ninth
through eleventh centuries to determine the authenticity of
relics was in reality a very pragmatic one: if the relics performed as relics—that is to say, if they worked miracles, inspired the faithful, and increased the prestige of the community in which they were placed—they had to be genuine.
Thus, after all the more "rational" means of authenticating
the relics of Helen had been exhausted—the agent who had
brought them having been interrogated, a map of Rome having been examined to determine whether his story was plausible, and investigators sent to the city itself—the relics were
finally verified by recourse to ordeal.[42] Bishop Erchambert of
Freising, uncertain about the authenticity of the relics he had
purchased from Felix, proclaimed a three-day fast to ask

God for a sign to show "if this above-mentioned Felix speaks the truth or not, and if he is deceiving us by a trick of the devil."[43]

❖

Clearly recipients of relics did not view the efforts of professionals in the same favorable light as they did thefts by men motivated by devotion and not by greed. Thus while thieves who stole relics for profit probably flourished throughout the central Middle Ages, they are rarely encountered in translation accounts except when their evil designs have been frustrated. Even if a church or monastery did buy relics from a thief, it was better to say that the thief had been an amateur and not a professional. It is important to keep this in mind as we examine the more common varieties of *furta* narrative. In many cases a more elaborate *translatio* that tells of a theft *causa devotionis* may in fact disguise the purchase of relics from a Deusdona, a Felix, or an Electus.

CHAPTER FOUR

Monastic Thefts

KINGS, emperors, and powerful ecclesiastics were the most common customers of professional relic thieves, but they were hardly typical of the Christians who needed relics during the centuries that followed the collapse of the fragile Carolingian Empire. With the exception of a few precocious Italian cities, Europe was predominantly rural during the tenth and eleventh centuries, and the centers of religious and cultural life were not cathedrals or palaces but rather rural monasteries. The vast majority of accounts of relic thefts describe monastic communities' efforts to acquire the remains of powerful patrons.

Across Europe hundreds of monasteries faced the same problems: loss of continuity resulting from destruction or dispersion at the hands of Viking, Arab, or Magyar invaders, threats against their property by local nobles no longer restrained by an effective central authority, and rivalry with other monasteries for the devotion and patronage of the laity.

Not only had the invasions of the ninth and tenth centuries destroyed personal property, but even more importantly they had destroyed documentation of monastic rights, and disrupted the continuity of local customs so vital for the preservation of oral traditions of rights and privileges. In the custom-bound world of the eleventh century, monasteries had to reestablish ties with a distant and ill-remembered past in order to maintain dignity and importance in the present.

Lay protectors appointed to look after the temporal concerns of monasteries had never, even at the height of Carolingian control, refrained from appropriating as much of the "temporalities" of the monasteries they "protected" as possible. Now, in the absence of royal supervision and constraint, they became little more than extortioners whose nominal Christianity was more than offset by their greed and willingness to take whatever of the Church's lands and rights they could.

Even other monasteries often presented more of a threat than a solace in these confused times. Local pride and particularism combined with a realization that in an underpopulated, near subsistence-level world, the prosperity of a religious community was a fragile luxury that could provoke intense rivalries between neighboring monasteries.

In reality, the monasteries had few resources to meet the challenges of this precarious existence. Lacking human protection in the forms of military or economic force, they looked to the protection of saints to reestablish lost prestige, intimidate local magnates, and outdistance other monasteries in the race for spiritual renown. A key ingredient in the development of the cult of a new patron was the acquisition of his or her relics; and possession of the remains of a popular saint could mean the difference between a monastery's oblivion and survival. Hence, the acquisition of relics was a real necessity, and, as ever, the only means of acquisition were purchase, gift, invention, or theft.

Particularly in the area of what is today southern France and in the west, stories circulated of the thefts of saints. But these stories bore little resemblance to the accounts of professional relic thieves—at least superficially. Unlike the professional jobs, they were said to have been perpetrated not by merchants but rather by pious monks motivated by their ardent love of the saints. Their expeditions to find relics took on the status of sacred quests, and the thefts themselves were revered as works of piety rather than of greed.

The historical accuracy of these accounts is impossible to determine. As we shall see in Chapter 6, many of them are formally related in a hagiographic tradition that owes more to a sense of how a relic should be stolen than to the particulars of the actual acquisition. But in those cases for which sufficient documentation exists, it is possible to see how both the acquisition of a saint and the literary tradition of the *furta sacra* met the particular needs of monastic communities. Whether the story of the theft disguised a purchase, a gift, or an invention, and whether or not it approximated the actual events, clearly certain crisis situations arose that called for thefts and not any other form of acquisition.

MONASTIC COMPETITION

The interior life of a monastery was that of an army waging a constant spiritual war for Christ; the external life of these communities was a constant war against the real or supposed encroachments of other monasteries and laymen. This posture naturally developed community pride, based on the "family" of the monastic community and rationalized as defense of the *honores* of its patron. Thus monastic pride differed little from the family pride of the laity from which the monks came. Moreover, this pride was intensified by a clear perception of the economic facts of life: in the ninth through the eleventh centuries monastic communities were luxuries in an impoverished Europe and depended on the good will and patronage of the local laity for their existence. Other houses in the area that threatened to compete for this patronage posed a threat that could hardly be taken lightly.

The proper defense against such threats differed from place to place and from time to time. Acquisition of a "new patron" could successfully reinforce a monastery's hold on lay devotion and charity. However, the reasons for stealing this new patron are not so readily apparent. The circumstances leading to the creation of the traditional account of the theft of Saint Foy from Agen to Conques show ways in which a stolen relic might best answer the needs of the moment.

The acquisition of Saint Foy appears to have been part of an effort to bolster the monastery of Conques against the increasing popularity and importance of another monastery, Figeac, which was more favorably located to attract the devotion of the laity. In time, the significance of Saint Foy and her theft reached beyond the confines of the local community. Certainly the irregularity of her acquisition was partly responsible for this success.

According to the two eleventh-century versions of the *Translatio Sanctae Fidei*, the monks of Conques had heard of the fame of the saint and determined to acquire her remains for "the health of the area and for the redemption of its inhabitants."[1] For the task they chose Arinisdus, a monk of Conques, who went to Agen posing as a secular priest and asked to join the religious community serving the church which contained the relics. He was admitted and spent a long time (ten years according to the one version of the *translatio*) in the church gaining the community's confidence. He finally was appointed guardian of the church's treasure, including of course Saint Foy's tomb. One night he was left alone in the church and seized the opportunity by breaking open the tomb, and taking the body of Saint Foy. He hurried back to Conques where he was received with joy.

The historical value and significance of these accounts has long been debated and it is unnecessary to pursue the details of this debate here.[2] Briefly stated, both Ferdinand Lot and Léon Levillain agreed that the translation must have taken place on January 14, 865 or 866, although they offer different reasons, while J. Angély has insisted that the entire story is fictional and that the translation never took place.[3] Regardless of the historical value of the *translationes* themselves, by 883 the monastery of Conques's possession of the remains of Saint Foy was recognized by those who counted most—donors and lay patrons of the monastery. Subsequent claims to possess the remains are immaterial even if the claims may have been legitimate. Throughout the Middle Ages, Saint Foy continued to work her miracles in Conques, not in Agen, and these miracles were what mattered to the thousands who went on pilgrimages there.

Although Agen sporadically tried to reassert its claim of possession, it finally recognized the translation of Saint Foy to Conques. A fragment of the prologue to the account of a miracle worked at Périgueux by the relics of Bishop Phebade, included in the proper of the mass in Agen on October 6, the feast of Saint Foy, documents Agen's capitulation:

> The city of Agen which once surpassed all the towns of Aquitaine in the illustrious patronage of its saints now remains widowed by almost all of them as a result of some unknown sin; some having been carried off by force, others by theft. You will find, visitor to Aquitaine, that which I have found. In diverse places there are those who tell you "Here is the body of Martyr so-and-so, translated from Agen; there such-and-such, a confessor or virgin, or such a portion of that saint."[4]

While it is impossible to determine the source for Conques's claims, the monastery direly needed the remains of a saint in the latter half of the ninth century. Angély correctly focuses on the rivalry between Conques and the neighboring foundation of Figeac as the proximate cause for the community's interest in Saint Foy. These two monasteries' relationship apparently was one of competition and animosity from the very foundation of Figeac in 838, and the documents that concern this relationship are a tangle of forgeries, interpolated texts, and fictions.[5] In spite of the existence of the original diploma of Figeac's foundation issued by Pepin I in 838, Léon Levillain, with good reason, hesitated long before opting for the authenticity of this document. Besides the numerous diplomatic irregularities and problems with the text, the account itself describes a very peculiar situation. Figeac was founded, according to the diploma, because Pepin judged that Conques was located in a place so narrow and so difficult to reach with supplies that it could not hold a larger population. Therefore Pepin decided to establish a new monastery to be called "New Conques" at Figeac, and he ordered the monks of the nearby community in Joanata[6] to move to this place to serve God along with "the other brothers coming from Conques."[7] The community was to remain under the authority of the abbot of Conques and his successors.

Pepin's attempt to unite the two communities and to reduce or abolish Conques obviously failed. Instead he managed to create a dispute over the proper authority exercised
in the two monasteries which smoldered until the eleventh
century when it erupted with new force. The controversy
and rivalry between the parent monastery and its new and
unwanted offspring created the need for an important pres-
tigious acquisition. Because its location placed Conques at a
real disadvantage it needed an attraction that would encourage pilgrims to dare the tortuous approach. Thus, in 855,
the monastery determined to acquire the body of an important saint. The first choice was not Saint Foy but rather Saint
Vincent of Saragossa. According to the *Translatio Beati Vincentii*,[8] Hildebertus, a monk of the monastery, had a dream
in which he heard a voice telling him to go to Valencia and
find the sepulcher and bring Saint Vincent back to Conques.
The voice described the saint's location in heartbreaking
terms: the church in which it lay had been destroyed by pagans, and now lay deserted, lacking even a roof to protect it
from the elements. Hildebertus determined to carry out the
task and enlisted the help of another monk, Audaldus, who
had heard a similar story concerning the tomb from a Spanish noble, Berta. With the permission of the abbot Blan-
dinus, the two set out, but Hildebertus soon fell ill leaving
his companion to carry out the mission alone. In Valencia
Audaldus found a Moor, Zacharias, who for a price agreed
to help him find the relics. He found the tomb in the church,
and that night returned, opened the tomb which gave off a
fragrant odor, and took the body. He then hid it in a sack of
palm branches. However, he was caught by the bishop of
Saragossa, Senior, and interrogated as to the identity of the
saint whose relics he was carrying. He insisted that they
were the bones of a relative until, under torture, he admitted
that they were relics, but invented a Saint Marinus so that
the bishop would not know whose body he had actually stolen. Senior believed his confession and, after confiscat-
ing the body, released the monk. Upon Audaldus's return to

Conques without the relics, his story was not believed and he was refused admittance. Thereupon he went to Castres where he was received into the community.

In 864 a Catalonian noble sent some of the community of Castres, including Audaldus, to the acting caliph of Córdoba and, pretending that the body was that of Salamon's father, bribed the caliph to force Bishop Senior to relinquish it to them. Thus the relics finally arrived not at Conques but at Castres.

Apparently the community of Conques realized their error in allowing Vincent's body to escape their grasp and determined to acquire another Vincent, that of Pompéjac in the area of Agen. This reaction would certainly have been reasonable, considering that in the eyes of the faithful one Vincent is as good as another. While there, the monks probably also stole the remains of Saint Foy, whose cult in time far surpassed Saint Vincent's in popularity, and by the eleventh century when the *translationes* were written in their final form, only the theft of Saint Foy was mentioned.

The monks of Figeac could not simply stay idle while Conques gained fame for its *furtum sacrum* and its possession of Saint Foy. In the tenth or early eleventh century, a monk of Figeac wrote a *translatio* describing his monastery's acquisition of the remains of Saint Bibanus, a Merovingian bishop of Saintes.[9] The text relates that some time under the abbotship of Haigmar, who "was always eager to acquire the bodies of saints by trickery or theft,"[10] scouts were sent to Saintes to see what they could carry off. They arrived at just the right time, since shortly after they arrived the Normans attacked Saintes and all of the inhabitants ran to the defense of their city.[11] The monks were able to use this moment of panic to carry off Saint Bibanus's remains which, after a number of miracles, arrived in Figeac.[12]

Possibly intending a riposte to this obviously spurious account, an unknown monk of Conques reworked the original account of the translation of Saint Foy to make the story more interesting and competitive. By this time Vincent had been all but forgotten in the tremendous growth of the cult of Saint Foy, and so, if he was originally included in the *translatio*, he was omitted in the final form of the *Translatio Sanctae Fidei*.

FINANCING CONSTRUCTION

An important source of funds for church construction, at least beginning in the eleventh century, was the practice of carrying the relics of a church's saints around the surrounding countryside while lay or clerical preachers told of their miracles and asked for alms.[13] With well-known saints, the lives and miracles would provide material for sermons to impress and inspire the faithful. Even obscure or unknown saints were used to inspire generosity; the miraculous and exciting tales of their acquisition made up for the lack of details concerning their lives and martyrdoms. If the acquisition was a theft from a distant land, the tale could resemble a popular adventure story, as is the case of the *Translatio Sanctae Lewinnae* written by Drogo of Bergues around 1060.[14]

The account of the arrival of Lewinna in the Flemish monastery of Bergues-Saint-Winnoc makes up in adventure what it lacks in detail of the saint's life. In 1058, according to Drogo, Balgerus, a monk of Bergues, set sail for England in the company of a group of merchants. The ship was blown off course and finally landed on the Sussex shore. Because the day was Holy Saturday, Balgerus set out to find a church at which to celebrate Easter Mass. Before long he came upon a monastery dedicated to Saint Andrea where he learned of their most prized possession: the body of Saint Lewinna. When he heard the account of her life and miracles he was seized with the desire to acquire the remains for his own monastery. He attempted to buy them but was rebuffed. Therefore he resolved to steal them, but his first attempts were thwarted by the miraculous intervention of Lewinna herself. Finally after much prayer and effort on Balgerus's part, the saint consented to be carried off. The relics were

smuggled on board and the boat presently set sail, but Balgerus's troubles were by no means over. While he was sent
ashore to buy fish for the ship's provisions, a wind blew the
ship carrying the relics away from shore so that it could not
pick him up. The merchants decided to complete their business, and left Balgerus to make his way home as best he
could. Lewinna's remains were entrusted to a sailor who
stored them in his home, along with the rest of Balgerus's
possessions. The monk arrived at the home in the sailor's absence and only after much pleading convinced the wife to
give him the most worthless-appearing part of his possessions—the relics. Thus he was able to bring them at last to
Bergues. After carefully inspecting the seals on the relics to
determine their authenticity the abbot and the community
joyfully received their new patron.

There is no mention of Lewinna in English sources. If
there was a cult of this saint in England prior to the translation, no trace remains. The *translatio* says that her life and
miracles were written around her shrine in Anglo-Saxon, but
provides no indication of the content of these inscriptions.
Even the location of the supposed Sussex monastery from
which she was allegedly stolen has been a point of strenuous
debate.[15] The author of the *translatio* also wrote a *Vita Sanctae Lewinnae* but nothing in it indicates that he drew upon
any pretranslation tradition alive in Sussex.[16]

Lewinna's obscurity—even in the eleventh century—may
well account for the unusually imaginative details of her
translatio. Dom Nicolas Huyghebaert pointed out that the
date of the translation coincides with the construction of the
new abbatial church of Bergues-Saint-Winnoc.[17] Moreover,
the second part of the *translatio* is composed of a series of
miracles worked by the saint during a tour of western Flanders made by her relics with monks of Bergues to establish
her cult in the area. Apparently, Huyghebaert suggests, the
tour was to raise funds for the construction, and the *historia
translationis* was part of the propaganda in favor of this
fund-raising project.

Given the obscurity of the saint and the use to which her relics were put shortly after her arrival in Flanders, a *translatio* that reads rather like an adventure story should have been quite useful. Nothing remarkable could be said about Lewinna's English past to inspire the faithful, but the very act of her acquisition captured the imagination of those who heard of it. The mysterious foreign monastery, the miracles, the adventures at sea and her final arrival in Flanders are details that would provide an otherwise obscure saint with an interesting past. If her renown did not begin until her translation, at least it began then with a good story.

RIVAL LOCAL TRADITIONS

Conflicting claims to possess the relics of important patrons were and are numerous, but most parties disdainfully ignored the position of rivals or simply created a plausible account of how one's own church acquired the remains of a saint. But at times either the rivalry was too intense or the claims of one's competitor too strong to ignore the divergent traditions. This was particularly true in rivalries between various monasteries founded by the same person, or in towns evangelized, according to tradition, by the same apostle. An ideal resolution was presented in the *Vita Sancti Abbani*. Two Irish monasteries on the verge of war over possession of the saint's remains were dissuaded when a miracle produced a second body so that each monastery could maintain its founder's remains.[18]

This method of resolution was rare. More commonly one of the disputants would admit that its rival's claims had been valid at one time but that the body had since been secretly stolen from its original resting place. The monastery of Saint Vanne in Verdun used this approach when, in the course of reform and expansion under its great abbot Richard (ca. 970–1046), Verdun needed to establish a claim on the body of Saint Sanctinus. Richard saw nothing contradictory or immoral about his theft or falsification of important relics. In fact, Richard's own interpretation of his role as religious reformer and administrator rendered such actions not only proper but necessary.

Richard's hagiographers unanimously portray him as a holy man, and he was indeed by contemporary standards. He, like the majority of his contemporaries, was principally concerned with the physical, the sensible dimensions of piety. He demonstrated this concern throughout his career in pursuit of a particular form of monastic life and in his passion for saints' relics.

The monastery of Saints Peter, Paul, and Vanne, which Richard entered as a young man, provided little that encouraged him in his pursuit of his monastic ideal. The church that housed the small community had been the original cathedral of Verdun although in 451 the bishop had moved his seat to Saint Mary's.[19] Until the middle of the tenth century a community of canons had occupied the church, but in 951 Bishop Berengar established there a Benedictine community under the patronage of Saint Vanne.[20] The first abbot, Humbert, was a native of Verdun, but by the time that Richard entered the monastery, if his *vita* is to be believed, the community consisted of seven Irish monks under the abbotship of their compatriot Fingenius.[21] The monastery's austerity and poverty reflected the Irish monastic ideal, but Richard was far removed in sensibilities from such a community. His ideal was rather the prosperous wealthy monastery of Cluny with its elaborate rituals, sumptuous vestments, and numerous monks. Shocked by the reality he found in Verdun, he went to Cluny to seek advice on transferring himself to a more appealing monastery. Abbot Odilo, however, insisted that he remain faithful to Fingenius at Saint Vanne.[22]

Richard obediently returned to Saint Vanne and entered the monastic life, but he did not have long to suffer under the old dispensation. Time and the sentiment of the younger monks were in his favor, and when Fingenius died in 1004, Richard succeeded him as abbot and immediately proceeded to realize his image of the ideal monastery. His success was due in part to his connections with the local nobility. A member of a noble family from the area of Reims, he had entered Saint Vanne with Frederic, the count of Verdun, who continued to be a lifelong friend.[23] He secured generous contributions from the local nobles as well as from people as far removed as William the Conqueror by instituting at Saint Vanne a necrology along the Cluniac model which carefully noted the benefactors of the monastery and included them eternally in the community's prayers.[24]

Although Saint Vanne was probably never formally affiliated with Cluny,[25] Richard clearly modeled his monastery after the great Burgundian house. His biographers considered his greatest achievements to be elaboration of the liturgy, the increase in revenues that made possible the acquisition of sacred vessels and sumptuous vestments, and the great reconstruction and renovation projects he carried out. Splendor, wealth, and sanctity were inseparable in his mind, and it was the monastery's role to reflect the triumphant glory of the Church on earth. His building projects were so extensive that even in his own day he was severely criticized by one great ascetic who did not share his enthusiasm for construction. Peter Damian, writing to the Roman prefect Cintheus some time after Richard's death, told of a vision of hell in which Richard had a prominent part: "After his death a certain man was taken up in spirit . . . to hell and saw diverse torments of retribution. Around those there he saw Abbot Richard of Verdun anxiously building towering machines as though constructed for besieging castles. For this abbot worked in death as he had lived, since he had expended almost all of his efforts in constructing useless buildings and had wasted much of the Church's resources in such frivolities."[26]

Public opinion was not behind Peter, however, and most saw Richard's efforts as the height of sanctity. Robert II of Normandy was certainly favorably impressed by Richard's efforts just as his son would be after him, and had generously contributed to the monastery.[27] Richard W. Southern has pointed out what it was that attracted men like William the Conqueror (and at the same time repelled those like Peter Damian):

> Briefly, they expected to find a busy, efficient, orderly community, maintaining an elaborate sequence of church services, which called for a high degree of skill and expert knowledge. They did not expect to find a body of ascetics or contemplatives, and they would have thought it a poor reward for their munificence if they had found marks of poverty in the buildings, dress or equipment of the monks. For them, monasticism was not a flight into desert places undertaken by individuals under the stress of a strong conviction; it was the expression of the corporate religious ideals and needs of a whole community.[28]

One of the most important of these religious needs was the remains of saints. As an integral part of his concern with the tangible evidences of the kingdom of God on earth, Richard craved material contacts with the kingdom of God in heaven. Just as his buildings proclaimed the monastic community's faith in God and his saints, the presence of many holy martyrs proclaimed the reciprocal concern of the saints for the community.

Reports of Richard's passion for relics reach back to his premonastic days in the church of Reims. The account of the miracles of Saint Gengulphus by Abbot Gonzonus of Florennes describes the young Richard as particularly devoted to the relics of Saint John the Baptist kept in the crypt of the cathedral.[29] Richard was charged with safeguarding these relics and evidently spent long hours in the darkened crypt meditating on his charge. This devotion did not prevent him, however, from giving a joint of the protomartyr to Gerardus of Florennes, later the bishop of Cambrai, so that he could build a church in the saint's honor.

It would be pedantic to argue the illegality of that gift, particularly since the story is apocryphal. But the accounts of Richard's youthful devotion to the relics and his disregard of the tenuous legal right of ownership exercised by any church over a saint's remains are certainly characteristic of his later life. The story of his acquisition of the arm of Saint Pantaleon for Saint Vanne is somewhat similar to the one above, except this time Richard was on the receiving end of the transaction. The relic was a gift of the bishop of Cologne to the church of Commercy acquired during his mission to Constantinople to arrange the marriage of Otto II. When Count Odo of Champagne sacked and burned Commercy in 1033 a priest was able to dash through the flames and rescue the arm. Richard was evidently on the scene or happened by shortly afterward and purchased the arm for one mark silver.[30] The arm was subsequently brought to Verdun where he placed it on the altar of Saint Vanne.

In his grandest reconstruction project, that of the church of Saints Peter and Paul at Saint Vanne, Richard was particularly concerned with providing for the physical remains of the church's spiritual protectors. Since the church had originally been the cathedral of Verdun, many of the earliest bishops of the town were buried there. In fact, the presence of these holy men was one of the major reasons that Richard had decided to enter this otherwise unattractive monastery in the first place.[31] Highlights of the renovation were the *inventiones* of the early bishops' tombs and either their restoration or removal to new places of honor. The chronicler Hugo mentions the discovery of the incorrupt bodies of Bishops Madelveus (d. 776) and Berengerius (d. 960), and the transferrals of the bodies of Bishops Hildinus (d. 846), Hatto (d. 870), and Dado (d. 923) to new tombs. Other tombs, such as those of Vitonus (d. 529), Firmin (d. 502), Puleronius (d. 470), and five other unidentified bishops, were left intact but restored and adorned.[32] The basilica's glory was its collection of early bishops and Richard spared no effort or expense to render these protectors the honor they deserved. He also adorned the tombs of the early bishops of Verdun in other churches in the town. Bishops Maurus, Salvinus, and Arator, respectively the second, third, and fourth bishops of Verdun, were properly honored in the church of Saint John which Richard also administered.[33]

The importance Richard attached to the physical presence of these bishops is revealed in his account of the life and miracles of Saint Vanne.[34] Since all of the earlier accounts of

Saint Vanne's life and works had been destroyed by fire, Richard found it necessary to construct a profile of the ideal clerical administrator in the purely hagiographical tradition and his account draws heavily on the *Vita Sancti Maximini abbatis Miciacensis*.[35] When the account reaches the posthumous glory of Saint Vanne, however, Richard presents his own view of the importance of saints' bodies. The universal acceptance of Vanne's sanctity was evidenced, he explains, in the number of foundations in his name not only in the diocese of Verdun, but elsewhere. These churches "rejoice" in the power of his relics even more than in their grants of immunity, "since the holy bishops, his successors, when they built new churches in his name sanctified them with relics from his body."[36] Richard's comparison of these relics with the legal protectors of religious institutions shows that he considered them the more potent weapons in a church's arsenal protecting it from spiritual or material encroachments. But these foundations, he continues, possessing as they do only fragments of the saint, are but dim reflections of the church which houses his tomb: ". . . how much more powerfully does the greatness of his sanctity shine forth in the sanctuary of this basilica in which the dust of his sacred body has been known since earliest times to be buried."[37]

What was true of the body of the titular patron of the monastery was true of the other bishops. Richard perceived them as allies against monastic enemies, spiritual or material. The proof of their potency was demonstrated by the miracles of healing they effected in behalf of pilgrims who came to Saint Vanne seeking their intercession.

The only bishop missing from Richard's collection was by far the most important—Saint Sanctinus, the first bishop of Verdun. This Sanctinus's background and literally every aspect of the history of his cult is clouded in obscurity. According to Hincmar of Reims, Sanctinus was a disciple of Saint Dionysius and the first bishop of Meaux near St. Denis.[38] Bertarius, the early tenth-century author of the *Gesta pontificum Sanctae Verdunensis ecclesiae*, states that this same Sanctinus was also the first bishop of Verdun. Writing

after the episcopal archives in Verdun had been destroyed by
fire, Bertarius names as his source a lost *Vita Sancti Servati*.
Concerning the location of the body of the saint, he states,
"Where however his body may now be buried, we have been
unable to discover, unless it be in Meaux."[39] The only other
independent document prior to the eleventh century which
connects Sanctinus with Verdun is the forged proceedings of
the false Council of Cologne, which were written in the
eighth century based on some earlier documents.[40] Here is
listed a bishop "Sanctinus Articlauorum aut Urbis Clauo-
run," a location identified by Yvette Dollinger-Leonard as
Verdun.[41] Although various scholars have tried to identify
two men in this confusion, to deny the existence of one or
the other of these "little saints," or to dismiss both as spurious, a decisive definitive solution is impossible and, for our
purpose, unnecessary.[42] In Richard's day Sanctinus was acknowledged to have been the first bishop of Meaux and of
Verdun. Moreover, Richard and his contemporaries knew
that no less an authority than Bertarius had stated his belief
that Sanctinus was buried in Meaux, where in fact a monastery existed under his patronage.

As dynamic and enterprising a man as Abbot Richard
would hardly have remained deprived of the relics of the
first evangelist of Verdun, and, in fact, by 1039 a donation
to Saint Vanne mentions the presence of Sanctinus's body in
the monastery church of Saint Peter and Paul.[43] Just how he
got there, if indeed he did, is uncertain.

Neither of Richard's hagiographers mentions the transfer
of Sanctinus to Verdun—a surprising omission considering
its importance. However, a manuscript from Saint Vanne
written in the late eleventh century tells a remarkable story
of Sanctinus's translation.[44] According to the text a certain
monk of Saint Vanne, Richard (not necessarily Abbot Richard), was traveling to Chartres and found it necessary to
spend a night in Meaux. There he met an old priest who,
upon learning that Richard was from Verdun, asked him if
he knew of Sanctinus. When Richard replied affirmatively,
adding that his body was believed to be at Saint Vanne, the

priest agreed and told him how it came to be transported there from Meaux. He related that there had been a famine in Meaux so great that the town was deserted by everyone except four priests, himself among them, who had been appointed by the bishop to guard the relics and other ecclesiastical valuables. Shortly thereafter merchants of Verdun returning from Spain stopped in the town and asked to be allowed to spend the night in the church. As they spoke with the priests, their conversation turned to the relics stored there, and when they learned that one was the remains of Sanctinus, they asked the priests to sell them the body of Verdun's first bishop. Won over by the size of the bribe, the priests broke their oath and handed over the relics to the merchants, who returned joyously to Verdun praising and glorifying God.

This text's importance has long been recognized by economic historians since it mentions Verdun merchants returning burdened with riches from Spain. But its historicity is questionable. Various theories have been offered. In the nineteenth century Clouet suggested that the purchase had taken place in 954 during the Hungarian invasions.[45] In disagreement, Dauphin points out that the tenth-century enumerations of the bodies venerated at Verdun make no mention of Sanctinus's presence there.[46] He suggests instead that the translation took place immediately prior to the composition of the document mentioning his presence in Verdun, that is to say before 1039, and further suggests that the translation took place during a famine in the year 1032. Dauphin objects to dismissing the entire story as a fabrication since in the thirteenth century Meaux gave some of Sanctinus's relics to St. Denis.[47]

On its own merits, the account is either a fabrication or at least a highly inventive version of what actually happened. First, its complete lack of chronological information, omitting names of historical personages such as the bishop of Meaux, or even the day of the year on which the translation was supposed to have taken place makes it suspect. Second, its reliance on such hagiographical *topoi* as the *senex*, the account of the famine, and the arguments of the merchants, indicates that it belongs to the realm of hagiography rather than history. But the most telling indictment is the very neatness with which it reconciles the two towns' traditions concerning Sanctinus. The author was obviously familiar with the tradition that made Sanctinus first bishop of Verdun and of Meaux. Likewise, he knew that Meaux had a strong claim to possess the body of the saint, a claim strengthened by the testimony of a priest of Verdun, Bertarius. Rather than denying Bertarius, then, the author makes Sanctinus the evangelist of both towns and acknowledges that he was buried in Meaux. In order to establish a claim for Verdun's possession of the body, he fabricates the story of the purchase and, in a neat turnabout of the *Gesta*, attempts to lend it credibility by putting the entire account in the mouth of a priest of Meaux.

Of course, Abbot Richard may have acquired the body, or at any rate a body, from merchants returning to Verdun. The route passing from Verdun to Reims, Meaux, and Paris, and then south through Orléans, Poitiers, Bordeaux, and then into Spain was well known and used in the eleventh century.[48] Slaves were the principal items of commerce, but returning merchants would certainly have been willing to provide a wealthy and eager abbot with so valuable an item as the remains of Sanctinus. As is clear from his *vita*, Richard was eager to purchase relics whenever he had the opportunity, and of all the relics that might have been offered to him, this one was the most desirable.

The relative value of relics varies as that of any valuable commodity existing in a very limited number: as the number of these objects already owned increases, the relative value of those needed to complete the collection also increases. At Saint Vanne or in other churches in Verdun, Richard had the remains of all the other great bishops of the town. He could hardly have refused the opportunity to purchase or "invent" the body of the last and most important bishop. Given his faith in and dedication to the remains of Verdun's saints, Richard was almost certainly responsible for the *Translatio Sancti Sanctini*.

EVOLUTION OF RELIGIOUS SENTIMENT

Traditions of *furta sacra* did not always originate in monasteries lacking powerful patrons. In some cases the monasteries involved in the creation of these traditions were forced by changing fashions in saints to acquire the remains of a new patron more attractive to popular tastes. New cults appeared at established devotional centers, and in time these new devotions became focused on purported relics of the honored saint. The religious institution which housed these relics then had to explain how the saint's body had arrived. The evolution of the cult of Mary Magdalene at Vézelay during the eleventh and early twelfth centuries clearly exhibited this twofold pattern of evolution: first, the Gallic saints replaced Roman ones in popularity, and second, the resulting cult of the Magdalene initially produced the saint's body and then a series of increasingly elaborate accounts of how it had arrived in Burgundy.

Victor Saxer has traced the various stages of the cult of this composite saint from its origins in the early eleventh century, into the first quarter of the twelfth when it takes on its widespread importance, and even further to the end of the Middle Ages.[49] The devotion to Mary Magdalene at Vézelay, which apparently already existed in the 1020's, received a major impetus during the abbacy of Geoffroy (1037–1052). The abbot may have first developed a personal devotion to this composite saint[50] as a result of his association with Erminfroi of Verdun, a contemporary of Richard of Saint Vanne of Verdun and founder of a church dedicated to her in 1022.[51] Thanks to the efforts of Geoffroy, Leo IX agreed to the issuing of a bull on April 27, 1050, naming Mary Magdalene as one of the patrons of Vézelay.[52] Rapidly she became the only patroness of the monastery, eclipsing, in the manner of Saint Foy of Conques, Saints Peter, Paul, Andeolus, Pontian, and even the Virgin Mary. The Magdalene could not remain patroness in spirit alone, she had to be physically present. By 1050 a second papal bull had recognized the presence of her remains at Vézelay.[53]

At first, the manner in which the saint had reached Vézelay was not known. The earliest hagiographical text that recounts Geoffroy's efforts on her behalf and the cult's development explains that these details are not important. To people who asked how the relics of the saint were transferred from Judea to Gaul, one could answer simply that "all things are possible with God."[54]

This explanation may have sufficed for the monks of the community, but more critical minds soon sought a more detailed explanation. By 1024–25 the *Gesta episcoporum Cameracensium* explained that the monk Baidilo had brought the body with him from a pilgrimage to Jerusalem.[55] Today this account might appear as good as any other but by the twelfth century it was no longer adequate. According to Sigebert de Gembloux, Count Girard carried the relics to Vézelay from Aix-en-Provence in the year 745 in order to protect them from the Saracens.[56] In its final form, elaborated and perfected during the course of the twelfth century and affected by the popularity of Count Girard in the *chansons de geste*,[57] the *translatio* takes on all of the characteristics of the Aquitanian accounts, as follows. Sometime in the mid-eighth century, during the rule of Louis the Pious (!), Provence is laid waste by the Saracens. (Or alternately the time is the rule of Carloman and Pepin, and the devastators may be the Normans.)[58] Count Girard of Burgundy and Abbot Heudo of Vézelay (founded in 858)[59] send the monk Baidilo to Aix-en-Provence to acquire the remains of the saint. He arrives to find the town filled with pestilence and death. Baidilo spends only a few moments weeping at the sight and proceeds to the main church where he finds a group of old men. He inquires after the remains of the

Magdalene, and in return for food the men lead him to it. Later he returns by night and finds the body incorrupt and giving off a fragrant odor. A vision of the saint assures him that she approves of the removal from the destroyed city and so he takes the body and returns home.[60]

Just how Mary Magdalene had gotten to Provence in the first place is recounted in the *Vita apostolica beatae Mariae Magdalenae*.[61] After the ascension, Lazarus and his two sisters were driven from Palestine by Jewish persecution and landed in Marseille. Mary went into solitude to live a life of penance in the surrounding wilderness, but near the end of her life she returned to civilization and was buried in Aix. As a matter of fact, as early as 1102 there was a devotion to Saints Maximus, Lazarus, and Mary Magdalene in Provence.[62] A superficial examination of the two stories would suggest that the *translatio* served, as did the *Translatio Sancti Sanctini*, to appropriate the legend of Mary Magdalene in Provence for Vézelay's benefit. But as Saxer points out, the *Vita apostolica*, far from being a creation of the south, in fact emanates from Vézelay itself.[63] Aix's claims to possess the body rest on a late twelfth or early thirteenth-century forgery claiming to be an encyclical of Bishop Rostan d'Hyeres (1056–1082) mentioning the tombs of Maximus, Mary Magdalene, and Lazarus.[64] Why, then, did the hagiographers of Vézelay feel called upon to alter the original account of the acquisition of the body from Jerusalem and to substitute an account of a theft? The answer probably lies in the great appeal of the theft account and its correlation with two related phenomena: the popularity of Gallic saints and the pilgrimage to Saint Foy of Conques.

The rising popularity of Mary Magdalene had effaced that of Saints Andeolus and Pontian as patrons of Vézelay. According to tradition, the remains of these saints had been acquired in the ninth century by the founder of Vézelay, Count Girard of Vienne, from Pope Nicholas I.[65] The popular basis for this belief was the popularity of Roman relics in the ninth and tenth centuries. But by the eleventh and twelfth centuries, the vogue of purely Roman martyrs was clearly on the decline in France, and the most desirable relics were those of Frankish saints, or at least of those saints who in their lifetimes had been associated with Roman or Merovingian Gaul. This tendency began with Saint Dionysius, identified throughout the Middle Ages as the disciple of Saint Paul. In the eleventh and twelfth centuries more and more saints of the Apostolic Church were credited with at least a visit to Gaul. Among these were Lazarus, Mary Magdalene, and Joseph of Arimathea. This phenomenon might result from an increasing sense of regional identity on the part of the French, and a related desire to establish a direct connection between their homeland and the apostolic heroes. More realistically, Victor Saxer suggests that the popularity of these saints in Provence was the result of an effort on the part of ecclesiastical officials to promote the recovery of churches severely damaged by the Saracens in the tenth century.[66] Another important factor, particularly in Burgundy, was the desire to compete with Compostela and its Apostolic shrine. Not only had James been buried in Spain, but he had been the first Apostle to the Iberian peninsula. Through the eleventh and twelfth centuries Burgundy, primarily through the agency of Cluny, had provided many of the pilgrims to Compostela as well as the knights who participated in the reconquest.[67]

The pilgrimage from Burgundy towards Compostela provides the second important element in the origin of the theft account—the popularity of Saint Foy. Pilgrims to Compostela passed through Conques, which was one of the most important shrines on the Auvergne route to Spain.[68] As early as 1086, pilgrims and donations from Burgundy bore witness to the popularity of Conques in the west of France.[69] By the middle of the eleventh century, pilgrims to Conques had introduced a devotion to Mary Magdalene at Conques inspired by that of Vézelay.[70]

The two cults had similarities which help to explain their popularity. Both were established around thaumaturgia, both were established in the semimythical Carolingian age, both were on the pilgrimage route to Compostela. However, Conques had something more in its favor. Saint Foy was a Gallic saint associated in her lifetime with the early days of the Church in Gaul. Her life and death had been recently celebrated in a vernacular *chanson* which, while incomprehensible to pilgrims from the north and west, certainly showed her widespread popularity. One need not see any willful deceit on the part of the hagiographers of Vézelay in suggesting these lines of thought: all truly great saints and patrons of France were associated in their lifetimes with France. Mary Magdalene was such a great patroness. On the other hand, Vézelay did not exist in the early Christian period. Hence, Burgundian hagiographers explained, she must have been first in Provence. For details on how she arrived in Burgundy, they looked to the widely known account of the translation of that other great saint of the eleventh century, Saint Foy.

LAY ENCROACHMENT

Monasteries feared the loss of their *spiritualia* to other monasteries; they feared the loss of their *temporalia* to local nobles. Here too a new patron often proved a valuable weapon against the monastery's enemies. How the theft of a saint might work to combat this threat can be seen in the circumstances that led to the composition of the *Translatio Sancti Maiani*, yet another furtive *translatio*.[71]

According to the *Vita Sancti Maiani*[72] the saint had been in his lifetime a staunch defender of his church in Gascony where he settled after a pilgrimage to Compostela. He protected his flock both from the devil, who ravished the countryside in the form of a dragon, and against godless nobles whom he prevented from sacking his church. The *translatio* tells how, sometime after his death, two monks from the Bitterois monastery of Colognac who had heard about the many miracles brought about through the intercession of Maianus decided to go in search of his relics. With the permission of their abbot they traveled into Gascony and, locating the church where Maianus was buried, professed a desire to settle in the area. They remained working the land and cultivating vineyards until the local populace had accepted them without suspicion. Then one night they secretly entered the church, opened the tomb and took the relics. When the inhabitants realized what had happened, they set out after the two but lost the trail in a great forest. The two monks then proceeded to their monastery where the relics were joyfully received. The name of the saint spread throughout the Bitterois and in time the monastery changed its name to *Vallemagnae* in his honor.

The *translatio*, although it presents details that were intended to place the date of the translation in the ninth century, is a fabrication. The date is impossible, the story concerning the name of the monastery is false, and other evidence points to a date of composition no earlier than the beginning of the eleventh century.[73] The text was probably written at Villemagne in an effort to establish a claim on the remains of a saint who had proven himself a match for the local lord, Viscount William of Béziers.

A number of miracle accounts follow the *translatio* itself, the principal one taking place at the monastery of Saint Tiberius to which the relics had been brought by monks of Villemagne attending a local synod. Also present was a "Guillelmus viscomes Biterrensis" whose servant was miraculously cured through the intercession of the saint.

Although there was no Viscount William of Béziers in the ninth century, there was one from ca. 979 until 993[74] who was certainly involved with the monastery of Saint Tiberius, although his dealings with it were not always amicable. He apparently had confiscated considerable property from the monastery and toward the end of his life, in 990, he returned what he had taken along with other properties before setting out on pilgrimage to Rome with his wife.[75] Before leaving, he attended a synod at Narbonne convened for the purpose of condemning lay seizure of church property.[76] Probably at this synod, overcome with remorse or fearing his imminent death, he made out his will which included donations to a number of local ecclesiastical institutions, among them Saint Tiberius.[77]

In this same year William's wife Arisnid wrote her will which included a donation to the monastery of Saint Martin of Villemagne, but contained no mention of Saint Maianus or of his cult.[78] William's will mentioned the cult in the diocese of Béziers, but not in connection with either of the two abovementioned monasteries. William made a donation "to Saint Peter's of the city of Agde, the manse which is in the villa of Maianus, with its fields and vineyards and all those equipages which pertain to that manse."[79] Maianus did not become a titular patron of Villemagne until some time during the next fifteen years.[80] By the time that Villemagne was claiming the saint, both Saint Tiberius and the castle of Rojan were also claiming him. The reason for this sudden popularity of Maianus around Béziers may well be related to the cure of Viscount William's retainer and his change of heart.

To suggest that Maianus was responsible for the viscount's return of the lands he had expropriated from Saint Tiberius is not necessarily to imply that William was simply overcome with gratitude and gave up his sinful life. The reality was certainly much more complex. William was at a local synod attended by clergy and nobles. Also present was Saint Maianus (whether accompanying the delegation from Villemagne, Saint Tiberius, or some other party is not certain). Furthermore, Maianus had had in his lifetime a reputation for vigorous defense of the Church against its opponents. No indication of the business of the synod was given, but one can imagine that the dispute between the monastery and William was on people's minds. And then one of William's retainers was brought before the relics of the saint and miraculously cured. Such a public display of grace accorded the viscount by the power of religion could hardly go unreciprocated; the opinion of those present would have been too greatly outraged by such a show of ingratitude. And if Maianus could work miracles to cure William's followers, he could just as easily work curses to injure them. These and similar considerations reinforced at the Council of Narbonne, probably led him to his decision to undertake his pilgrimage to Rome, and before leaving to restore to their owners the properties he had confiscated.

But what was the relationship between Maianus and Saint Tiberius? Why should the saint have intervened on behalf of another monastery if he was the patron of Villemagne? In all likelihood his cult was not localized in Villemagne in the late tenth century, but existed at Saint Tiberius, Rojan, and elsewhere. Saint Tiberius's monastery claimed to possess the body by virtue of an eighth-century donation of an oratory in Lombez wherein lay the body of Maianus.[81] The diploma is a forgery of the tenth or eleventh century, but nevertheless is evidence of Saint Tiberius's claim. Finally, the *translatio* mentions that the castle of Rojan was also claiming to have obtained the body.

Thus as the reputation of Maianus grew as a defender of the church after the conversion of the viscount, several locations sought to appropriate the saint and his growing reputation for knowing how to deal with feudal lords. Saint Tiberius, which probably had the prior claim since the miracle was worked at that institution, did so by means of a forged diploma. Villemagne accomplished the same thing with the story of a *furtum sacrum*. By insisting that the relics were stolen rather than acquired by some other ordinary means, Villemagne could circumvent the claims of the monastery of Saint Tiberius to have received the original tomb of Maianus from the count of Aquitaine, without having to prove either that the document on which Saint Tiberius rested its claim was false or that at some earlier date the monks of Tiberius had been willing to part with these relics. The *furtum* account was equally effective against the claims of Rojan. Since the theft had been done long ago in the semimythical Carolingian period, these more recent claims would lack authority.

Conclusion

Need for funds, competition with other monasteries, spiritual protection against lay excesses, shifts in religious sentiment—one could multiply examples of these general cases many times over without significantly altering our perception of what sort of circumstances might have given rise to a furtive *translatio*. If, however, one goes beyond the particulars of local history which set the scene for the creation of these *translationes* and considers analytically the entire corpus of monastic thefts, characteristics emerge that unite most of these *translationes* into one of three groups according to location: the Rhineland, southern France, and the northwest—Normandy, Brittany, and Flanders. Each of these groups is defined by more than mere geographical coincidence, since each betrays a distinctive cultural and religious unity.

The Frankish elite's preoccupation with Italy and especially with Rome that was so evident in the Carolingian Empire continued in the Rhineland throughout the central Middle Ages. Given the focus of the empire politically and culturally, this continuity is natural. Virtually all of the thefts are from Italy and repeatedly the particular account is adopted directly or indirectly from Einhard's *translatio*: a German abbot or monk goes to Italy on business; there he is inflamed with the desire for a certain saint's remains; he enters a church at night and with greater or lesser difficulty is able to remove the body of the martyr, which he brings back with him to his monastery.

The saints throughout the period are very similar to those sought in the 820's. They are early Christian saints and martyrs: Pope Callistus, Gregory the Great, the Empress Helen, Chrysogonus and Anastasia, Epiphanius and Speciosa.[82] They are well known saints with long-established cults. For the imperial Church just as for the imperial government, Roman tradition will remain the source of spiritual direction.

The differences between the Rhineland and the south and west are immediate and striking. Clearly the religious ideals of Einhard and Hilduin were alien to these older areas of Gaul. In the south, the saints worth stealing were exclusively local or Spanish: Vincent, Fausta, Foy, Maianus, Bibanus.[83] Apparently, in order to inspire the local population to devotion and generosity, monasteries sought to establish ties with the glorious past of Aquitaine's ancient faith and to return to the roots of that faith via the saintly contemporaries of Sulpicius Severus and Gregory of Tours. These saints were not outstanding abbots or bishops, but rather, with the exception of Bibanus, bishop of Saintes, virgins and confessors whose religious excellence was apparently outside of the Church hierarchy.

The saints of the northwest coast were likewise local saints, with the exception of Lewinna. Here they were bishops of the early Christian period in Normandy and Brittany: Nicasius, Sulpitius, Ebrulfus.[84] In these regions, continuity with early Christianity was apparently sought in the episcopal hierarchy rather than in confessors and virgins.

Yet another striking contrast between the Roman saints favored in the east and the local saints of the west was that most of the latter appear to have been extremely or even totally obscure at the time of their alleged translations. In Aquitaine Fausta and Maianus were entirely unknown while Foy and Bibanus were, even at the time of their supposed thefts, relatively obscure. In the west this obscurity is even more profound: Lewinna was quite unknown, even in Sussex; Sulpitius cannot even be attached to an authentic pretranslation tradition that would make him bishop of Bayeux. The same darkness settles on the Norman saints who were the objects of English thefts.

These saints may have enjoyed a much wider popularity and devotion in the early Middle Ages than our documents indicate, but this is unlikely. Even the monastic communities to which the saints were said to have been translated confused them with saints with similar names or described them in *vitae* that, even for hagiographical texts, were unenlightening. Apparently these saints were as obscure then as now. This very obscurity may explain why they were said to have been stolen. As in the case of Lewinna, all knowledge of these saints began with their theft. Hagiographers could not report any more than the most typical details of their lives and their martyrdoms. Without pasts to give them appeal and authenticate their power, these saints appear on the scene with a flourish at the moment of their translation. Thus the accounts of their acquisitions had to be of the sort to excite the imagination of the faithful, both within and outside the community. The importance of this creative memory will again be critical when we consider the functions of the furtive *translatio* in communal histories.

A second preoccupation in the *translationes* from the south and the west are the Norman invasions. Between 856 and 862, and then sporadically over the next decades, Aquitaine was ravaged by repeated expeditions. The west coast of France was subjected to the most serious and long-range effects of efforts to pillage and then colonize the Atlantic seaboard. However, due to the nature of the historical sources on these invasions, students of the subject, at the turn of the century Lot[85] and Vogel,[86] and most recently Musset[87] and D'Haenens,[88] cannot say exactly what effect these sporadic invasions had on the economy and population of Aquitaine. To judge from the abandonment of rural and urban churches in the wake of these invasions, a phenomenon common enough that fictitious accounts of translations seemed plausible to subsequent generations, the effects would have been considerable. The *translationes* speak of the removal of relics from abandoned churches that lie without exception along the Garonne within thirty miles from the river. The burning of these churches is documented, and often chronicles speak of the desertion of monasteries or towns for years. These accounts are surely exaggerated, but they suggest a depopulation of this area with a shift in population toward Limousin, Auvergne, and Provence.

The actual facts of the Norman incursions are only part
of the explanation for the development of this historical-ha-
giographical tradition. More important was the magnified
recollection of these invasions during the following centuries. Because of the discontinuity of communal life and loss
of records, almost anything could have happened at the
time. Those hazy years were not only terrifying in the collective memory of future generations but also convenient for
dating uncertain or unlikely occurrences in the lives of religious communities. Destruction of written documents at the
hands of the invaders was in retrospect a most fortunate occurrence for, in many instances, the documents could be re-
produced with "more than total recall," guaranteeing privileges that monasteries had not had but felt they should have
had. From the safe perspective of the eleventh century, the
Normans were no longer the terrible invaders to be feared,
but rather, in a sense, allies against the pretensions of other
communities or hostile local lords.

These hagiographic traditions also point out the monasteries' real posture in relationship to the aristocracy of the surrounding areas. For a time, under the Carolingians, and
later in the twelfth and thirteenth centuries, the presentation
of diplomas of immunity or charters of donation would have
some force to preserve the rights of a religious institution in
the face of lay encroachment. But in the later ninth century
and certainly through the tenth and the beginning of the eleventh, law was not the most efficient way of preserving justice. Not in a position to use force, monasteries naturally
had to win lay support and respect by the spiritual prestige
of their patrons. For a person like Viscount William of Béziers, the advantages to be gained by enlisting the help of Saint
Maianus to intercede for him would undoubtedly have been
more persuasive than were charters to make him restore to
the monastery of Saint Tiberius the property he had annexed
from it. A monastery without a powerful patron had little
hope of justice at the hands of those who understood only
force, whether physical or spiritual. In a dispute between

two religious communities, as between Conques and Figeac or Solignac and Beaulieu, the monastery particularly favored by the presence of the remains of a great miracle worker was undoubtedly in the stronger position.

A final important element that contributed to the development of the Aquitanian group of *translationes* was the growth of pilgrimages to and through the south of France. By the twelfth century, the routes to Compostela were a primary source of income and prestige for those monasteries which, like Conques and quite possibly Villemagne, were located on them. During the preceding centuries, as these routes were being defined, the acquisition of a saint's miracle-working remains that might attract some of these pilgrims was vital. Thus the struggle for preeminence between Conques and Figeac was not merely a spiritual competition, but also a dispute over who would benefit from the vast numbers of pilgrims on their way to Compostela.

As the pilgrim traffic grew in the eleventh and twelfth centuries, the accounts of earlier thefts spread, and thus the fame of a stolen virgin's body served to promote the fame of a distant converted prostitute, Mary Magdalene.

We have examined the motivations that prompted elaboration of *furta sacra* legends in the rural monastic world of transalpine Europe. But below the Alps a very different kind of medieval world was developing—a world based on commerce and composed of small, highly competitive cities. Here too thefts of relics had their place in the life of Christian communities. The function of these thefts and the forms in which the thefts were recorded were in marked contrast to those of the north.

CHAPTER FIVE

Urban Thefts

J UST AS THE emerging character of feudal Europe produced a special, localized *furta sacra* tradition, the Italian cities—preoccupied as they were with the East during the central Middle Ages—produced their own type. Most of the translations beyond the Alps were effected by monks in behalf of their monasteries; in Italy, the agents were usually laymen bent on acquiring patrons for their towns. The victims of these thefts were eastern Christians, particularly Greeks, for whom the Italians displayed a mixture of envy and distrust.[1] But since this disdain for Greek customs, dress, and liturgical practice was accompanied by a firsthand knowledge of the Byzantine Empire, Italians were in a position to take advantage of the increasingly weakened position of the Byzantines. In particular, Italian envy of the East's great store of saints resulted in a number of thefts culminating in the sack of Constantinople in 1204 when the Venetians carried off the city's choicest relics.[2] But the events of 1204 were the climax of a tradition already four centuries old, which had seen relics stolen from the empire not only by Venice but by other Italian towns.

The most significant thefts of relics perpetrated by the Italian cities during the central Middle Ages, both for their local history and for the history of the cult of saints in the West, were the translations of Saint Mark from Alexandria and of Saint Nicolas from Myra. Although these events were separated by over two centuries, they were similar both in the details of the accounts and in the events that led up to their being written. Considered together, they indicate much about the relationships between the religious devotion and the secular preoccupations of Italian merchant communities, which greatly differed from those of their northern rural contemporaries.

Equally remarkable both in these *translationes* and in the account of the attempted theft of the remains of Saint Appianus from Comacchio is the corporate nature of these enterprises. Instead of two men working alone on behalf of their community as in monastic thefts, these thefts were perpetrated by groups of citizens who thoroughly organized their expeditions in a carefully planned and coordinated effort to achieve their goals. In Bari, the group involved in the theft of Saint Nicolas, known soon after as the *Societas Sancti Nicolai*, even went on to become the dominant social, political, and religious body of that town.

For northern monasteries, the theft of relics had been a solution to their problems of monastic rivalry or threats from local lords; Italian communities faced other crises which led them to *furta sacra*. These towns were struggling toward autonomy, both from the Byzantine Empire and from the dominant power in Italy at the time: in the ninth century, from the Carolingians; in the eleventh century, from the Normans. Economic rivalry was another serious problem, and the presence of a widely honored saint could provide the means of establishing or maintaining economic power and a competitive position vis-à-vis other cities.

"Translatio Sancti Marci"

The political and economic precocity that characterized Venetian history throughout the Middle Ages is evidenced in the acquisition of the body of Saint Mark from Alexandria in 827. Although the Venetians, like their northern contemporaries, reacted to crisis by claiming to have stolen the remains of a saint, the circumstances in which Venice found itself in the year 827 and the particular literary account that purported to describe their response to this crisis both indicate the very different, cosmopolitan world of ninth-century

Venice. Over two centuries later, when another Italian city, Bari, reached a somewhat similar level of sophistication, it looked to the Venetian example for a solution to another grave crisis. Every aspect of the translation of Saint Mark has been studied with greater attention than has any other relic theft because of its acknowledged pivotal importance in the history of Venice. A century of scholarship has established an acceptable account of this famous theft.[3]

In 827 Venice was, as usual, attempting to maintain the maximum possible independence from Carolingian Italy on the one hand and from the Byzantine Empire on the other, without completely giving up good relations with either. The Carolingians currently presented the graver threat. Over the past several decades, Charlemagne and his son Louis had failed to gain political and military control over the Venetian estuary, but they had not given up hope of gaining at least ecclesiastical control. In 827 the Carolingians scored a major victory over the Greek Churches of the Adriatic, particularly the Venetian, at the Synod of Mantua.[4] The occasion of the synod was an effort to end the centuries-old conflict between Aquileia and Grado for episcopal primacy. The details and arguments of the earlier phases of the dispute need not concern us here, but the Church of Grado argued that when Patriarch Paul of Aquileia fled to Grado in the face of the Lombard invasion, taking with him the relics of the church, he had permanently established the patriarchate in that city. Since Venice claimed that a similar flight from Grado to the Rialto had been the occasion of her foundation, the question of the preeminence of the two sees was ultimately the right to the title of patriarchate and thus, ultimately, to ecclesiastical independence. At Mantua the Aquileian party appeared with a staggering array of falsified documents and spurious arguments designed to show that their Church had never lost its right to primacy over the region.[5] Not surprisingly, the Carolingian bishops meeting in Carolingian Mantua decided in favor of Carolingian Aquileia, particularly since, aside from the historical and ecclesiastical arguments put forth, the bishops particularly considered

... that the clerics and the lay nobles chosen by the people of
Istria came to the holy synod asking that they, freed from the
most pernicious bond of the Greeks, might return to Aquileia,
their metropolitan city to which they had been subject in ancient times, because those elected and ordained had first to
swear fealty to our most pious imperators [Louis and Lothair]
and then to the faith of the Greeks, and hence they said themselves to be burdened and insisted that they were unable to
serve two masters.[6]

Obviously, the Carolingian emperors were not concerned about establishing the relative merits of rival historical claims but rather with the question of ecclesiastical and
hence political domination of the area. Louis, whose policy
everywhere in his empire was to establish conformity in religious and liturgical practice, would not abandon the people
of Istria, and thus of the entire area, to the Greeks.

Venetian reaction to the ecclesiastical argument used to
support the political decision ultimately resulted in the deter-
mination to steal the body of Saint Mark. By the time of the
synod it was believed that the founder of the Church of
Aquileia had been none other than Mark the Evangelist, sent
from Rome by Peter himself to convert northern Italy. Hence
it was the most venerable see of northern Italy in spite of its
later abandonment in the face of Lombard invasions, and it
was to this patriarchate that Grado (and hence Venice) owed
allegiance.

This decision in favor of Aquileia, had it gone unchal-
lenged, would have amounted to a major setback for the Venetians' efforts toward autonomy. Naturally, the Doge Gius-
tiniano Particiaco and his churchmen could not countenance
such a defeat. Particiaco looked for the most effective
method of neutralizing this synodal decree, and he found a
way in the acquisition of the body of Saint Mark. The choice
could not have been better; the benefits of this acquisition
only began by allowing a claim of superiority by the church
possessing the body of a near-Apostle over one merely
founded by him.

First, the importance of Apostolic sees was well established, and in Italy belief in the superiority of churches possessing the remains of Apostles had a venerable tradition by
the ninth century. Most obvious of course was the Apostolic
character of the Church of Rome with the tombs of Peter
and Paul. But since the time of Saint Ambrose, northern Italian towns which could not claim Apostolic foundation for
their churches had been carefully acquiring relics of apostles
for religious and political reasons. The bishop of Milan
began this tradition himself; he placed Apostolic relics in his
own church and then made gifts of these relics to the
churches of Concordia, Aquileia, Lodi, and Brescia.[7] In the
following century Ravenna received relics of Andrew, John
the Evangelist, Peter, and Paul.[8] In an effort to bolster the ecclesiastical importance of Ravenna vis-à-vis Milan, Rome,
and Aquileia, in the mid-sixth century Maximus translated
to Ravenna relics of John the Baptist, John the Evangelist,
Andrew, Thomas, and four other Apostles.[9] Venice was following a long-accepted tradition in seeking out the body of
Mark.

Apart from the choice of Mark because of his
identification with the church of Aquileia, the decision was
important in another sense; it was clearly a step away from
Byzantine influence in the city. Mark was preeminently the
Italian evangelist. His gospel had been written in Rome for
Italians and he was honored as the apostle to a major portion of the Italian Church. When his body arrived in Venice,
it was clearly destined for great things since it was not
placed in any of the city's preexisting churches but was evidently kept in the ducal palace. A special chapel was built to
house the saint, located between the palace and the chapel
dedicated to Saint Theodore, the Byzantine equivalent of
Saint George and patron of the doges.[10] Mark was intended
to replace Theodore as patron of Venice, and this progressive replacement is evidenced in the following centuries by
the gradual eradication of all memory of Theodore. Following the destruction of the ducal palace and chapel in the re-
volt of 976, the chapels were rebuilt,[11] but the Byzantine war-

rior was allowed to vanish entirely in the restoration of 1094.[12]

It is impossible to say what actually took place in 827 when the relics were acquired. The first mention is found in the will of Doge Particiaco (died 828) in which he directed "concerning the body of blessed Mark, I wish that my wife build a basilica in his honor within the territory of Saint Zacharias."[13] Modern scholars disagree on the value of this text as evidence of the presence of the body in Venice in the ninth century. Silvio Tramontin is convinced that the text is genuine,[14] but Antonio Niero suggests that it is either a later interpolation or that it refers to something other than the actual presence of the body of Saint Mark in Venice.[15] If genuine, the text is the only ninth-century evidence of the translation. However, the destruction of the Venetian archives in the tenth century[16] makes it impossible to argue *ex silentio* that the translation did not take place. The only other pertinent source which may date from that century is a statement of a certain Bevado who made a pilgrimage to the Holy Land around the 850's and later wrote an account of his journey.[17] On his return home he claims to have stopped in Alexandria hoping to visit the tomb of Mark, but was unable to do so because the body was in Venice. Even if one suspects interpolation in the text, the fact that the earliest manuscript of the account dates from the tenth century proves at least that by that time the story of the translation was well known.

The *Translatio Sancti Marci*, composed some time prior to the eleventh century, gives a complete account of the relics' arrival in Venice.[18] The text begins with a recapitulation of the tradition that made Mark the apostle to Aquileia and describes how, at the time of the Lombard invasion, Patriarch Paul fled to Grado with the bodies of Saint Hermacora and the other patrons of the Aquileian church. Later, according to the introduction, a similar flight to Venice took place in the face of subsequent Lombard attacks. The body of the text recounts that, in the time of the Doge Particiaco, two Venetian merchants, Bonus and Rusticus, were in Alexandria when the Saracen rulers of that city decreed that marble columns and tablets might be taken from Christian churches for the construction of a new palace. The custodians of the church of Saint Mark were saddened by the thought that their church might be destroyed, and when the Venetians heard the reason for their sorrow, they offered to take the body and the two most important custodians—the monk Stauricius and the priest Theodorus—home with them to Venice. The two Greeks were properly shocked by this suggestion and reminded the Venetians that Mark had been the first apostle to Alexandria. Then Bonus and Rusticus replied by telling the story of Mark's mission to Aquileia and asserted that they were Mark's first-born sons since they had first received the gospel from him. The discussions went on secretly until, after one of the custodians had been seized and whipped by Saracens for hiding a marble tablet from the church, the two Greeks agreed to cooperate with the Venetians. At night they secretly removed the body of Mark and replaced it with that of Saint Claudia. The body gave off a fragrant odor which spread throughout the city. The inhabitants were suspicious and checked the tomb, but finding the body of Claudia they failed to detect Mark's removal. The Venetians put the body under pieces of pork and returned to their ship. On the way they were stopped by Saracens who, on examining their cargo, saw the pork and left in disgust. The Venetians sailed for home accompanied by Stauricius and after a miraculous voyage arrived at the island of Umago, where they hesitated for fear that the doge would be angry with them for having gone illegally to Alexandria. Naturally, when the doge learned of the treasure they brought with them, he welcomed them into the city as his sons and the body was placed in the doge's palace. He intended to build a chapel to house the remains, but death interrupted the plan. The task was completed by his brother John.

The proximity of the composition of the *translatio* to the events it purports to describe cannot be established with certainty. Its editor N. McCleary placed it between 1050 and 1094.[19] However, the Bollandist Baudouin de Gaiffier discovered a tenth-century manuscript of the *translatio* copied in Fleury and now in Orléans, thus pushing back the date of composition by as much as a century.[20] Therefore, by the tenth century the standard version of the acquisition was widely known, but given the entire lack of supporting documentation it is impossible to say to what extent the *translatio* is historically accurate. As an index of Venetian policy and interests, however, the text is invaluable. The obvious familiarity with the East and particularly with Alexandria, the fact that merchants and not monks are said to have effected the translation, and the civic pride of the author all point to a very different mentality from that of contemporary northern hagiographers.

There is little doubt of the ultimate success of the venture, regardless of the text's historicity. The universality with which the Venetian claims were accepted in subsequent centuries indicates that Venice accomplished, with the help of her new patron, exactly what she had set out to do: achieve superiority over the towns of the northern coast of the Adriatic, and independence from her Byzantine "masters."

"TRANSLATIO SANCTI NICOLAI"

It has been recently suggested concerning Saint Nicolas that "chances are that when, if ever, the available evidence is codified, the most popular saint in Christendom may prove to be the least essentially religious saint of all."[21] This judgment is harsh, not only on the saint whose body was translated from Myra to Bari in 1087 but, I suspect, on medieval religion in general. While the cult of Saint Nicolas may fail to measure up to post-Reformation definitions of "religious," the reality of widespread devotion to the saint from the eleventh century on cannot be doubted. In the absence of such devotion to Nicolas throughout the Mediterranean world, the translation would have been meaningless and the proliferation of his cult in merchant communities would have been unthinkable. This religious basis of Nicolas's cult made the translation an important political and economic event throughout the West. Only his status as a great and important saint could have made the theft of his body appear to be an answer to the economic crisis in which the citizens of Bari found themselves at the end of the eleventh century. The secular importance of the translation was not something added after the fact, but rather logically and chronologically simultaneous with the religious devotion that led to the translation.

The events of 1087 took on increasing significance in the local history of Bari as the twelfth century progressed, although the issues arising from these later developments have obscured the original context of the translation. Rival jurisdictional claims over the church of Saint Nicolas built to house the relics, giving rise to a host of spurious documents concerning the foundation of the church and its privileges, have led some scholars to interpret the translation as a stage in the factional disputes of the citizens.[22] With more enthusiasm than scholarship, Giuseppe Praga reduced the causes of the theft to the overriding necessity of finding a saint around whose standard the pro-Norman merchants of Bari's middle class could rally in opposition to the pro-Byzantine noble faction led by Archbishop Ursone under the patronage of Saint Sabatino.[23] As an extreme consequence of his theory Praga obscured the considerable merits of his research by insisting that the translation must have occurred in 1071, immediately after the success of the Norman siege of Bari (August 5, 1068–April 16, 1071). His primary argument for this date is the *a priori* reasoning that it was at this time and not fifteen years later that the translation was needed.

In reaction to Praga's mechanistic and somewhat distorted view of the event, Francesco Nitti di Vito, archdeacon of the basilica of Saint Nicolas and editor of the *Codice diplomatico barese*,[24] established the main outline of the twelfth-century disputes and the role of forged documents and altered *translationes* in these disputes.[25] He also demonstrated conclusively that the date given in the Latin versions of the *translatio*, as well as in contemporary chronicles,

1087, is correct;[26] Praga's suggested date for the arrival of
the relics in Bari, May 7, 1071, is impossible because at that
time Myra had not yet been taken by the Turks.[27] Nitti also
reacted strongly against Praga's suggestion that the translation was essentially a clever power play on the part of the
pro-Norman merchants, and he insisted that it should be
viewed as the fruition of long devotion to Nicolas on the
part of Bari's citizens to which had been added retrospec-
tively political and economic significance.[28]

Praga's failure to understand the events surrounding the
translation is more fundamental than his confusion over the
date. His vision of a pro-Norman merchant class opposing a
pro-Byzantine noble class is neither reasonable nor supported by what is known of the men who actually participated in the translation. Unfortunately, Nitti's explanations
are not altogether acceptable either; despite his great erudi-
tion he failed to recognize the place of the three *translationes
Sancti Nicolai* in the hagiographic tradition of furtive *translationes*. Before presenting still another interpretation of the
translation, therefore, it is necessary to summarize briefly the
three versions of the *translatio*.

The first text is found in a manuscript of the Vatican written in the first half of the twelfth century.[29] The author pro-
fesses to be a monk of Bari, Niceforus. He recounts that certain men of Bari had gone to Antioch to sell grain, when
they heard rumors that a group of Venetian merchants in Antioch planned to go to Myra and steal the body of Nicolas
and had even brought iron instruments to use to break open
the marble tomb. The Bari merchants resolved to beat the Venetians to the prize and hurried to Myra. Once there, they
asked the curators of the shrine to show them the tomb.
Thinking that the merchants wanted to worship, the monks
showed them the place from which flowed oil sacred to Nicolas, but soon grew suspicious and asked the visitors if they
were planning to steal the body. The Barians admitted the
truth, claiming that the pope had sent them on the mission.
An argument almost leading to violence resulted, in which
the monks insisted that they did not really know where the

tomb was. Finally, when the merchants threatened to destroy the church and its guards if the monks were not cooperative, one of the guards admitted that the body did lie beneath the place from which flowed the sacred oil and that the saint had recently appeared in a vision and announced that he wished to go to another place. The guard added, however, that in the past many emperors and other powerful persons had attempted to move the body but that no one had been able to do so. Unconcerned, the merchants broke open the tomb and had no trouble removing the relics.

A wonderful fragrance spread throughout the area, reaching even into the town of Myra several miles distant. The monks took this success as a sign that the saint did indeed wish to go with the merchants to Bari. Leaving the church, the band of merchants encountered a large number of inhabitants who had been aroused by the fragrance and had realized its meaning. While holding off this crowd with arms, the Barians explained that Myra had had the honor of possessing the saint long enough and that they had been ordered to remove his remains by a divine revelation. The inhabitants were disconsolate, but the merchants made good their escape. After various difficulties they arrived at the port of Saint George the Martyr four miles from Bari where they constructed a small chapel to house the relics. A great number of townspeople soon gathered to view the wonder and an argument broke out over what was to be done with them. Some insisted that the relics should be taken to the archbishop who was then absent; others said that they should be taken to Helias, abbot of the monastery of Saint Benedict. A decision was made that finally gained the consent of the archbishop and all the people to place the body under the care of the abbot. The *translatio* concludes with the statement that the translation was accomplished the ninth day of May, 1087, and recounts a series of miracles performed in Bari through Nicolas's intercession.

The second *translatio*, ostensibly written by Archdeacon John of Bari at the command of Archbishop Ursone of Bari, contains many of the same details as the Niceforus *transla-*

tio.[30] Bari merchants in Antioch heard how the Turks had taken Myra and cruelly mistreated its defenders. Then a group of Venetian merchants arrived in Antioch with plans to take the body of Nicolas from Myra. Discovering the plot, the merchants of Bari decided to beat them to the prize, "not so much for their own glory and honor and the greatness of their own fatherland . . . but because of the disgrace and evil which they hoped to expose." Quickly wrapping up their business in Antioch, they hurried to Myra and stole secretly to the church. There, having been shown the source of the oil which was the principal remembrance given by the custodians to pilgrims, they announced that they had been sent by the pope to carry the body back to Bari. The reaction of the custodians was as described by Niceforus: at first they objected, insisting that the body could not be removed against the saint's will, but finally reluctantly recognized the will of the saint when the merchants were able to remove the relics. The scene at the shore as the merchants faced the angry crowd, and the subsequent return to Bari were the same as in Niceforus's account. There, the relics were entrusted to the abbot of Saint Benedictus who kept them three days in his church. Then the citizens of Bari began to argue concerning where the relics should finally be placed, but with the arrival of the archbishop they were placed in the church of Saint Stephen, although they remained under the protection of Abbot Helias.

Although the two accounts correspond closely in all details except for the question of the final disposition of the relics, Nitti found both accounts suspect. He was convinced, and probably rightly, that the original account, possibly written by Niceforus, had contained the same basic outline of the story but had ended differently. Some time in the twelfth century, when the dispute between the cathedral and the monastery was raging over jurisdiction of the basilica of Saint Nicolas, both accounts may have been altered to reflect the positions of the different parties.[31] Nitti thought that he had found the original account of the translation preserved in a fourteenth-century Russian manuscript that gives a somewhat different account of the translation.[32] This *translatio* begins with a description of the destruction of the Byzantine Empire as far as Antioch by the "Ismaeliti" and the resulting desolation of the tomb of Saint Nicolas. Shortly after, the saint appeared to a priest of Bari and asked that his body be moved to that city. The story of this vision spread through town, and three ships were prepared for the expedition. Under the guise of grain merchants, the representatives of Bari sailed to Antioch. While the merchants were selling grain there, they learned that the Venetians were also planning to steal the body and carry it home to Venice. The Bari merchants then hurried to Myra where they seized the body and returned home accompanied by two of the four Greek monks who had been guarding the shrine. In Bari, the remains were first placed in the church of Saint John the Baptist at the Sea. Three years later, the *translatio* continues, Pope Gurmanus (Urbanus) visited Bari and officiated at the deposition of the relics in the new church of Saint Nicolas.

Urban II did in fact participate in the consecration of the new church of Saint Nicolas in 1089.[33] If the Georgian monk and bishop Efrem (died 1103), who developed a great interest in the life and cult of Nicolas during his exile in Constantinople, was the author of this *translatio* then the date of its composition must be close to the actual event.[34] Nitti thought that this proximity guaranteed the account's accuracy, particularly its assertions that the expedition was planned before the merchants left Bari, that the nature of the translation was peaceful as evidenced by the accompaniment of two monks back to Bari, and that the body was deposited in the church of Saint John.[35] Two difficulties cast doubt on this suggestion. First, it is impossible to demonstrate that the Russian account actually dates from the early twelfth century. The chronological details are accurate, and no textual evidence suggests composition in the thirteenth or fourteenth century, but neither is there any proof that this text is not an altered version of a now lost original.[36] More importantly, the text's version of events cannot be taken literally because the account is so clearly within the tradition of the fictionalized *furta sacra* genre, especially since it was composed under the inspiration of the *Translatio Sancti Marci*.

The evidence for this influence is overwhelming. First, the description of the desolation of Myra is tellingly similar to that of Monte Cassino in the *Translatio Sancti Benedicti* and to the descriptions in all the *translationes* in the northern group. Nicolas's appearance to the holy priest of Bari is likewise the most traditional of all justifications for thefts. The monks' willingness to accompany the body to Bari is lifted directly from the account of the translation of Saint Mark.

This analysis is also applicable to the two Latin *translationes*. Even if they had not been altered or expanded in the course of the twelfth century, they would not be valid sources from which to reconstruct the actions of the Bari merchants on their fateful expedition to Antioch. When the hagiographic commonplaces are discounted, only three original elements common to the three accounts remain: the expedition of merchants to Antioch to sell grain, the report that a group of Venetians were after the body of Nicolas, and the removal of the body to Bari. These three elements, properly understood, provide a key to understanding the importance of the translation in the life of late eleventh-century Bari.

In order to explicate these elements, we have to return to Praga's thesis that the translation resulted from a class struggle within Bari between a pro-Norman merchant class and a pro-Byzantine noble class. Just why the merchant class should have been pro-Norman in 1071 or even 1087 is not clear. Bari had long been an important Byzantine port and its merchants had participated in Mediterranean trade through the transport of grain from Apulia to the Levant. Termination of Bari's status in the Byzantine Empire would have been a great blow to the city. If Praga's assumption is correct—that an important portion of the population was willing to embrace the Normans—why didn't they simply open the gates of the city during the three terrible years of siege? The merchants had nothing to gain and everything to lose by embracing the Norman cause. Besides, Praga's distinction between nobles and merchants in Bari is economically inaccurate. Landholders in Apulia were not categorically separated from merchants; Bari was the only Italian seaport in the empire with a large hinterland, even more than in Venice and Amalfi, and excess capital from agriculture was invested in trade. Moreover, the grain produced on estates of nobles was exported through the intermediary of merchants. Thus a close symbiotic relationship existed between merchants and nobles, and the line that separated the two "classes" was extremely fluid.

Research into the backgrounds of the individuals who formed the *Societas Sancti Nicolai*, those sixty-two men who, at least by 1105, were officially recognized as the heroes who brought the body of Nicolas to Bari,[37] bears out these speculations about the community of interests in Bari. After simple sailors, the largest group represented in this *societas* was *nobiles homines* or *boni viri* who provided thirteen members, three more than even the *mercatores*.[38] Not all of these men are mentioned in other sources so they can not be studied in any detail, but an excellent study of this society by Francesco Babudri demonstrated that at least three, Melis de Caloiohanne,[39] Leo de Guisanda,[40] and Leo de notario Iacobo de Guiscanda,[41] were important nobles of Byzantine origin.

All these individuals probably did not accompany the merchants on their voyage to Myra. The expedition was organized much like any merchant expedition, and these thirteen nobles participated by financing the venture. Nonetheless, their backing is sufficient to warn one against supposing that the translation resulted from any clear-cut political conflict between merchants and nobles.

The translation was rather a reaction to the external threat posed to Bari's economy by those very merchants they determined to beat to the theft—the Venetians. The Norman conquest of Bari and the continuing wars against the Byzantines posed a serious threat to Bari's traditional economy. They both disrupted normal trade between Bari and the East, and resulted in a relative rise in the status of Venice, whose merchants competed with those of Bari for the transport and marketing of Apulian grain. Since the beginning of the century, Bari had served a twofold purpose in Venetian trade: it had become a convenient stopover for ships going to and from the East, and it was a source of grain to be traded in Constantinople, Antioch, and other eastern cities.[42] Certainly by the mid-eleventh century Venice's preeminence was obvious, but the wars between the empire and the Normans provided the Venetians with an opportunity to acquire unprecedented trading privileges in the empire, culminating in the Chrysobull of 1082 which exempted Venetian merchants from all tariffs and secured both *de jure* and *de facto* her economic supremacy.[43]

Of course, as long as there was any hope of a Norman victory in their war with the Byzantines, represented at sea by the Venetian fleet, the citizens of Bari may have held some hope for an improved position won through force of arms. But the Normans' defeat off the coast of Butrinto in 1085[44] and the death of Robert Guiscard on July 17 of that same year[45] ended any possibility of the Bari merchants controlling the grain trade between their city and the East. Evidence from Venetian commercial documents confirms that Venice played a major role in this commerce through the end of the century and during the next. Venetians made voyages to "Lombardia" and then on to Constantinople in 1089,[46] they shipped Apulian grain to Antioch in 1104,[47] and sent expeditions to Dalmatia and Constantinople from Bari in 1119.[48]

Bari could not compete with Venice in economic activity, but it sought to compete in prestige and in a different sort of economic pursuit—pilgrimage. The sack of Myra gave the Barians an opportunity to acquire a patron who in the East was at least as important as Venice's Saint Mark. It is quite likely that the Venetians had their eyes on the same body, so the Bari merchants' coup was a clear victory in the competition for fame and religious importance. The mere fact that the Venetians might want it made it an irresistible prize for Bari. The similarity in the accounts of the two translations is surely no accident.

The acquisition of Saint Nicolas meant more to Bari than mere one-upmanship. From the saint's first arrival in the town he was intended to attract pilgrims. This is evident in the architecture of the basilica of San Nicola already under construction by 1089. The large crypt and the carefully designed stairways leading to the crypt from the aisles, all of which were completed by 1089, are proof that its designers expected to accommodate great numbers of pilgrims.[49]

Obviously the Bari efforts were a success. While the merchants were never able to rival Venice, they did manage to retain a share of the trade, and the pilgrim business to the shrine gained momentum through the twelfth century. The Venetians were sufficiently envious of the town's growing fame as a shrine to "rediscover" their own patron with great fanfare only a few years later,[50] and early in the twelfth century even went so far as to claim to have acquired for themselves a part of the relics of Nicolas from Myra along with the body of Nicolas's uncle.[51] A similar claim was advanced by Benevento as early as 1090.[52] Bari basked in the reflected glory of its new patron, and throughout Europe, from the Mediterranean to the Baltic, merchant communities envied the success of the *Societas Sancti Nicolai.*[53]

"VITA SANCTI APPIANI"

A third Italian theft account repeats certain characteristics of the *translationes* of Saint Mark and of Saint Nicolas. It too concerns the efforts of merchants, this time salt traders from Pavia, to acquire the remains of Saint Appianus from Comacchio.[54] But both by its literary form and by the resolution of the action—for once, the thieves are frustrated—the text stands outside the hagiographic subgenre of furtive *translationes.*

The story is reported as one of nine miracles performed posthumously by Saint Appianus, a monk of the monastery of San Pietro in Ciel d'Oro in Pavia who at an unknown

date had been sent by his abbot to live in Comacchio and supervise the collection of salt for the Pavian monastery. Appianus evidently became involved in the religious life of the
town, and after his death he was revered as a saint by the inhabitants. Some time later, according to the *vita*, citizens of
Pavia came to Comacchio to gather salt. They secretly entered the small chapel dedicated to Appianus and removed
his body, planning to bring it back with them to Pavia. The
saint however did not want Comacchio to lose his patronage
and protection, so he miraculously prevented the ship from
sailing. The sailors were terrified when they found that no effort could move it. Realizing that the saint himself was inter-
vening, they ceased trying to sail and allowed the ship to
drift where it would. It floated to shore near the church of
Saint Maurus and the citizens of Comacchio carried the
body into the church.

This brief report of a miracle performed by a saint in
order to remain in a chosen place is almost identical to others appearing in books of miracles across Europe.[55] But even
so this story reveals particular characteristics that illuminate
both the author's probable reasons for including it in this collection, and the relationship between the mentality which
produced this text and the ones which produced the other
more famous Italian theft narratives.

First, the author is concerned to show that Appianus is a
great saint and that Comacchio is particularly blessed over
all the cities in the world in possessing his remains. He demonstrates this importance by emphasizing miracles performed on people who had traveled to Comacchio from
other towns. Some had even been cured by Appianus after
they had failed to obtain help from other relics: a blind
woman from Lucca received her sight, a possessed man from
a neighboring town was freed of his devil, a cripple from Poitiers was made whole, a woman whose injured arm could
not be cured by Saint Justina in Padova was referred to Appianus by Justina herself, and a possessed woman who could
not obtain relief even in Rome was freed from her tormentor
by Appianus. In this context, the suggestion that merchants

from Pavia would want Appianus badly enough to steal him
is consistent with the intent of the other stories. The idea
that he was worth stealing, coupled with the insistence that
Appianus was unwilling to leave his beloved Comacchio,
heightened the saint's importance and the town's fame.

There is a second type of continuity within the nine miracles. In three of the nine—well over three-fourths of the entire text—Appianus inflicts paralysis on people who would
dishonor or disobey him. The immobilization of the ship containing the body of the saint already described is one of
these texts. The story immediately preceding it tells of a girl
who had gone to play with her friends in the churchyard
where, unknown to them, Appianus had recently been buried. When the girl had to answer a call of nature, she unfortunately went to do so next to the saint's tomb. For her disrespect she was paralyzed in this embarrassing position until
the bishop, clergy, and laity of the town came to the site and
prayed for Appianus's pardon.

The eighth episode tells of a poor paralytic from Poitiers
who vowed that if Appianus would cure him, he would
never leave his church. The saint complied with the prayer
and the pauper remained in the service of the church until,
one day, he grew lonesome to see his parents. After much
pleading his bishop agreed to allow him to visit them, but as
he stepped out of the church he was immediately struck with
worse paralysis than before. Witnesses of the miracle picked
up the paralytic and carried him to the altar of Saint Appianus. There he remained until vespers when Appianus once
more restored his health.

Since the author of the *vita* was clearly concerned with
the saint's power to intervene and stop certain activities, he
chose this particular frustrated theft story as an ideal illustration of the exercise of such power. Just as Appianus was
able to freeze people, he was able to stop inanimate objects
such as the ship. Thus the hagiographer was probably less
concerned with the question of theft than with the display of
Appianus's power.

A third reason for the inclusion of the theft story can be

found in the historical circumstances at the time the *vita* was written. The complete lack of supporting evidence from the ninth and tenth centuries makes it impossible to go beyond mere hypothesis but if there were claims that Pavia possessed Appianus's remains, the miracle story may be Comacchio's indirect rebuttal of such claims.

The date the account was written cannot be determined. The text is part of a late eleventh or early twelfth-century manuscript which contains 131 other hagiographical texts from all parts of Italy.[56] However, the salt trade is described with such accuracy in the *vita* that the account may have been written at a time when Comacchio was an important source of salt for Pavia and other cities of Po, that is, in the eighth and ninth centuries.[57] Unfortunately, owing to the successive destructions of Comacchio by the Venetians in 854 and 946, no records remain of the cult of Appianus in the town[58] and there is apparently no tradition, other than the vita, to suggest that he remained buried there.

On the other hand, Pavia has claimed since the thirteenth century to guard the remains of a Saint Appianus, said to have been a bishop of Africa whose body was brought to San Pietro along with that of Saint Augustine.[59] There is no convincing evidence that the two Appiani are one and the same saint.[60] However, if there had ever been a popular belief that Appianus returned to his monastery in Pavia after his death, the passage from the *vita* might represent an effort to counter such a rumor by admitting the effort had been made, but had failed. This hypothesis is merely a possibility, but accords well with other similar translation accounts.

Regardless of the actual circumstances that gave birth to this miracle story, its similarities to the other Italian thefts are striking. Just as in Venice and Bari, the perpetrators are merchants. They arrive in Comacchio on business, and determine to remove the town's patron. Again, the enterprise is to some extent corporative rather than the efforts of one individual. And finally, although the text is not explicit on this point, the thieves act on behalf of their town and its prior claims, and not on behalf of a particular religious institution. Thus, even if the *miraculum* has no basis in history, the hagiographer adjusted his story to fit the characteristics of the emerging merchant world of maritime Italy.

CHAPTER SIX

Justifications

Some uncertainty is inescapable when trying to determine how or even if a thief carried off a saint's remains. As we have seen in the above chapters, Electus, the English relic merchant, may never have existed; the alleged thief of Mary Magdalene's remains certainly never did. Limited as we are by our sources, we are never quite sure whether or not a particular theft took place, much less how the thief, if he existed, might have viewed or justified his actions. But if we cannot evaluate the justifications and rationalizations of the thieves, we can analyze those of the hagiographers who recorded the thefts. Actually, these latter are of more interest to historians because they reflect quite accurately the moral horizons of their contemporaries. This accuracy is assured both by the intention of the authors (to codify the communal tradition concerning the acquisition of a new patron) and by the function of these texts (as we have seen, the *translationes* became formal parts of the public liturgy and as such were shared by the entire community).

It is possible, then, to understand how various communities of the central Middle Ages viewed theft as an appropriate means of relic acquisition. Were they in fact seen as true thefts, morally reprehensible and hence sinful, or were they but one more acceptable way of acquiring a saint? The answer to this question is that they were seen as both, sometimes simultaneously, and hence the *translationes* exhibit a certain tension which is the result of hagiographers' efforts to justify and glorify a tradition with which they were not altogether comfortable.

Because of the ambivalent feelings of many hagiographers, historians have tended to emphasize only one side of the evidence, the one which implies that furtive translations were not even considered thefts. Heinrich Fichtenau has suggested that since people were convinced that saints were living powerful individuals, theft of their relics against their wills was inconceivable. If the saint did not wish to be removed then no power on earth could move him.[1] Klaus Schreiner took this suggestion even further and argued that the term *furtum* did not necessarily imply a theft at all.[2] Using the example of a properly conducted translation of Saint Eugene from St. Denis to Brogne by Gerhard of Brogne in the tenth century, he pointed out that this translation was called a *laudabile furtum*.[3] Because any translation removed a wonder worker from a locality, it was a sort of "slipping away." Schreiner also cited the sermon of Rather of Verona on the theft of the body of Saint Metro to show that, before the twelfth century, the good intention of the thief absolved him from guilt.[4]

Both of these examples in part justify Schreiner's conclusions, and in part contradict them. True, Gerhard of Brogne had the right to remove Saint Eugene, but the translation was done secretly in order to avoid the wrath of the local populace. Thus the translation was done in a deceitful manner. This use of *furtum* is in accordance with the medieval etymology of the word accepted since Isidore of Seville: "Furtum is the clandestine appropriation of the property of another, so called from the word *furvo*, that is, dark, because it is done in obscurity."[5]

Normally, translations were solemn, public events, not covert operations. Thus if the translation of Saint Eugene was not a true theft, neither was it an ordinary translation, and Schreiner's argument that "lawful relic recruiting" could also be termed *furta sacra* remains to be demonstrated.

Similarly, his example taken from Rather of Verona is not completely satisfactory. Rather's purpose in delivering his diatribe was not to discuss the morality of relic thefts but rather to chastise the citizens of Verona. Furthermore, the difficult and argumentative bishop is hardly a typical hagiog-

rapher. As we shall see, reference to the intention of the thief
was one means of justifying relic thefts, but it was by no
means the only one, or the most common.

LEGALITY OF RELIC THEFTS

Legality and morality are seldom the same: the mere illegality of unauthorized translations is not proof that perpetrators or recipients considered them wrong. This is especially
true since monks could cite abundant precedent from the
Old Testament for instances in which the divine will was effected through lying, stealing, trickery, and other similar
means. Nor did mere legality satisfy communities destined to
lose their saintly protectors through entirely regular means.
Even official translations had to be justified to the populace
and to the religious of their old communities, and these
justifications often resembled those presented for thefts. Nevertheless, by the ninth century civil and ecclesiastical law
had established proper procedures for translating saints, and
hence those who benefited from stolen relics knew that these
bodies had been acquired illegally.

The first legislation concerning relics' translations developed from Roman funerary law, and forbade the transport
of martyrs' bodies altogether. From earliest times, altars and
oratories had been erected on the tombs of martyrs, and
with the advent of religious toleration, devotion at these
tombs increased greatly.[6] Along with this increase in devotion came the desire to have bodies for veneration in areas
where none were to be found. Translations of relics into
churches became common, and so too did all sorts of abuses
including thefts and frauds. In the early fifth century, Augustine complained of unscrupulous individuals who were
going about selling what they claimed to be relics of martyrs.[7] The Theodosian code attempted to prevent such
abuses by forbidding translations altogether, though it is
doubtful that this prohibition had any real success in curb-
ing these excesses of piety.

Translations, particularly those unauthorized by any civil or ecclesiastical authority, remained suspect and objectionable to churchmen throughout the next four centuries. But to judge from the vigor and frequency of their denunciations, the practice must have continued to flourish.[8] Gregory the Great, as bishop and protector of Rome, was particularly concerned with the unauthorized removal of martyrs from the city and forbade the practice.[9] Gregory of Tours also condemned the theft and sale of relics perpetrated in Gaul during his day.[10]

Although translations were common enough throughout the history of the early Church—more common, in fact than narrative sources would suggest, to judge from inventories of relics and altar dedications—it was only toward the end of the eighth century that the phenomenon grew enormously as a result of the changes in Frankish society and religion we examined in Chapter 2. The result was the Carolingian Church's efforts to regularize and direct the means by which relics might be moved about. The resulting legislation, particularly the canon of the Council of Mainz in 813 requiring that no translations should be made without the advice of the prince and/or (vel) the permission of the bishops and the holy synod,[11] sought to establish the proper procedures to control translations. It is in the context of controlling translations and not primarily of establishing a means for canonization, as Herrmann-Mascard wrongly suggests, that this canon must be viewed.[12]

Theoretically, then, from the beginning of the ninth century there was a right and a wrong way to acquire relics. When a hagiographer reported that a relic had been removed in the dead of night from a neighboring church or had been purchased from a custodian, the author was quite aware that such action was condemned by ecclesiastical law. On rare occasions when thieves were caught, they were threatened with stringent penalties if they did not return the relics to their rightful owners. Bishop Stephen of Cambrai, for example, threatened the religious of Maubeuge with excommunication if they did not return the body of Saint Gislenus they had stolen from a nearby monastery.[13] Hagiographers knew that their community's gain was another's loss; relic thefts were seldom victimless crimes, since the inhabitants of the area from which the saint was taken were deprived of their patron's protection.

An even more impressive example of the extent to which the theft of relics, far from being generally condoned by society, was in fact seen as a serious crime to be punished whenever possible, is that of the thefts of the relics of Saint Oricolus recently published and examined by François Dolbeau.[14] The remains of Oricolus were venerated in the church of Senuc near Autry (modern dép. de la Marne) which had been restored in the late eleventh century by Manasses of Autry. Two Norman clerics appointed by Manasses to serve the church stole the relics and were heading for Verdun when they became lost in the Argonne forest. They were captured near Clermont-en-Argonne and the confiscated relics were placed in the chapel belonging to Hubert, the local lord. Manasses and Abbot Heirmarus of St. Remi attempted in vain to force Hubert to return the relics. Finally, Archbishop Gervasius of Reims excommunicated Hubert, and after five years he returned the relics. Even though Saint Oricolus himself appeared undisturbed by the theft (he continued to work miracles at Clermont just as he had at Senuc), both the original theft and the failure to restore the confiscated relics were condemned and severely punished by human authorities.

RATIONALIZATIONS

These legal and moral considerations did not lead hagiographers to condemn thefts or even to disguise them, but they did motivate authors of *translationes* to offer some sorts of explanations which, while explaining why the theft was proper, also indicate that the thefts were in need of some sort of justification. Although they did not usually appeal to universal criteria of right and wrong or to legal or theological principles as did Rather, in their justifications the hagiographers betray a way of thought centered on their religious communities, the respect due to the saint or saints in question, and the religious or miraculous world that entered constantly and without disruption into the world of daily experience, and was in fact part of that world.

The literature on thefts of relics can be separated naturally into two groups, distinguished by the situation of the author: with few exceptions he is either one of the victims or one of the victimizers. But whether praising or condemning the theft, he uses a set of moral referents that apply equally well to condemnation and justification. If one author defends a theft on the grounds that the rightful possessor already had too many other relics, another will praise the ambitious collector and quote Luke 19:26, "He that has will be given more, and he that has not, even that which he has will be taken from him."[15] If one writer says that relics were removed from a church to avoid desecration by pagan pillagers, another asserts that relics were properly removed to a place in danger of destruction, because the relics' very presence would serve to ward off the invaders.[16] The variety of principles of justification used throughout the three centuries under consideration indicate that Schreiner's explanation does not go far enough and that other justifications of relic thefts were also important in the central Middle Ages.

Fichtenau observed that the impossibility of stealing a relic without the permission of the saint is one major means of justifying (or condemning) a theft. We have seen that the deacon Peter appeared to Einhard's agent and helped him remove his own and Marcellinus's remains. Similarly, Balgerus could not steal the body of Lewinna until he received her permission. This sort of story is a commonplace in hagiography and certainly reflected the conviction that the saint was in control of his own fate. It is, therefore, not surprising that when thefts failed, the failure too would be attributed to the saint's will. The account of the attempted theft of Saint Appianus of Comacchio examined in the previous chapter is typical of these stories. Direct action of the saint usually frustrates the thieves in these episodes: they are paralyzed[17] or struck dead, or a tremendous storm[18] or an earthquake[19] alerts the guardians of the relics.

Because this justification was based on the saint's power to exercise his will over his body even after his death, a key element in the cult of saints we shall examine below,[20] it frequently occurs in furtive *translationes*. But there are other more specific ways hagiographers justified their thefts.

Throughout the three centuries, apologists justified many thefts by reference to the security of the relic itself. In the case of the supposed translation of the body of Mary Magdalene from Provence to Vézelay, Count Girard of Burgundy and Abbot Hugo of Vézelay were said to have sent a monk Baidilo to get the relics, which were in danger of desecration at the hands of the Saracens (or the Normans, depending on the manuscript) and bring them to safety in Burgundy.[21] Similarly, the translations of relics from Spain and Aquitaine accomplished by theft in the latter half of the ninth century were justified by the poor state of the churches in which they lay exposed to the ravages of the pagans as well as of the weather.[22]

Such concern for the proper veneration of relics could, however, have quite the opposite results. In the *vita* of Saint Tigria, the archdeacon of Archbishop Rufus of Turin was visiting the church of Maurienne when he found there the finger of John the Baptist. The archdeacon was dismayed to find so great a relic in an obscure church and spoke with the archbishop of the desirability of removing it to a place where it would receive proper veneration. The archbishop wanted no part in the undertaking, so the archdeacon attempted to carry it off alone. Evidently the baptist didn't appreciate his effort for according to the *vita* the archdeacon was immediately struck dead.[23]

An equally important theme of justification of thefts appealed to the good of the community to which the relic was translated. This justification is present to varying degrees in almost all of the accounts. The body of Saint Foy was stolen from Agen and brought to Conques "for the health of the area and the redemption of many.[24] A nearly identical statement appears in the eleventh-century account of the translation of the head of Saint Valentinus to the monastery of Jumièges in France.[25] The priest who perpetrated the theft was "not attracted by any desire of profit, but rather eager that the ultramontane province might rejoice and be made famous."[26]

In the tenth and eleventh centuries, a new theme appeared in the justification of thefts: the spiritual and moral state of the individual perpetrator. Simply stated, the action of a good man was good, although the same act performed by an evil man would be bad. Of course, this judgment usually depended on whether or not the author was predisposed to approve of the action, so that the "justification" was transparently forced. Even so, in accounts such as the life of Saint Bertulfus, the actions of Electus, the official from eastern Brittany who stole the body of Bertulfus for King Athelstan of England, was objectionable on the grounds that he was a "sacrilegious official."[27] Similarly, the thieves from Maubeuge who stole the body of Saint Gislenus from Mons were condemned as evil people motivated by greed.[28]

But these same motives in "good men" could be interpreted as laudable. Archbishop Anno of Cologne, for example, was described as constantly eager in acquiring and honoring the relics of saints. Hence, when he secretly removed the relics of Saints Innocent and Vitalis from Rome to the monastery of Siegburg, he was praised for his piety.[29] Similarly, a priest in the entourage of Bishop Otwinus of Hildesheim who stole the bodies of saints Epiphanius and Speciosa from Pavia escaped censure because he was "advanced in age, of a most simple nature, devoting his time to prayers, fasts and vigils."[30] Obviously such a man could do no wrong, and after the theft was discovered Otto I refused to acquiesce to the demands of the townsmen and allowed the thief to keep the relics.

The three foci of moral discussions examined above, the

relic itself, the place to which it is to be translated, and the agent of the translation, are found in the great majority of furtive *translationes*. But several others merit examination. Some hagiographers looked beyond the immediate situation to consider the proper relationship between relics of saints and those places which were influenced by the life of the saint whose relics they were. This problem is raised in the life of Saint Abbanus, a sixth-century Irish saint. Upon his death in the monastery of Magh-Arnuidhe which he had founded, citizens of Ceall-Abbain, his birthplace, came and stole his body. The result was almost a war, but the two opposing forces met and presented their arguments before coming to blows. The spokesman of Ceall-Abbain asserted his community's right to the saint's remains because its members had been his first followers. The second community replied that the many years the saint had lived in their monastery and his death there made their claim to the body the strongest.[31] Neither side carried the day however, because a miracle provided each community with an identical body of the saint. A similar situation occurred in Cologne when a priest of the church of Saint Cunibert found one of the many holy virgins adjacent to his church. The nuns of the church of Saint Ursula claimed that although the body had been found elsewhere, it should be removed to their church because it was proper that it should be placed with the remains of the other holy virgins. Naturally Saint Cunibert's clergy insisted that the body should remain in their church near where it had been found. Once again neither side's argument proved decisive because yet another virgin was found and her body was carried to the church of Saint Ursula.[32]

A final and typically medieval justification for the theft of relics was the argument from tradition. This argument, which formed the basis for so much of medieval theology and law, was actually used to justify at least one theft, that of the remains of Saint Prudentius to Bèze.[33] The author of this *translatio*, writing at the end of our period, around 1127, looked back on the previous *translationes*, and

equated the theft of the remains of Prudentius to the translations of Stephen from Jerusalem to Constantinople, of Nicolas from Myra to Bari, Mary Magdalene from Provence to
Vézelay, and Benedict from Monte Cassino to Fleury.[34] Thus
by the twelfth century, *furta sacra* were considered, at least
by some, as a legitimate part of the venerable tradition
handed down from the age of the Fathers.

A number of general observations are in order to conclude this investigation of attitudes towards thefts. First,
these actions were not universally accepted or condemned
and hence there was no single "medieval attitude" toward
relic thefts. Secondly, even though authors of *translationes*
may have approved of the actions, they felt compelled to
offer some justification for what was clearly an extraordi-
nary means of acquisition of sacred relics. These explanations or apologies owed little to learned theological or legal
considerations and, with a few exceptions, made no general
appeal to a universal system of values or of propriety. For
the most part they centered on the object itself, the locations
involved, and the agents of the theft. Finally, these same
basic justifications, repeated in more or less the same form
throughout the literature, evidently are *topoi* that owe little
to the concrete situation in which the thefts occurred. They
tell hardly anything about why the thefts actually did take
place or why fabricated thefts were said to have taken place.

What they do indicate is that their authors definitely recognized these *translationes* to be unusual. Although acts of virtue, they still needed some justification or explanation to dif-
ferentiate them from other, impious thefts. This recognition
was influential in determining the narrow limits of the literary tradition within which accounts of thefts were couched.
The translation of Saint Prudentius was laudable precisely because it could be assimilated to a venerable tradition of relic
thefts. True, it was a theft, but these earlier thefts had been
meritorious, and since that of Prudentius resembled these
others, it shared in that tradition. This desire to avoid innovation, to participate in an accepted form of recourse when

one needed relics, produced in time a more or less standard narrative that sought to establish the legitimacy of the theft through conformity to traditional models.

THE FORMATION OF A LITERARY TRADITION

Einhard's *Translatio SS Marcellini et Petri* provided the model for the subsequent development of furtive *translationes*. Imitators soon spread it across Europe, and in the following two centuries this literary tradition developed into three basic forms: the closest to Einhard's original were the accounts of thefts from Rome; the second was the group of *translationes* that told of thefts from Spain and Aquitaine; and the third, thefts from Normandy and Brittany.

Einhard's *translatio* contains the basic elements that would characterize the *furta sacra* narrative. As he told the story, it was not an account of the business trip Deusdona's journey surely was, but it was the story of the cooperation between Einhard's high-minded servant and the two saints. Constantly Einhard minimized Deusdona's role in the successful acquisition of the desired relics and presented the entire story as though Deusdona had nothing to do with the translation.

Quite early on the journey to Rome, Ratlecus's servant Reginbald became ill and, according to Einhard, had a vision of a deacon (evidently Peter). This deacon told him that Deusdona would have little or nothing to do with their mission and pointed out the church in Rome that was to be their goal. The boy reported this vision to Ratlecus. Upon arriving in Rome, Deusdona found that he was unable to supply the relics he had promised because they were in his brother's home, and his brother, as was mentioned above, was in Benevento on business. Left to their own devices, Reginbald and Ratlecus first sought out Marcellinus's tomb and removed his ashes, and then returned with Hilduin's emissary for the bodies of Peter and Tiburtius, this time assisted by a Greek monk whom they persuaded to help them find their way back to the church.[35]

From an historical point of view, this account is hardly credible. Deusdona had promised Hilduin the body of Tiburtius.[36] Deusdona was surely aware of the fact that it lay in the basilica of Saint Helen on the via Labicana with the bodies of Marcellinus and Peter.[37] He would not have passed up a chance to acquire the bodies when he went with the Frankish agents to remove Tiburtius's relics. It was hardly chance that led them to this particular church. Moreover, if Deusdona had really been as inefficient and useless as Einhard makes him appear in the *translatio*, he would hardly have enjoyed the confidence that Einhard, Hilduin, and Hrabanus Maurus showed him in the following decade. No, Einhard actually attempted to combine two conflicting accounts of relic acquisitions, and was only partially successful. The first strain Einhard incorporated was the account of Deusdona and his family's business. Einhard commissioned him to acquire certain relics for his new foundation and sent his secretary along to make sure that the relics were genuine. Deusdona accomplished this mission as instructed, but later Abbot Hilduin claimed that *his* agent had acquired the relics by deceit. This deceit necessitated the writing of a *translatio* to justify the relics' acquisition. The other strain is one that became familiar in the next few centuries. Two monasteries in Frankland sent monks to acquire the relics of some important saints from Rome. On the way to Rome one had a vision informing him how to proceed and disclosing the location of the relics to be stolen. Upon arrival in Rome, the monks sought out the aid of a local inhabitant (in this case the Greek Basilius) and with his help found their way to the martyr's tomb. By night they secretly opened the sarcophagus, removed the ashes, and hurried back to their monastery pursued by papal agents and by the frenzied Roman populace (the legates sent out from Rome to Louis the Pious, mentioned in the *translatio*, were of course not concerned about the theft, but their mention adds some excitement to the account).[38] It is little wonder that of the two accounts, the latter captured the imagination of contemporaries and began a hagiographic tradition that could be altered and adapted to fit the particular circumstances of later generations.

The first hagiographer to be influenced by the account was Adrevald of Fleury, the mid-century author of the *Historia Translationis Sancti Benedicti* and the *Miracula Sancti Benedicti*.[39] As a young boy, Adrevald had been greatly impressed by the translations from Rome that occurred in the third decade of the ninth century. In the *Miracula*, he recalled the excitement at Fleury when Hilduin gave Abbot Boso of Fleury some of the relics of Sebastian that he had recently acquired from Pope Eugenius. The enthusiasm of the laity was so great that a special wooden structure had to be built outside of the cloister in which the relics could be placed on Sundays so that women could come to visit them.[40]

Adrevald admired Einhard's writing, and in his *Miracula* he is more indebted to him for style and material than to any other author.[41] Whether his knowledge of the general outline of the account of the translation of Marcellinus and Peter came from Einhard's *translatio*, from the Soissons version that gave possession of the relics to that monastery, or merely from hearsay cannot be determined, but the presence at Fleury of the oldest manuscript of Einhard's *translatio*, a ninth-century copy, would indicate Adrevald had a firsthand familiarity with the text.[42] In any event, when Adrevald undertook the task of recounting the translation of Benedict from Monte Cassino to Fleury, he reshaped the eighth-century traditions concerning this translation to conform to the ninth-century theft narrative.

The tradition alive in Fleury and throughout the West concerning the translation of Benedict prior to Adrevald's account can be reconstructed from two independent accounts, one from an eighth-century manuscript of the monastery of Saint Emmeram of Regensburg,[43] the other from Paul the Deacon's *Historia Langobardorum*.[44] As Henri Leclercq has shown,[45] between 690 and 707 a group of monks from

Fleury arrived at Monte Cassino, which had lain abandoned for over a century, and carried off the relics of Benedict and Scholastica. In the account from Saint Emmeram, the monks were aided in their search by a swineherd, and the actual discoverer of the tomb was the expedition's cook.

Adrevald retains the basic outline of this tradition, but altered it in the style of the theft narrative. He named Aigulfus, the first abbot of Lérins,[46] as the head of the expedition and placed the translation under the abbacy of Mummolus.[47] En route to Italy, the monks were joined by citizens from Le Mans who were likewise on their way to Monte Cassino, having been told in a vision to bring back to their city the body of Scholastica. As in the Einhard *translatio*, the two expeditions united, though there was trouble later. Upon arrival in Rome, the monks from Le Mans tarried to transact some business, possibly related to the purchase of relics, but Aigulfus hurried on to Monte Cassino.[48] There he was aided by a *senex* who, for a price, showed him around the ruins and told him how to go about finding the tombs. At night, the tombs' location was miraculously revealed, and the next morning the monks broke open the tombs from the side and removed the remains of Benedict and Scholastica. Shortly thereafter the expedition from Le Mans arrived, and not wishing to share the relics, Aigulfus and his monks hurried back to Fleury. They were pursued by the pope and Lombards who had been miraculously warned of the theft, but the monks' escape was made good by a miracle. The inhabitants of Le Mans heard of this success and came to Fleury to demand the body of Scholastica. After consultation, Aigulfus was persuaded to part with the remains of Benedict's sister.

The similarities of this account to Einhard's are evident: the two expeditions, the dalliance in Rome, the dreams revealing the location of the tomb, the assistance, the deception on the part of one of the groups, the pursuit by the pope, the final revelation of the deceit, and the settlement of all claims to the relics.

The *Translatio Sancti Benedicti* was extremely popular

throughout the central Middle Ages, owing to the importance Frankish Benedictines placed on the tradition that the
founder of their monastic life had chosen Gaul as his home.
In the following centuries, monasteries throughout Francia
and Rhineland adopted the structure of the *translatio* to describe their own acquisitions of Roman or Italian relics.[49]

The fact that the literary convention used to describe these
translations was clearly borrowed does not necessarily indicate that the translations or thefts never took place. Throughout the Middle Ages, monasteries acquired relics through the
efforts of monks on pilgrimage to Rome. Surely some were
purchased, others given them by Italian or Roman clergy,
and probably some actually were stolen. Significantly, the
form of the two earlier *translationes* was used to describe
these acquisitions.

If Benedict had allowed himself to be translated from
Monte Cassino to Fleury-sur-Loire, surely the saint's cooperation in the translation made it a glorious, respectable,
means of acquiring a new patron. By casting the account of
a monastery's acquisition of the remains of a Roman saint in
the tradition of Einhard or Aigulfus, the new saint and the
new monastery shared in the glory of these ancient heroes.
Moreover, such assimilation was only natural since if every
saint is a model of Christ, then every saint should resemble
every other, not only in his life and death, but in his posthumous activities. The glorious translation of Marcellinus
could equally be reported of Callistus.

The Aquitanian *translationes* also took their inspiration
from the *Translatio Sancti Benedicti*, but indirectly through
the *Translatio Beati Vincentii* of Aimoinus. The monk of
Saint Germain des Prés retained the earlier story's basic elements: the dream vision, the abandoned state of the tomb,
the help from a mysterious stranger, the quest, the actual
theft, and adventures on the return journey. However, he
transferred the scene from Italy to Spain in accordance with
information provided him by the monks of Castres who commissioned him to write the *translatio*.

ies of the saints, which will not rise until the last day. But various descriptions and treatment of relics by the faithful, lay and clerical alike, bear out this identification.

Hagiographers, writing for their communities, attributed to the eucharist and to relics identical miracles. If struck, the eucharist was likely to bleed, a sign of its identity with the living body of Christ. Relics too often bled when mishandled. Invariably bodies are described as incorrupt, exuding a fragrant odor rather than the stench of death. Through human agents they moved about at will, even changing their residence from one church to another as they wished. They made their pleasure or displeasure known in no uncertain terms and, like the eucharist, tolerated no disrespect.

Relics even had legal rights; they received gifts and offerings made specifically to them and owned churches and monasteries, which were technically the property of the saints who lay in their crypts. At solemn occasions they were present to witness oaths and attend councils. In other words, relics were described and treated as though they were saints themselves living in the community and participating in its life.

If we keep in mind this concept of the "living relic," then it is easier to understand why they would become involved in social, political, and economic affairs of the communities in which they lived. Certainly thefts of relics (or rather kidnappings)[56] were irregular, even illegal. But the saints could understand the tremendous drive, the absolute necessity that led men to the act. In their desire to help their devotees, saints allowed themselves to be moved about from place to place, and were willing to add their spiritual strength to their followers' mundane causes.

Sacred History and Communal Pride

The historical significance of the *translationes* is drastically altered if the relics are recognized as living persons. The theft of such relics then becomes a ritual kidnapping and the *trans-*

latio becomes the story of how an important powerful individual leaves his home, wanders through many dangers, and finally is welcomed into a position of honor and authority in a new community. The "heroes" of the *translationes* were not the thieves, but the saints themselves.

Regardless of the immediate circumstances of the acquisition of new relics, the official memory of the event in the collective history of the community acquired the characteristics of what anthropologists call a ritual of elevation. As the historical details of the actual theft or translation dissolved under the influence of the *furta sacra* model, the *translationes* increasingly embodied precisely those elements which characterize such rituals. Hagiographers presented in their official versions of the saint's passage from another community to theirs those formal and symbolic elements which emphasized the proper means by which this passage had occurred.

In his classic study of rites of passage, Arnold van Gennep defined these rites as "all the ceremonial patterns which accompany a passage from one situation to another or from one cosmic or social world to another."[57] Whether the passage is from one culturally defined status to another or from one community to another, the rites of passage are marked by three phases: separation, margin, and aggregation. As the anthropologist Victor Turner explains, each of these phases has its characteristic structures, both in the sense of social structure and in Lévi-Strauss's sense of logical categories and the relations between them. The first phase, separation, includes the behavior that indicates that the individual or group undergoing the ritual is being detached from its original place in the social structure or from a fixed set of cultural conditions. During the second marginal or liminal period, the subject is characterized by ambiguity as he exists in a cultural "realm" that has little resemblance to the past or future states. This is often a period of loss of identity, danger, and uncertainty. In the final phase, aggregation, the subject is incorporated into a new stable state in which he has new rights and obligations of a clearly defined and "structural" type.[58]

Examination of the furtive *translationes* in their more detailed examples reveals this tripartite structure and these very characteristics.

The first phase, separation is obviously the act of the theft itself. This central event, as we have seen, usually takes place at night and is accompanied by violence of some type—usually the breaking open of the tomb. It is the most dramatic moment of the *translatio* and has been prepared by the description of the quest for the saint and the sorry condition of the shrine.

The second, liminal phase characteristically exhibits ambiguity and marginality. The relics and the thief are often in physical danger from their pursuers or from other would-be thieves; the identity of the relics may be in doubt, as in the *Translatio Sancti Vincentii* when he is mistakenly identified as Saint Marinus. There may be danger of natural disaster such as the shipwreck in the *Translatio Sanctae Lewinnae*.

The final phase of the relic's passage is its reception and incorporation into its new community. This is accomplished by ritual: the saint and his thief are met, usually at some distance from the town or monastery, by the community. A solemn procession is formed with candles and incense, and the relics are transported to their new home by the entire community praising and glorifying God. Frequently, too, a new and more sumptuous reliquary is prepared for the remains, as befits their new, more elevated status.

The similarity among theft accounts is comprehensible if the evolution of the genre is seen as the gradual creation of an *ex post facto* rite of passage on three levels: first, there is the obvious spatial passage of a saint from one location to another. Second, there is the passage of the saint from an improper social role (neglect, physical danger, lack of proper veneration) to a proper one (honor, attention, devotion). Finally there is the transition of the saint from the periphery of religious devotion (either in the community to which he is brought or in the location from which he has come) to the center of importance as a chief patron and protector of the community.

Obviously, many communities possessed or thought they possessed relics of saints whose provenance had been forgotten. Gradually, as with Mary Magdalene at Vézelay, the saint took on an important function in the community's life. At some point a fitting and satisfying memory of how she had arrived had to be formulated. Various unsatisfactory histories might be proposed before a community settled on a final version of the recollection of a theft.

Other communities knew how their relics had been acquired, but the memories were unsatisfactory, either because they included doubts as to the authenticity of the relics (which may have been simply purchased) or because they failed to provide a memory that would give the acquisition proper solemnity and perspective.

As Hubert Silvestre suggested some thirty years ago in his examination of the theft of relics, commerce was often considered synonymous with treachery.[59] Misrepresentation and fraud were thought to be essential aspects of commercial transactions. This was especially true in a society in which, as Philip Grierson has pointed out, the normal means by which goods were exchanged did not include trade.[60] Wealth circulated more importantly through exchanges of gifts and through pillage. Gifts of relics were certainly the normal means by which relics were distributed. But when a community, reflecting on the arrival of its patron, found this form of recollection unacceptable, the other obvious pattern of memory to employ was the *furta* account, which provided an appropriate remembrance of the translation and a popular focus for the community's pride and religious aspirations.

CHAPTER SEVEN

Conclusions

Investigation of the complexity of *furta sacra* has led us into an examination of two interrelated facets of the phenomenon. First, we have examined the specific historical contexts that gave rise to *furta* narratives within particular communities. Second, we have examined the manner in which hagiographers reflecting on the communal memory of these historical events, attempted to assimilate them into the ongoing functional history of their community in spite of evident moral hesitations. The product of these reflections was a specific literary tradition that continued to meet the needs of medieval communities.

Occasions for Composition

Thefts of relics, genuine or fictitious, were occasioned by one or a combination of six circumstances. What might be termed a seventh, pure economic opportunism such as that demonstrated by Deusdona, Felix, or Electus, should not be included in the list because it was simply an expedient, a means to an end, which would have been senseless without one or more of these other circumstances.

The first is that of new religious foundations. The Carolingian period furnishes numerous examples of this fundamental occasion for the production of relics. As religious communities developed, as parishes were established and populations increased, this basic need continued to be felt.

Secondly, in cases such as Mary Magdalene at Vézelay, and Sanctinus at Verdun, an equally fundamental situation can be discerned: the gradual tendency to make the possible actual and the abstract concrete. Just as in other aspects of medieval life, devotion to a saint over a period of time in a particular location tended to produce the physical remains of the saint as center of this devotion.

Political turmoil, such as that evidenced at Saint Tiberius, also occasioned translations. In a time when stark force of a physical or spiritual nature was the only right, religious communities felt a real need for protection against secular powers, so they brought in an outside protector—the relics of a saint.

Religious competition also spurred translations. This category could include rivalries of a more administrative nature such as that between Conques and Figeac, although monks of either community would have found it difficult to separate such differences from "genuine" religious differences. Religious competition might also take the form of rivalry between cult centers as foci of contemporary piety, as Conques and Vézelay.

Obviously, communal prestige was often an important point of rivalry. The translation of Saint Mark clearly resulted from the competition between Venice and Aquileia.

An effort to channel popular devotion could result in claims of stolen relics. Such efforts were evident at Conques and Villemagne in the eleventh century and at Dijon in the ninth. In the former cases, channeling should be taken literally, since the streams of pilgrims toward Compostela had to be channeled to the churches in question.

Finally, the possession of really important relics could compensate for defects in other areas. In Bari economic problems were alleviated when possession of a famous relic brought pilgrims. The tourist trade of the Middle Ages and the income from this trade offset to a certain extent loss of revenues in other areas.

These circumstances occurring singly would not normally culminate in a relic theft. In varying combinations these conditions existed in many places that never knew relic thefts. But in each of the cases in which a theft occurred, there were one or more accompanying reasons why normal responses or regular means of relic acquisition were closed or not as at-

tractive. Relics were often scarce in areas of new foundations. This situation, frequently in fact solved by the simple
purchase of relics, is referred to by Silvestre, who concluded
rightly that stolen relics had greater contemporary claim to
authenticity than purchased ones.[1] But there were other
quite different circumstances that combined with the situations above to inspire stealing. Competition with prees-
tablished claims compelled many thefts. The relics of
Sanctinus could not be "found" at Saint Vanne unless the
Meaux tradition was in some way dealt with, and since the
church of Meaux was not likely to part freely with its founder's remains, the theft story was a most convenient explanation. Sheer chance occasionally put individuals in a position
to remove relics or at least to say that they had removed
them. The Norman and Saracen incursions disrupted historical continuity and gave individuals the opportunity to prof-
fer such claims. Finally, the very popularity of theft accounts
gathered its own momentum and should not be discounted
in considering the *translationes* of Fausta and Prudentius.
Possession of stolen relics came to be regarded as a mark of
prestige in itself.

The traditional form of the theft narrative as it developed
in the ninth and tenth centuries seems to have greatly affected the variety of furtive *translationes*. Many of the narratives' conventional parameters were self-imposed, revealing
the lingering moral hesitations of their authors throughout
the period. With few exceptions, relics were removed from
one of five places: Rome, Aquitaine, Spain, North Africa, or
the Near East. Of these five, Rome was the only entirely
Christian source of stolen relics, and as the primary store-
house of the remains of martyrs, naturally occupied a peculiar place in the West. The other four lay outside the disposition of narrow, community-centered orthodoxy. Spain,
North Africa, the Near East (and also Aquitaine since according to the *translationes* the thefts occurred during times of
pagan disruption) clearly were outside western orthodoxy.
Each of these areas had its own Christian community, of
which the hagiographers were well aware. Nevertheless,

these communities were not considered to be entirely worthy of the honor bestowed by the residence of a great patron. But this chauvinistic attitude was not confined to communities outside of Christian political control; relics could be stolen from Anglo-Saxon communities by continental monks or *vice versa*, possibly because even those communities were, in the minds of the hagiographers and their communities, sufficiently different in custom, tradition, and culture, to be lumped in the same category as Mozarabs and Byzantines.

Another reason for locating the targets of these thefts in distant lands and cultures may have been the lure of the exotic and the difficulties of communication between these and other Christian communities. Much of the entertainment value in the story of the theft of Mark or Lewinna derives from descriptions of the foreign lands, strange languages, and perilous voyages. Moreover, since distant Christian communities seldom communicated with the areas to which the relics were brought, refutation of the thieves' claims by the supposed victims was unlikely.

Moral hesitations, rather than a lack of imagination on the part of the authors, account for the standardization of the *translationes*. Stealing relics was a spiritual exercise hallowed by generations of hagiographers, but there was a very specific form in which these thefts were remembered. Without the previous desolate condition of the shrine, dream visions, assistance from mysterious elders, etc., a theft might more resemble the shoddy operations of Felix than the pious efforts of Aigulfus, the translator of Benedict to Fleury. Thus, even before the hagiographer set down his *translatio*, it is likely that the Christian community had, in the retelling and recollection of the acquisition, already gone far in standardizing its memory of the theft. The standardization reflected both what was a natural organization of the events into their three components—preliminal, liminal, and postliminal—and a conformity to the mode in which other communities had recorded the same sort of translation.

A real conviction that the relic was the saint, that the relic was a person and not a thing, undoubtedly helped mitigate the more blatantly immoral aspects of stealing. Paralleling the custom of ritual "kidnappings" of brides by their prospective husbands, the theft of relics was at once a kidnapping and a seduction; overcome by the force of the thief's ardor and devotion, the saint allowed himself to be swept away to a new life in a new family.

Thus the formal tradition of *furta sacra* provided an appropriate memory of how and why a particular community came to be graced with the presence of a powerful new patron. It demonstrated the saint's love of the community and his concern with its problems while simultaneously showing the lengths to which the community was willing to go in order to bring the saint to live with its human members.

Throughout this study one might have sought an answer to what appears today a fundamental question: "how could actions recognized as thefts by their reporters and publicized for political and economic reasons be reconciled with high religious sentiment?" Increasingly, in the centuries that saw the massive influx of relics from the crusades and the growth of rational and legalistic thought in the rediscovery of Roman law and Aristotelian logic, the apparent contradictions would become more troublesome. Even ordinary religious and laity proved capable of distinguishing the relics from the saints themselves, and when relics were perceived more as object than subject, these contradictions could not so easily be ignored. But during the central Middle Ages, the contradictions, if they existed at all, were easy to accept. They would become serious problems only for those who stood outside the world in which relics were alive, moving about as they wished, and helping those they chose.

The subject of this study has been a state of mind, a way of thinking exemplified by the faithful monk guarding the relics of his monastery through the night. Alone with them in the silent crypt, listening to the steady breathing of the saint asleep in his tomb or perhaps alternating psalms with him in the darkness, the guardian's presence symbolizes the faith, avarice, and apparent contradiction of the entire phenomenon of relic thefts. He knows that he is guarding what can only be stolen by the will of the saint. And if the saint wills to be removed, then a mere man will be powerless to prevent it. At the same time, he is convinced that his vigilance will protect the community from the loss of its most vital animating force, unless of course he should be persuaded by eloquent argument or rich bribes to give it up. Whatever contradictions may be present in this image must be accepted for what they are—part of the fabric of human life no more preposterous than the contradictions future generations may see in our own society.

Critique of Texts

I. "TRANSLATIO BEATI VINCENTII"

While the date of Aimoin's *translatio* can be established with precision as 869,[1] it is impossible to determine with any degree of certainty the facts of the text's account. On the one hand, the information it provides concerning Bishop Senior of Saragossa and Count Salamon of Cerdagne is accurate. Senior is known from a letter of Bishop Eulogius of Toledo,[2] while Auzias has shown that Salamon, whose name appears not only in Aimoin's *translatio* and in the highly fictive *Gesta comitum Barcinonensium*,[3] but also in an act of 868,[4] was the individual appointed to govern the newly created Spanish March by Charles the Bald in 865.[5] But on this historical basis, Aimoin has built an historical fiction which cannot be properly evaluated.[6]

If one can believe Aimoin, Castres was offered the opportunity to acquire the remains of Vincent quite by chance—a chance the monks seized eagerly. But Castres was by no means the only religious institution eager to possess Vincent's remains around the middle of the ninth century. Audaldus had of course originally set out on his quest from Conques, according to the *translatio*. And as Aimoin reports in his *Translatio SS martyrum Georgii monachi, Aurelii et Nathaliae*,[7] the original purpose of Usuard's expedition had been to obtain the same body for Saint Germain des Prés, where Vincent had been honored since Childebert had brought his stole to that monastery in 527.[8] In Viviers, Usuard learned that the body had already been translated to Benevento in Italy.[9]

This rumor, which Aimoin dismisses as false (since according to his *translatio* between 855 and 864 Vincent's remains

lay in Saragossa venerated under the name of Saint Marin),
presents a curious problem; not that the body should have
been translated from the same place more than once—as was
seen above this was a frequent occurrence—but rather that
there was no tradition of the possession of Vincent's relics at
the monastery of Saint Vincent of Volturno near Benevento
to which the remains were said to have been translated.

True, Sigebert's life of Archbishop Theodoric of Metz reports what would appear to be such a tradition. He tells
how in 970, while traveling with Otto I in Italy, Theodoric
obtained the body of Vincent from the bishop of Arezzo.[10]
According to the bishop, the body had originally been at the
monastery of Saint Vincent but when this was destroyed by
Saracens in the ninth century,[11] the body had been removed
to Cortona and had not been returned when the monastery
was rebuilt.[12] The bishop went on to explain that it had been
secretly acquired by two monks who had brought it from
Spain.[13] But none of the records of that important monastery
report any tradition of the possession of the body, either before or after its destruction.[14] It is much more likely that the
bishop of Arezzo, pressed by the credulous Theodoric for
some valuable relic, and not daring to displease the close
companion of Otto, used the proximity of the monastery of
Saint Vincent to invent a relic that would certainly please the
German.

From the time of Aimoin on, there continued in Francia a
strong tradition associating Vincent and Castres. The cult of
the saint quickly spread throughout the area and pilgrims
came from the surrounding Cerdagne, Toulousan, and
Rouergue. A primary force behind the cult was Bishop Elisa-
char of Toulouse (861–863) who instituted a pilgrimage to
the monastery and led the faithful himself barefoot the final
nine miles to Castres.[15]

The memory of Vincent's translation to Castres was also
maintained at Saint Germain des Prés, as shown in B.N. ms.
lat. 13760, a ninth and tenth-century collection of hagiographical texts from that monastery. Fols. 148r–186v contain
Aimoin's *Translatio B. Vincentii* which was divided into les-

sons and used as a liturgical text. The translation was also commemorated in a tenth-century sermon for the feast of Vincent added at the end of the *Passio B. Vincentii* found in the same manuscript.[16] After a brief reference to the Passio, the homilist goes on to recall the manner in which the provinces of Gaul received the saint's relics, first his cloak and later his body:

Childebertus quoque et Clotharius Francorum reges dum Hispaniam uastant Cesaraugustam circumdantes obsident, sed ciues tunicam Vincentii martyris circumferentes misericordiam Domini rogabant. Qua de re flexi reges Childebertus et Clotarius pace composita in munere stolam beati Vincentii martyris a Cesaraugustanis acceperunt. Parisius Childebertus reuersus aecclesiam in ueneratione beati martiris Vincentii ibi constructam, eandem ipsam stolam in eandem ipsam aecclesiam reposuit. Laudino quoque danato haud procul a muro urbis (in marg.: eius nominis basilica a Brunechilde quondam regina ut fertur) est edificata.

Aecclesia autem que super sancti Vincentii corpus constructa fuerat post multum tempus a paganis ob malignorum ciuium et circumhabitantium prauam conuersationem destructa est, ibique corpus sanctum absque ullo religionis honore nullo excepta matre tellure obstante tegmine imbre humectabatur aethereo. Domino autem reuelante repertum est corpus eius a quodam uenerabili monacho Audaldo nomine et in cenobio beati Benedicti quod Castrum cognominatur situm in partibus Aquitanię translatum est. Ibique corpus sancti leuitę et martiris Vincentii a uiro religioso domno Gisleberto abbate caeterisque fratribus sub eo degentibus post altare pii patris Benedicti condigne sepultum est. Quo in loco coruscat rite assiduis uirtutum signis prestante domino nostre Ihesu Christo cui est honor et gloria in saecula saeculorum. Amen.

All documentation on Castres during the century following the translation is lacking, but when it is again available, around the middle of the tenth century, the cult of Vincent is on a par with that of Benedict. No longer is the monastery referred to as *Bella cellula* or *monasterium Sancti*

Benedicti, but rather *Monasterium Sancti Benedicti et Sancti Vincentii.*[17]

II. "TRANSLATIO SANCTAE FIDEI"

Without hoping to bring to a final, satisfactory close the arguments which have raged for a millennium concerning the translation of Saint Foy to Conques, it is possible to arbitrate between the two major traditions of historical and hagiographical investigation: that of Ferdinand Lot and Léon Levillain who saw the *translatio* as a fairly accurate historical text, and that of J. Angély, who considered the entire tradition a fabrication.

The *terminus ante quem* for the composition of the *translationes* (for the prose and verse versions are clearly the same account and are closely related) is the twelfth century, since at least one manuscript of the verse *translatio* is of that period.[1] In order to date the composition more accurately, Ferdinand Lot pointed out that since the prose *translatio* refers readers to a "codex miraculorum" which he identifies with the *Liber Miraculorum* of Bernard of Angers composed after 1020[2] this text must be later than the first quarter of the eleventh century. Following the editor of the *Liber Miraculorum*, A. Bouillet, Lot identifies the author of the *translatio* with the continuator of the *Liber* who wrote around 1060.[3] Finally, Lot dated the verse *translatio* after 1034 since the author had clearly relied on Ademar of Chabannes's (died 1034) *Chronicon* for his erroneous cognomen applied to Charles the Simple: *Carolus minor.*[4] Léon Levillain agreed with Lot and pointed out in addition that the verse *translatio* mentions the dispute between Conques and the nearby monastery of Figeac which only began again in earnest after 1060, hence reinforcing the hypothesis that the two texts date from the mid-eleventh century.[5]

If there was substantial agreement on the date of composition of the *translationes*, there was much less on the method of establishing the date of the translation itself. Both schol-

ars accepted the details of the *translationes*, and used these
details, the cartulary of Conques,[6] and the martyrology of
Ado of Vienne to construct their arguments.[7]

Briefly stated, Lot's argument ran as follows. Supposing
that the reference in Ado to the presence of Foy in Conques
is not an interpolation, the translation must have been prior
to 875, the date of Ado's death. The Carolus minor spoken
of in the *translationes* is Charles the Young who reigned in
Aquitaine from 855 to September 29, 866. The last donation
to Conques that does not mention the presence of Saint Foy
is that of Count Bernard and his wife Ermengarde dated "in
mense julio, XII kalendas augustas, anno VII regnante Karolo rege Francorum et Longobardorum."[8] This obviously erroneous title should be corrected to read "regnante Karolo
rege Francorum et Aquitanorum." Thus the date would be
July 21, 862. But since Bernard should hardly have carried
the title of count prior to the death of his predecessor (Count
Stephen, killed by the Normans in December 863), the diploma must be of July 21, 864. Between that date and the
death of Charles in 866, the only possible dates for the translation would be January 14, 865 or 866.[9]

Levillain objected to Lot's arguments on several grounds.
First, admitting that the title *minor* comes from Ademar, is it
necessary to see this confusion pointing to Charles the
Young? Could it not be equally Charles the Bald? Secondly,
Lot's correction of the title in charter 153 to read "rege Francorum et Aquitanorum" is arbitrary; Levillain, the editor of
the royal Aquitanian diplomas, pointed out that the Aquitanian kings never referred to themselves as "rex Francorum." Moreover, Bernard did not take the title of count in
863 since, as the *Annales Bertiniani* suggest, Stephen was
not killed until the following year.[10] Finally, the abbot Bigo I
mentioned in the charter could not have been abbot both in
852 and 862 or 864 since the *Translatio B. Vincentii* of
Aimoin, who should have been well informed, named the
abbot in 855 Blandin.[11]

In place of Lot's arguments, Levillain proposes his own
which ultimately suggest the same possible dates. First he

identifies the Carolus of charter 153 with Charles the Bald
and dates it 854, reckoning from Charles's consecration at
Orléans in June 848, a common practice in Aquitanian pri-
vate charters. He then suggests that in 855, when the monks
of Conques failed to obtain the relics of Vincent, they looked
to another nearby Vincent, that of Pompéjac near Agen.
While there, the monks stole the remains of Saint Foy. Taking the verse *translatio* literally and supposing that the monk
actually remained ten years in Agen waiting for an opportunity to steal the bodies, or at least supposing that the mention of the ten-year period indicated that "their desires were
not realized until after ten years of efforts," one is led to the
years 865 or 866. If the Carolus minor referred to in the
translationes is Charles the Young, then the date of the theft
must be January 14, 866.[12]

More recently, the local hagiographer of Agen, J. Angély,
has strenuously objected to the entire approach of these two
outstanding historians, insisting that the entire story is a fabrication and that the translation never took place. Although
Angély's purpose is above all to demonstrate that his home
town is still in possession of both Foy and Vincent, his arguments are worth considering.[13] He argues first that the date
implied in the two *translationes* as well as in the *Chronicon*
of Conques places the translation in the year 884, an obvious impossibility in view of a charter of Conques dated 883
which mentions the presence of Saint Foy in Conques. He re-
jects the dates proposed by Lot and Levillain, 865 or 866, because by then the church of Saint Foy in Agen had been destroyed by the Normans and the monk of Conques could
not have joined a religious community there at that time. Secondly, he insists on the similarity between the *Translatio S.
Faustae* and the *Translationes S. Fidei* and contends that the
similarity proves a direct dependence of the latter on the former, negating any possible historical value in the accounts.
Finally, he insists upon the uninterrupted possession of Saint
Foy's remains throughout the Middle Ages and modern period, offering as proof the account of a visit to Agen by a
monk of Saint Gallen in the eleventh century.[14]

By way of arbitrating between these arguments, several observations are in order. First, Angély is quite right in pointing out the essentially literary nature of the *translationes*. Although there is no compelling reason to ascribe the *Translatio S. Faustae* as the primary model for the *Translationes S. Fidei*, they clearly belong to the tradition growing out of the *Translatio S. Benedicti*, probably by way of the *Translatio S. Vincentii*. On the other hand, the cartulary demonstrates that between 854 and 883 Conques came into possession of what were widely taken to be the remains of a Saint Foy and quite probably of a Saint Vincent. Angély's insistence on the destruction of Agen by the Normans completely misses the point. The destruction of the town and the church of Saint Foy would have been exactly the sort of circumstances to result in a theft or a claim of a theft by more fortunate neighbors.

In the final evaluation, the facts of the case are these: by 883 Conques was recognized to be in possession of the remains of Saints Foy and Vincent, and so recognized by those who counted most—donors and patrons of the monastery. Just how this possession came about may well not have been decided for almost two centuries. It is immaterial that Agen may have continued to claim possession of the remains, or even that this claim may have been legitimate. Throughout the Middle Ages, Saint Foy continued to work her miracles in Conques, not Agen, and this was what mattered to those thousands who made the pilgrimage there.

III. "TRANSLATIO SANCTAE FAUSTAE"

According to the *Historia translationis S. Faustae*,[1] in the same year that Saint Vincent found his way to Castres, Duke Arnald of Aquitaine gave permission to the monks of the monastery of Solignac, which had been destroyed by the Normans, to go south in search of a relic in the area recently abandoned after the Norman pillaging. Two persons were chosen for the mission, a priest named Aldarius and a nephew of the duke, Gotfried. The two had traveled a great distance and had almost despaired of finding a suitable relic when they happened upon a church in the area of Vic Fésenzac dedicated to Saint Fausta which had been burned by the Normans. That night, Aldarius and Gotfried went secretly into the church where they found the saint's tomb. Opening the tomb, they were all but overcome by the fragrant odor which it exuded, but they recovered sufficiently to remove the body and hurry back toward Solignac. After a journey marked by miracles performed by Fausta, they arrived at Brivezac, a priory of Solignac, and placed the relics in its church.

Unlike many other *translationes* which are pure fiction, the *Translatio S. Faustae* is probably a fairly accurate account of what must have been a frequent occurrence in the later ninth century: following the destruction of churches by invaders, secular and religious leaders gave permission for other religious communities to remove the saints' remains from these churches. But the author of the *Translatio S. Faustae* apparently attempted to disguise a legal translation as a theft. Why this was done and why the possession of Saint Fausta was necessary at all can be answered by an examination of the monastery of Solignac in the second half of the ninth century.

The translation of Fausta appears to have been part of an effort by the monks of Solignac to preserve their monastery's position of prestige and importance in the face of two very serious threats. To this end they determined that they needed a new patron, and with the help of the count and his *nepos* they found this patron in Fausta.

The first threat was the destruction of the monastery by the Normans. There can be no doubt that this event was of catastrophic proportions for the community. Besides the loss of life and property that must have resulted from the burning of Solignac, the monks were further harmed by the apparent loss of all records of the monastery's possessions and privileges. This latter loss, or supposed loss, seems to have been particularly significant for the monks. In 865 Charles the Bald issued a diploma acknowledging the destruction of these records and reconfirming the ancient privileges granted by his predecessors.[2] The following year Abbot Bernard of Solignac appeared at the Synod of Soissons and described in moving terms the state of the monastery after its destruction and the utter loss of all its records. Evidently moved by the account, the synod reaffirmed the privileges of immunity and tutelage granted the monastery by the kings and emperors of the Franks.[3]

But strangely enough, the accounts of the destruction of the monastery's archives were greatly exaggerated. In fact, today at least six privileges for the monastery issued prior to its destruction are preserved either in original or in transcription.[4] Either the account of the total destruction of the monastery was exaggerated by the abbot, or, as is more likely, the monks were able to flee with their charters; in either case one must wonder why Bernard felt it necessary to pretend that his monastery had been more severely damaged than it had been, and why he had chosen to ask for a reconfirmation of its rights at this particular moment.

The reason is to be found in the threat presented by the rapid expansion of a nearby rival monastic foundation. In this instance the competitor was the monastery of Beaulieu, which had been founded in 855 by Archbishop Rodulf of Limoges and his family, the counts of Turenne, as a dependency of Solignac.[5] Originally the new monastery had been placed under the authority of the abbots Burnulf and Cunibert of Solignac, and twelve monks of the latter monastery formed its first community.[6] But very quickly the new foundation, located near the castle of the counts of Turenne and particularly favored by Count Gotfried and his descendants, became independent of Solignac and grew rapidly in wealth and prestige. This development was aided by the fact that the new monastery was not destroyed by the Normans, and so was able to continue its growth while, for a time at least, the community housing its superior had ceased to exist.

Solignac enjoyed the support of the dukes of Aquitaine as well as that of the Carolingians. Hence it was in general in a

relatively secure position. But in the immediate area of
Turenne its rights were particularly in jeopardy, and this
was the location of Brivezac, the priory to which the body of
Fausta was brought. This priory, which had been a place of
refuge after the destruction of Solignac itself, was in the center of the area rapidly becoming dominated by Beaulieu.[7] As
protection against the ascendancy of the new monastery, the
monks of Solignac needed a reconfirmation of their temporal
rights that would guarantee their possessions after their reconstruction. This reconfirmation was found in the documents issued by Charles the Bald and by the assembled bishops at Soissons. But equally important was reconfirmation
of its spiritual importance, and this was found in the power
of Saint Fausta.

The choice of Fausta seems to have been mostly chance.
Her identity is far from certain, and the *translatio* offers little help in identifying her. There is no extant *vita* of an Aquitanian virgin and martyr of that name, and evidently she
was confused, even within the diocese of Limoges, with the
Saint Fausta who was martyred in Cizic under Maximianus
and whose feast is celebrated September 20.[8] Even at Solignac, where the feast of her translation, May 15, was celebrated as a first class feast with octave,[9] her feast was celebrated September 20 and, at least by the seventeenth
century, the only *Vita S. Faustae* known in the monastery
was that of the other Fausta.[10]

In the diocese of Auch, from which her remains were supposedly removed, even less was known of her in the century
immediately following her translation.[11] But the location of
the ruined church in Fésenzac and a mention of relics of the
Virgin Mary and of Saint Martin also removed from the
church by Aldarius suggest a highly speculative but attractive hypothesis concerning the saint's identity. There was a
sixth-century bishop of Auch, Faustus (died 585) mentioned
by Gregory of Tours,[12] who is probably the same Faustus
praised by Venantius Fortunatus as the founder of the basilica of Saint Martin in Auch.[13] A confused and obviously spurious tradition, in evidence in the diocese of Auch in the elev-

enth century, named Clovis as the founder of this church and counted among his many donations to the church the tunic of the Virgin.[14] The church appearing in the *translatio* is probably that of Vic Fésenzac, the location of the church of Saint Martin supposedly associated with Bishop Faustus. Given the possibility of the combined traditions of a Faust, a relic of the Virgin and one of Saint Martin in this same church, it is not entirely impossible that the account of the translation concerns the removal of relics from this church after its destruction by the Normans.[15] If the church really was abandoned, Aldarius and Gotfried could have learned little about the identity of its saintly patron. In the course of the translation, therefore, the Faustus, whose name was probably unfamiliar to the monks of the diocese of Limoges, changed sex and emerged as Fausta.

As in the case over a century later with Lewinna, since nothing was known of the saint, the account of her arrival had to make up for her obscurity. By attaching the story of Fausta's translation to the tradition of *furta sacra*, the monks of Solignac could emphasize that this saint, although obscure, was important and powerful, even important enough to steal, and thus could exert her spiritual power in behalf of the monastery of Solignac.

IV. "TRANSLATIO SANCTI MAIANI"

Although it purports to record a ninth-century translation, the *Translatio S. Maiani* is almost certainly an eleventh-century composition. In Chapter 4 we saw that the cult of Maianus did not appear in the area of Béziers until the extreme end of the tenth century. Additional evidence that the *translatio* is a later composition is provided in the opening lines of the text which date the *translatio* as follows: "Caroli principis junioris nepotis magni Ludovici Karoli imperatoris filii, ac Theodardi ecclesiae Narbonensis archiepiscopi egregii, nec non et Gilberti ecclesiae Biterensis episcopi temporibus." The conflict between the chronological and genealogical ele-

APPENDIX A

ments of this text suggests that it was written in the eleventh
century.

First, the episcopal years of Theodardus (885–893)[1] and
of Gilbertus (886–897)[2] would suggest that the translation
took place between 886 and 893. Since only one Charles
was king during this period, Charles the Simple (893–923),
the chronological information would date the translation in
the year 893. However, there are two difficulties with this
thesis. First, Charles the Simple was not the grandson of a
Louis and great-grandson of a Charles (or, if one reads filii
Ludovici to refer to Carolus junior, a son of a Charles).
Charles was rather "nepos Karoli, filii Ludovici." Moreover,
Charles was not referred to as "junior" before the eleventh
century.

The only Carolingian who could fit this genealogical information was Charles the Fat who was king of the West
Franks from 885 until his deposition in 887, but he was
never known as "Carolus junior." Thus it would appear
that the translatio's author wrote at a sufficiently distant
time to confuse Carolingian genealogy, combining elements
of various Carolingian Charles'es. He probably obtained the
names of Theodardus and Gilbertus from the proceedings of
a council, for example that of Porta in 887 at which both
were in attendance.[3]

Finally, the appellation "junior" probably comes from the
chronicle of Ademar of Chabannes (988–1034). In at least
one redaction of the Chronicon, Charles the Simple is called
"junior."[4] If the author of the translatio, writing in the second third of the eleventh century, had before him the proceedings of the Council of Porta and the Chronicon of
Adémar, then the confusing chronological and genealogical
information becomes understandable.

Who was Saint Maianus? The translatio provides only a
vague indication of the place from which the relics were stolen and no information about the saint himself. It only mentions that the church was in "Vasconia" and that to return
to Villemagne the monks had to traverse the forest of
Buchona.[5] The Bollandists attempted to identify the saint

with Merwinus, the seventh-century cult venerated in Brittany as Saint Méen.[6] But this identification is clearly erroneous considering the Gascon location and the fact that while Saint Méen's feast is June 21, Maianus's falls on June 1.[7]

Surprisingly, none of the scholars who have examined the cult of Saint Maianus have given serious attention to a most vital piece of documentation: the same manuscript from the monastery of Eysses that provided the text of the *translatio* also contained a *Vita S. Maiani* which, while hardly an historical account, is an important indication of whom Maianus was believed to have been in the Middle Ages. The manuscript disappeared during the French revolution, but not before Dom Claude Estiennot copied it along with the *translatio*. This copy, now in B.N. ms. lat. 12699, was used by Mabillon for a short notice on Maianus in his *Acta Sanctorum Ordinis Sancti Benedicti* but he did not publish it.[8] The Bollandists must have known of the text as well since it was probably responsible for the confusion with Saint Méen, although the two are clearly distinct.[9] However, they also chose not to publish it. Perhaps the reason that the *vita* was virtually ignored is that while, as we have seen, scholars have tended to consider the *translatio* an "historical" account of the ninth or tenth century, the *vita* is clearly much later. Moreover, although Maianus bears no resemblance to Méen in his origins or life, the two saints both were dragon-slayers. The Bollandists may have considered this similarity sufficient evidence to consider the two saints as one.

Maianus, according to the vita, was a monk from Antioch, who came first to Rome and then to Compostela on pilgrimage. Passing through Gascony he came to a place called "Longuierris" and, finding there a church dedicated to the Virgin, decided to lead a hermit's life in this lonely place. In time his reputation attracted a wide following in the area and when the devil began to ravage the countryside in the form of a dragon, the inhabitants came to him for help. He easily destroyed the beast by throwing his ring into its mouth, and after this victory people from far and near came to him to be miraculously cured.

Even after his death Maianus continued to protect the area, working miracles and in one instance preventing the sacking of the church by the count of Astarac.

The *vita* is poor evidence for the existence of an historical Maianus, but it does show that he was believed to have been an easterner, a hermit, and associated with a Gascon church dedicated to the Virgin. This last bit of information is similar to that found by Mabillon in a forged charter of the eleventh century.[10] Thus, whoever Maianus was, by the eleventh century he was honored as a Gascon hermit of eastern origins with a reputation for protecting his faithful from human and superhuman threats.

Handlist of Relic Thefts

The following is a handlist of relic thefts said to have taken place between ca. 800 and ca. 1100. The phenomenon is so common in hagiographic literature that there are almost certainly instances which I have overlooked. Nevertheless, I provide this list of those theft accounts which were examined in the preparation of this study, and when possible their approximate dates of composition, in order to make my data base available to readers.

Abbanus, Abbot of Magh-Arnuidhe. Inhabitants of Ceall-Abbain, the birthplace of Abbanus, steal his body from Magh-Arnuidhe, the monastery he had founded and in which he had lived for the latter part of his life. Date uncertain, eighth or ninth century? *Vita, AASS Oct.* XII, pp. 276–293. *BHL* 1.

Appianus, Monk of Pavia. Citizens of Pavia are in Comacchio to procure salt and attempt to carry off the body of Appianus. They are miraculously prevented from so doing. Ninth century? *Vita S. Appiani, AASS Mart.* 1, p. 320. *BHL* 619.

Arnulfus. Monks of Saint Médard try to steal relics of Arnulfus from Oldenbourg. ca. 1090. Hariulfus, *Vita Arnulfi episcopi Suessionensis, MGH SS* XV, p. 900. *BHL* 703.

Auctor, Bishop of Trier. Auctor appears to Gertrudis, Marchisa of Saxony, and asks that his remains be removed from Trier to Braunschweig in 1113. She complies. *Translatio Brunsvicum saec.* XII, *AASS Aug.* IV, pp. 48–52. *BHL* 748.

Bartholomew. Relic-monger Felix sells the body of Bartholomew, which he has stolen from Italy, to Bishop Erchambert of Freising. 830's. *PL* CXVI, col. 32.

Benedict of Nursia. According to Adrevald of Fleury, Aigulfus of Lérins removed the body of Benedict from Monte Cassino to Fleury in the early seventh century. *Translatio in Galliam saec.* VII, Mabillon, *Vetera Analecta*, 211–212. BHL 1116.

Bertulfus, Confessor Ghent. Electus steals the body of Bertulfus from Boulogne-sur-Mer where it had been placed temporarily for protection from Viking raids. He is caught and forced to return it. Tenth century. *Vita auctore Blundiniensi monacho, AASS Feb.* I, p. 682. BHL 1316.

Bibanus, Bishop of Saintes. Monks of Figeac carry off the body of Bishop Bibanus from Saintes to Figeac during the Norman destruction of Saintes. Ninth century. *Translatio S. Vivani episcopi, Anal. Boll.,* vol. 8 (1889), pp. 256–277. BHL 1327.

Boniface, Bishop of Mainz. In 758 Saint Hildulphus of Milan steals the body of Boniface from Stier and brings it to Milan. *Libellus de S. Hilduphi successoribus, MGH SS* IV, pp. 86–92. BHL 3949.

Callistus, Pope. Abbot Nanterus of Saint Michaels in Verdun goes to Rome, arranges to steal the body of Pope Callistus and returns with it to Verdun. ca. 1020. *Chronicon S. Michaelis in pago Virdunensi, MGH SS* IV, pp. 82–83.

Saints Chrysogonus and Anastasia, Martyrs. Gottschalk, a monk of Benedictbeuern, is in Verona in 1053 and visits the church where Chrysogonus and Anastasia are buried. He enters, steals some of their relics, but is caught returning for more. He begs the guard in Benedict's name for the relics and is given them. *Chronicon Benedictoburanum, MGH SS* IX, pp. 226–227.

Davin, Pilgrim of Lucca. A canon of the church of Lucca attempts to steal a finger of Davin but is paralyzed until the community prays for his forgiveness. He confesses and returns the finger. Before 1142? *Vita et miracula, AASS Iun.* I, pp. 322–325. BHL 2114.

Deodatus. Giso steals the body of Deodatus from diocese of Reims and brings it to Paris. ca. 870. Flodoard, *Historia Remensis ecclesiae, MGH SS* XIII, pp. 534–535.

Dodo. Abbot of Wallers-en-Fagne. Winigisus, an inhabitant of Tongres, steals a reliquary containing relics of Dodo as it is carried through Brabant. He is paralyzed and forced to return it. Tenth century. *Vita Dodonis, AASS Oct.* XII, pp. 634–637. *BHL* 2207.

Ebrulfus. Herluinus, chancellor of Duke Hugo of Orléans, and Radulfus of Dragiaco steal the relics of Ebrulfus from the monastery of Saint Ebrulfus and take them to Rebais. Many of the monks of the monastery of Saint Ebrulfus follow the relics to Rebais and establish their monastery there. 943. Ordericus Vitalis, *Historia ecclesiastica*, liber II, vi, ed. Marjorie Chibnall. *BHL* 2375.

Epiphanius and Speciosa. In 964 Bishop Otwinus of Hildesheim is in Pavia. Landwardus, a priest in his party, steals the bodies of Epiphanius and Speciosa. The citizens of Pavia appeal to Otto I who allows Landwardus to keep the relics for Hildesheim. *Translatio Sancti Epiphanii, MGH SS* IV, pp. 248–251. *BHL* 2573.

Fausta, Virgin martyr in Aquitaine. In 969 a priest of the monastery of Solignac, Aldarius, and Gotfried, nephew of Duke Arnald of Aquitaine, remove the body of Fausta from a church in Fésenzac and bring it to Brivezac, a priory dependent on Solignac. *Translatio S. Faustae, AASS Ian.* I, pp. 1090–1092. *BHL* 2832.

Florbertus. Monks of Saint Bavon in Ghent claim to have secretly stolen Florbertus's body from Saint Blandin. ca. 1050. Lantbertus, *Libellus de loco sepulturae Florberti abbatis contra monachos S. Bavonis, MGH SS* XV, pp. 641–644. *BHL* 3031.

Foy, Virgin martyr of Agen. In the 860's, the body of Saint Foy is stolen from Agen to Conques by a monk of that monastery. *AASS Oct.* III, pp. 294–299. *BHL* 2939, 2941.

Gislenus, Abbot in Hainaut. In 930 nuns of Maubeuge steal the body of Saint Gislenus from Mons but are forced by the bishop to return it. *Inventio et miracula, AASS Oct.* IV, pp. 1034–1037. *BHL* 3554.

Gorgonius. In 765 Chrodegang of Metz is returning from Rome with relics of Gorgonius given him by the pope. At

Saint Moritz the monks of that monastery steal the relics from him. He complains to Pepin who orders that the relics be returned. The monks refuse and Chrodegang begins to destroy the reliquary of Saint Moritz until the monks return the relics. *Vita Chrodegangi, MGH SS* x, pp. 553–572. *BHL* 1781.

Gregory I, Pope. In 826 Rodoinus of Saint Médard of Soissons enters Saint Peter's and takes the remains of Gregory the Great. He returns with them to Saint Médard. *Translatio SS Sebastiani et Gregorii I Papae, AASS Ian.* II, pp. 642–659. *MGH SS* xv, pp. 379–391. *BHL* 7545.

Helen, Imperatrix. In the 840's a monk of Hautvilliers goes to Rome and secretly removes the body of Helen and returns to his monastery with it. *Translatio S. Helenae ad coenobinm Altivillarense, AASS Aug.* III, p. 602. *BHL* 3773.

Innocent and Vitalis. Anno, Archbishop of Cologne, enters a church in Rome and, bribing the guards, steals the relics of Innocent and Vitalis. He returns with them to Cologne and builds a church to house them. ca. 1069. *Vita Annonis archiepiscopi Coloniensis, MGH SS* xi, pp. 462–514. *BHL* 507.

James. Adalbert of Bremen had acquired a tooth of Saint James, possibly stolen, from an Italian bishop in the eleventh century. Adam of Bremen, *Gesta,* III, 67. *MGH SS* vii, pp. 363–365.

John the Baptist. The archdeacon of Archbishop Rufus of Turin attempts to steal the finger of John the Baptist from Maurienne and is struck dead. Early ninth century? *Vita S. Tigriae, AASS Iun.* v, pp. 72–77. *BHL* 8290.

Justus. Liuthardus of Malmedy goes to Koniensi (unknown location), bribes the guard of the church who allows him to steal the body of Saint Justus, is himself almost robbed on his way home, but arrives at last in Malmedy with the relics. ca. 900. *Translatio Malmudarium, MGH SS* sv, pp. 566–567. *BHL* 4594.

Lewinna. In 1058 the monk Balgerus of the monastery of Bergues-Saint-Winnoc steals the body of Lewinna from an unidentified church on the southeast coast of England. *Historia translationis ex Anglia*, AASS Iul. v, pp. 608–627. *BHL* 4902.

Maianus. Around 893 two monks of Colognac travel to Gascony and remove the body of Saint Maianus from its church and return to Colognac. *Translatio S. Maiani, HGL* v, cols. 5–8. *BHL 5946.*

Marcellinus and Peter. In 827 Einhard sends his servant with Deusdona to Rome to acquire the bodies of Marcellinus and Peter for Heiligenstadt. *MGH SS* xv, pp. 239–264. *BHL 5233.*

Mark. In 827 or 828 merchants of Venice steal the body of Mark from Alexandria and return with it to Venice. *Translatio S. Marci*, ed. N. McCleary, "Note," pp. 223–264. *BHL 5283–5284.*

Martin, Hermit in Montemarsico. A monk of Saint Martin's tries to steal the body of Saint Martin. He is interrupted by an earthquake and stopped by Abbot Hilarius who had been warned by a vision of Saint Martin. Tenth century. *Vita translatio et miracula*, AASS Oct. x, pp. 835–840. *BHL* 5604.

Mary Magdalene. The body of Mary Magdalene was said to have been brought from either Palestine or Provence to Vézelay in the late ninth century. *Translatio Vizeliacum*, i, ii; Faillon, *Monuments inédits sur l'apostolat de Sainte Marie-Madeleine en Provence*, 2 vols. (Paris: 1848) ii, pp. 741–752. *BHL 5488–5489.*

Metro, Priest of Verona. The body of Saint Metro is stolen from Verona by inhabitants of a nearby town. ca. 960. *Invectiva Ratherii episcopi Veronensis*, PL cxxxvi, cols. 471–476. *BHL 5942.*

Modaldus, Bishop of Trier. In the eleventh century (?) a Frenchman enters the church of Saint Symphorianus in Trier and attempts to steal the body of Saint Modaldus, but he is foiled when the body begins to bleed. *Vita auctore Stephano Abbate S. Iacobi Leodiensi*, AASS Mai iii, pp. 50–78. *BHL* 5985.

Nicasius. Stolen from Tournai to Reims. ca. 900. Jean Cousin, *Histoire de Tournay,* vol. 3 (Douai: 1619), pp. 49–52.

Nicolas, Bishop of Myra.

1. Nicolas is translated from Myra to Bari in 1087 by merchants of that city. *Translationes,* Nitti, "Leggenda." *BHL* 6179, 6190.

2. Venetians steal relics of Nicolas and his uncle, another Nicolas, from Myra and bring them to Venice. ca. 1100. *Historia de translatione monachi anonymi Littorensis, RHC,* vol. 5, pp. 253–292. *BHL,* 6200.

3. Beneventans steal body of Nicolas and bring it to Benevento. ca. 1105. *Adventus Sancti Nicoli in Beneventum,* G. Cangiano, ed., *Atti della società storica del Sannio,* vol. 2 (1924), pp. 131–162.

4. The body of Nicolas is stolen from Bari and brought to the village of Porta in Lotharingia. ca. 1105. *Qualiter reliquiae B. Nicolai ad Lotharingiae villam quae Portus nominatur delatae sunt, RHC,* vol. 5, pp. 293–294.

Oswald, King of Northumbria. Balgerus, a monk of Saint Winnoc, steals the arm of King Oswald in the early eleventh century. *AASS Aug.* II, pp. 87–88.

Pantaleon, Martyr of Nicomedia. Abbot Richard of Saint Vanne buys relics of Saint Pantaleon from a soldier who has taken them during the sack of Commercy in the early eleventh century. *Translatio reliquiarum Virodunum saec.* XI, *AASS OSB* VI, i, pp. 471–472. *BHL* 6443.

Prudentius. Bishop Geylo of Langres, returning to Bèze from Compostela in 841, steals the body of Prudentius from a town on his route. *Passio, translationes, auctore Teobaudo, AASS Oct.* III, pp. 348–377. *BHL* 6979.

Reginswind. In the ninth century, a man attempting to steal the relics of Reginswind from her church in Würzburg is prevented by an earthquake, lightning, and thunder. *Vita, AASS Iul.* IV, pp. 92–95. *BHL* 7101.

Sanctinus. Merchants of Verdun returning from Spain steal the body of Sanctinus from Meaux. Eleventh century.

Translatio S. Sanctini, Subsidia Hagiographica no. 56, pp. 161–165.

Severus, Bishop of Ravenna. Felix, a relic-monger, steals the relics of Severus from Ravenna and sells them to Archbishop Otgarius of Mainz. *Litolfi vita et translatio S. Severi*, *MGH SS* xv, pp. 289–293. *BHL* 7682.

Stephen I, Pope. A monk from Trani goes to Rome in 1160 and steals the relics of Saint Stephen for his monastery. *Translatio ad coenobium Columnense prope Tranum, AASS Aug.* I, p. 131. *BHL* 7847.

Sulpitius. Stolen from Normandy to Mons. ca. 986. *Translatio S. Sulpitii in monasterium S. Gisleni, AASS Ian.* II, p. 788. *BHL* 7935.

Taurinus. Stolen from Normandy to Laon. ca. 1000. *Translatio ad Castrum Laudosum et ad coenobium Gigniacense, AASS Aug.* II, pp. 645–650. *BHL* 7995.

Valentine. A priest of the monastery of Jumièges goes to Rome ca. 1020 and steals the head of Saint Valentine which he brings home to his monastery. *De veneratione capitis S. Valentini martyris, AASS Feb.* II, pp. 758–763. *BHL* 8461.

Vincent, Deacon of Saragossa. In 855 a monk of Conques, Auoardus, goes to Valencia, steals the body of Saint Vincent, and after much difficulty it arrives in the monastery of Castres. *Translatio in monasterium Castrense, AASS Ian.* III, pp. 13–18, *PL* CXXVI, 1101–24. *BHL* 8644–8645.

Eleven thousand Virgins of Cologne. Four stories written around 1100 tell of efforts to steal relics of some of the Virgins by a priest, a merchant, a traveler, and a mad woman, each of which is foiled by miraculous intervention. *Translatio trium corporum. AASS Oct.* IX, p. 239. *BHL* 8445.

Wandrille. The guards of the monastery of Saint Pierre au Mont-Blandin are suspected of having stolen the relics of Saint Wandrille, but the location of the body is indicated by a miracle and the monks are cleared of the charge. *Ex sermone de Adventu SS Wandregisili, Ansberti, Vulfranni. MGH SS* xv, p. 628. *BHL* 8810.

Wicbertus. Adechus, monk of Gembloux, attempts to

steal body of Wicbertus from Gorze. ca. 962. Sigebertus, *Vita Wicberti, MGH SS* VIII, p. 515. *BHL* 8882.

Theft of *unidentified relics* from Cartagena by Frankish monks. ca. 1024. Aḥmad ibn 'Umar ibn Anas al-'Udhrī, *Fragmentos geográfico-históricos*, edición crítica por 'Abd al-'Azīz al-Ahwānī (Madrid: 1965). Second version of the same theft: Lévi-Provençal, ed. and trans., *La Péninsule ibérique au moyen âge, d'après le Kitāb ar-rawd al-mi'tar fī habar al-aktār d'Ibn 'Abd al-Mun'im al-Mimyari: texte arabe des notices relatives à l'Espagne, au Portugal et au sud-ouest de la France* (Leiden: 1938), p.182.

❖ *Notes* ❖

PREFACE (1990)

1. I have discussed my view of the past two decades of studies of hagiography in "Saints, Scholars, and Society: The Elusive Goal," *The Cult of Saints in the Middle Ages and Early Renaissance: Formation and Transformation*, ed. Sandro Sticca, Medieval and Renaissance Texts and Studies, (Binghamton, N.Y.: in press).

2. A theme that I develop in "Sacred Commodities: The Circulation of Medieval Relics," in *Commodities and Culture* ed. Arjun Appadurai (Cambridge, Cambridge University Press: 1986), pp. 169–191.

3. A topic I discuss in "The Saint and the Shrine: The Pilgrim's goal in the Middle Ages," *Wallfahrt kennt keine Grenzen* ed. Lenz Kriss-Rettenbeck and Gerda Möhler (Munich: 1984), pp. 265–274.

PREFACE

1. *AASS Oct.* III, p. 353

CHAPTER ONE
RELICS AND SAINTS

1. Patrice Boussel, *Des reliques et de leur bon usage* (Paris: 1971).

2. František Graus gives an excellent introduction to the history of hagiographic studies and to the methodological difficulties in the use of *vitae* as historical sources in his *Volk, Herrscher und Heiliger im Reich der Merowinger. Studien zur Hagiographie der Merowingerzeit* (Prague: 1965). His conclusion is quite accurate: "The legends are certainly not 'historical works' in the sense of the nineteenth century; they are rather 'literature,' and more particularly propaganda literature." p. 39.

3. Hippolyte Delehaye, *Les légendes hagiographiques* (Brussels: 1955) pp. 202–217.

4. Martin Heinzelmann, *Translationsberichte und andere Quellen des Reliquienkultes*. Typologie des sources du moyen âge occidental 33 (Turnhout: 1979) esp. pp. 34–101. For a brief, earlier introduction to *translationes* which retains its value see R. Aigrain,

L'Hagiographie: Ses sources, ses méthodes, son histoire (Paris: 1953) pp. 186–192.

5. For example, see the translation of Saint Gratianus in *Historia Francorum, MGH SSRM* I, p. 443.

6. Ambrose, *Oratio de obitu Theodosii, PL* XVI, cols. 1462–1466.

7. *AASS Feb.* II, pp. 758–763.

8. H. Silvestre, "Commerce et vol des reliques au moyen âge," *Revue belge de philologie et d'histoire,* vol. 30 (1952) pp. 721–739.

9. *AASS Oct.* III, p. 353.

10. *Chronicon Benedictoburanum, MGH SS* IX, pp. 226–227.

11. Christopher Brooke, *Europe in the Central Middle Ages 962–1154.* 1st ed. (London: 1964).

12. See the more detailed discussion of relics in Carolingian Europe in the following chapter.

13. *PL* CXX, col. 1608.

14. See Georges Duby, "Lignage, noblesse et chevalerie au XIIᵉ siècle dans la région mâconnaise. Une révision," *Annales,* vol. 27 (1972) pp. 803–823. Reprinted in *Hommes et structures du moyen âge* (Paris: 1973) pp. 397–422.

15. On Géraud d'Aurillac see the valuable study of Joseph-Claude Poulin, *L'Idéal de sainteté dans l'Aquitaine carolingienne d'après les sources hagiographiques (750–950)* (Quebec: 1975).

16. Lester Little, "Formules monastiques de malédiction au IXᵉ et Xᵉ siècles," *Revue Mabillon,* vol. 58 (1975) pp. 377–399, and "La morphologie des malédictions monastiques," *Annales,* vol. 34 (1979) pp. 43–60.

17. Nicole Herrmann-Mascard superficially describes the practice of humiliating relics in *Les reliques des saints. Formation coutumière d'un droit* (Paris: 1975) pp. 226–228. Heinrich Fichtenau, in his fundamental article on the cult of relics, "Zum Reliquienwesen im früheren Mittelalter," *MIÖG* vol. 60 (1952) p. 68, emphasized the practice of humiliation as a means of punishing the saint for failing to protect the community. Professor Fichtenau did not, however, overlook the propagandistic function of these humiliations. For a further study of the humiliation of relics, see P. Geary, "L'Humiliation des saints," *Annales,* vol. 34 (1979) pp. 27–42. Translated as "Humiliation of Saints," in Stephen Wilson, ed., *Saints and their Cults: Studies in Religious Sociology, Folklore, and History* (Cambridge: 1983) pp. 123–140.

18. Georges Duby, "Economie domaniale et économie monétaire: Le budget de l'abbaye de Cluny entre 1080 et 1155," *Annales,* vol. 7 (1952) pp. 155–171.

19. Herrmann-Mascard, pp. 173–174.

20. *PL* CXXXIII, col. 573; Herrmann-Mascard, p. 173.

21. Rodulfus Glaber, *Historiarum libri quinque*, ed. and tr. John France (Oxford: 1989), book V, 11, pp. 230–232.

22. On the growth of popular devotion to the eucharist see E. Dumoutet, *Le désir de voir l'hostie et les origins de la dévotion au Saint-Sacrement* (Paris: 1926). On the end of the practice of placing the eucharist in altars see Herrmann-Mascard, p. 167.

23. Gerd Zimmermann, "Patrozinienwahl und frömmigkeits-wandel im Mittelalter, dargestellt an Beispielen aus dem alten Bistum Würzburg," *Würzburger Diözesangeschichtsblätter* vols. 20/21 (1958/59) II, 103–104. Cited by Heinzelmann, *Translationsberichte*, pp. 24–25.

24. *Religion and the Decline of Magic* (New York: 1971), Chapter II, "The Magic of the Medieval Church," pp. 25–50.

CHAPTER TWO
THE CULT OF RELICS

1. "Dixit enim quod anno transacto duo quidam, qui se monachos esse dicerent, detulerint usque ad praefatam sancti martyris basylicam quaedam velut cuiusdam sancti ossa, quae se vel ex urbe Roma, vel ex nescio quibus Italiae partibus, sustulisse affirmabant: cuius tamen sancti nomen se oblitos esse mira impudentia dixerunt." *MGH Epist.* V, p. 363; *PL* CXVI, col. 77.

2. On the cult of relics in antiquity see F. Pfister, *Der Reliquienkult im Altertum* (Giessen: 1909–1912).

3. See P. Saintyves, *Les reliques et les images légendaires* (Paris: 1912) pp. 56–83, on the cult of relics in the non-Christian world.

4. For the most reasonable discussions of this complex subject see Hippolyte Delehaye, *Les origines du culte des martyrs* (Brussels: 1933) and *Sanctus: Essai sur le culte des saints dans l'antiquité* (Brussels: 1927). It could be argued, however, that Father Delehaye did not sufficiently emphasize the continuity of the Christian cult of martyrs with the Jewish.

5. On the conformity of Christian burials to Roman practice, see Delehaye, *Les origines*, Chapter II, "L'anniversaire et le tombeau," pp. 22–49.

6. The first translations of relics took place in the East. According to Delehaye, *Les origines*, p. 54, the earliest recorded is that of Saint Babylas. In the 350's Gallus attempted to improve the Christian community of Daphne by building a church there in which he placed the

body of this saint. Sozomenus, *Historia ecclesiastica* v, 19, *PG* LXVII, cols. 1120–1121. In the West, translations of corporeal relics as opposed to contact relics or *brandea* appear to have become common much later. See John M. McCulloh, "The Cult of Relics in the Letters and 'Dialogues' of Pope Gregory the Great: A Lexicographical Study," *Traditio*, vol. 32 (1976) pp. 145–184.

7. A particularly enlightening and critical investigation of the relationships between the emperor and Christ the King as implied in Carolingian architecture is that of Carol Heitz, *Recherches sur les rapports entre architecture et liturgie à l'époque carolingienne* (Paris: 1963).

8. Heinrich Fichtenau, *Das karolingische Imperium* (Zurich: 1949) pp. 180–181.

9. On Aldebertus see *MGH Concil.* II, *Concilium Romanum 745*, pp. 39–43. He is discussed at length in the valuable article of Leo Mikoletzky, "Sinn und Art der Heiligung im frühen Mittelalter," *MIÖG*, vol. 57 (1949) pp. 83–122.

10. Agobardus, *Epistola ad Bartholomaeum*, *MGH Epist.* V, no. 12, pp. 206–210.

11. *PL* CV, col. 460.

12. Richard Southern, *Western Society and the Church in the Middle Ages* (Harmondsworth: 1970) p. 31.

13. See above, p. 20.

14. Synod apud Celichyth, 816, "Ubi ecclesia adedificatur, a propriae diocesis episcopo sanctificetur: aqua per semetipsum benedicatur, spargatur, et ita per ordinem compleat sicut in libro ministeriali habetur. Postea eucharistia quae ab episcopo per idem ministerium consecratur cum aliis reliquiis condatur in capsula, ac servetur in eadem basilica. Et si alias reliquias intimare non potest, tamen hoc maxime proficere potest, quia corpus et sanguis est Domini nostri Jesu Christi." A. W. Haddan and W. Stubbs, eds., *Councils and Ecclesiastical Documents Relating to Great Britain and Ireland* (Oxford: 1872) vol. III, p. 580. On the similarities between the eucharist and the relics of saints see Marta Cristiani, "La controversia eucharistica nella cultura del sec. IX," *Studi Medievali*, vol. 9 (1968) pp. 167–233, esp. p. 216.

15. Herrmann-Mascard, pp. 159–160.

16. André Grabar, *Martyrium. Recherches sur le culte des reliques et l'art chrétien antique.* II *Iconographie* (Paris: 1946) pp. 356–357.

17. Ernst Kitzinger, "The Cult of Images in the Age before Icon-

oclasm," *Dumbarton Oaks Papers*, vol. 8 (1954) pp. 83–150, especially 118–119, 125.

18. On the philological problems involved in understanding the *Libri Carolini* see Gert Haendler, *Epochen karolingischer Theologie* (Berlin: 1958) Part B, Chapter V, "Die philologische Problematik," pp. 67–73.

19. *Annales regni Francorum, MGH SSRG*, ed. F. Kurze, 1895, p. 112. See Haendler, p. 68.

20. "Illi vero pene omnem suae credulitatis spem in imaginibus conlocent, restat, ut nos sanctos in eorum corporibus vel potius reliquiis corporum, seu etiam vestimentis veneremur, juxta antiquorum patrum traditionem." *Libri Carolini*, III, 16, p. 138.

21. Ibid., III, 24, pp. 153–154.

22. Ibid., III, 16, pp. 137–138.

23. *Capit. Aquisg. MGH Capit.* I, p. 170; Mainz *MGH Concil.* II, p. 270. In each parish feasts of the saints whose relics were to be found there were to be celebrated.

24. *Liber Diurnus*, ed. Theodor Sickel (Vienna: 1889) particularly the following formulae: "De condendis reliquiis intra monasterium," no. 16, p. 13; "De recondendis reliquiis inter episcopum," no. 17, p. 14; "Basilica que post ruinam iuxta ipsam alia constructa est," no. 28, p. 20.

25. Bede, *Historia ecclesiastica*, I, 30.

26. On Germanic oaths see Karl von Amira, *Grundriss des germanischen Rechts* (Strassburg: 1913) p. 270, and *Kulturhistorisk Leksikon for nordisk middelalder*, vol. 3 (1958) col. 517 for examples of oaths. I am in debt to the late Professor Konstantin Reichardt for advice on Germanic oath objects.

27. *Synodus Franconofurtensis*, 794, *MGH Capit.* I, p. 75.

28. J. M. Wallace-Hadrill, *The Long-Haired Kings, and Other Studies in Frankish History* (London: 1962) p. 24.

29. *MGH Capit.* I, 11, p. 118. "Omne sacramentum in ecclesia aut supra reliquias iuretur."

30. Ibid. The distinction between oaths sworn on relics and those sworn in church is more apparent than real. Since each church contained relics, swearing in church meant taking an oath on a relic. This is implied in the prescribed formula for the oath to be said in either circumstance: ". . . sic illum Deus adiuvet et sancti quorum istae reliquiae sunt, ut veritatem dicat."

31. *MGH Capit.* II, 853, p. 274.

32. Ibid., 860, p. 155.

33. Ibid., I, no. 28, ca. 42, p. 77.

34. See Heinrich Fichtenau's characteristically imaginative discussion of the lack of saints in the Carolingian empire in *Das karolingische Imperium*, p. 177.

35. Isidorus, *Etymologiarum Liber*, VII, xi, 1–4.

36. Numerous Carolingians, including Charles himself, were of course venerated as saints, but this did not occur until centuries later.

37. *MGH Capit.* I, 72, ca. 7, p. 163.

38. *MGH Concil.* II, p 272: "Ne corpora sanctorum transferantur de loco ad locum. Deinceps vero corpora sanctorum de loco ad locum nullus transferre praesumat sine consilio principis vel episcoporum sanctaeque synodi licentia." N. Herrmann-Mascard's efforts to interpret this canon as directed specifically toward regulating translations, in the sense of elevations of new saints, is not supported by contemporary documentation, nor is it reasonable given the concerns of the Carolingians we have considered above. See *Les reliques des saints*, p. 84.

39. On the political background see L. Halphen, *Charlemagne et l'empire carolingien* (Paris: 1947) pp. 221.

40. W. Hotzelt, "Translationen von Martyrerreliquien aus Rom nach Bayern im 8. Jahrhundert," *Studien und Mitteilungen zur Geschichte des Benediktiner-Ordens* vol. 53 (1935) pp. 286–343. See also Klemens Honselmann, "Reliquientranslationen nach Sachsen," *DEJ*, vol. 1, pp. 159–193.

41. *Ex Odilonis Translatione S. Sebastiani, MGH SS* XV, p. 386.

42. H. L. Mikoletzky in "Sinn und Art" (pp. 97–102) lists over 30 such translations in the decades following that of Sebastian. Roman Michalowski has recently examined these translations from Rome in terms of gift exchange and the significance of the donation of relics for the establishment of *amicitia*, that is, of a positive, mutual relationship of obligations, between parties. "Le don d'amitié dans la société carolingienne et les *Translationes sanctorum*," in *Hagiographie cultures et sociétés IV–XIIᵉ siècles*, Actes du Colloque organisé à Nanterre et à Paris 2–5 mai 1979 (Paris: 1981) pp. 399–416.

43. Gregorius Turonensis, *Historia Francorum* II, 29, *MGH SSRM* I, p. 133.

44. E. P. Colbert, *The Martyrs of Córdoba (850–859)* (Washington, D.C.: 1962).

45. Baudouin de Gaiffier, "Les notices hispaniques dans le Martyrologe d'Usuard," *Anal. Boll.*, vol. 55, pp. 268–283.

46. *MGH Capit.* I, *capitulare missorum* of 803, p. 115 no. 6. Charles's successors were even more specific in their complaints

about wandering pilgrims; Synod of Pavia in 850, *MGH Capit.* II, ca. 21, p. 122: "Quidam clericorum vel monachorum peregrinantes per diversas vagando provincias et civitates multiplices spargunt errores et inutiles questiones disseminant decipientes corda simplicium: de his decrevit sancta sinodus, ut ab episcopo loci detineantur et ad metropolitanum deducti discussione aeclesiastica examinentur. . . ."

47. *Concordia regularum*, III, vi; *PL* CIII, col. 748.

48. J. Guiraud, "Le culte des reliques au IXᵉ siècle," in *Questions d'histoire et d'archéologie chrétienne* (Paris: 1906) pp. 235–261.

CHAPTER THREE
THE PROFESSIONALS

1. "The Diffusion of Cultural Patterns in Feudal Society," *Past and Present*, vol. 39 (1968) p. 3.

2. See E. Dupré-Theseider, "La 'grande rapina dei corpi santi' dall'Italia al tempo di Ottone," *Festschrift Percy Ernst Schramm*, vol. 1, (Wiesbaden: 1964) pp. 420–432.

3. Deusdona and his associates appear in the *Translatio SS Marcelli et Petri* of Einhard, *MGH SS* XV, pp. 239–264 and in Rudolphus's *Miracula Sanctorum in Fuldenses ecclesias translatorum*, *MGH SS* XV, pp. 329–341.

4. *MGH SS* XV, p. 240.

5. Ibid.

6. Ibid.

7. Hagiographers of St. Médard produced two versions of *translationes* of Marcellinus and Peter, both relying on the *translatio* of Einhard. See Marguerite Bondois, *La Translation des saints Marcellin et Pierre. Étude sur Einhard et sa vie politique de 827 à 834* (Paris: 1907). These two texts are part of a larger tradition at St. Médard of extravagant hagiographical claims. See Ernst Müller, "Die Nithard-Interpolation und die Urkunden- und Legendenfälschungen im St. Medardus-Kloster bei Soissons," *Neues Archiv*, vol. 34 (1909) pp. 683–722; and Wilhelm Levison, *England and the Continent in the Eighth Century* (Oxford: 1946) p. 211, note 1. The *Translatio S. Sebastiani, MGH SS* XV, p. 386, by Odilo of St. Médard is part of this tradition.

8. Einhard, *Translatio*, p. 241.

9. Guiraud made this suggestion based on the deacon's familiarity with the catacombs. However, judging from the range of his operations in collecting relics (see below, notes 17 and 18) he was not limited to any one ecclesiastical area.

10. Rudolphus, *Miracula sanctorum, MGH SS* xv, p. 332.
11. Ibid.
12. Ibid.
13. Ibid., p.336.
14. Einhard, *Translatio*, p. 241.
15. Ibid., p. 240.
16. Rudolphus, *Miracula*, p. 332.
17. The tombs of Tiburtius, Marcellinus, and Peter were in the cemetery of Marcellinus and Petrus joined to the church of Helen, mother of Constantine, on the via Labicana. On modern excavations carried out at this site, see Franchi de'Cavalieri, "Il sarcofago di S. Elena prima dei restauri del secolo XVIII," *Nuovo bolletino di archeologia cristiana*, vol. 27 (1921) p. 29 sqq.
18. The traditional locations of the tombs of the martyrs sold by Deusdona in 835 can be determined from Usuardus's martyrology, ed. Jacques Dubois (Brussels: 1965), and from the early itineraries of Rome, edited in *CCSL* CLXXV, *Itineraria et alia geographica* (Turnhout: 1965. Using these two sources one can demonstrate that each year Deusdona provided saints who were geographically associated. Thus in 835 we find:

Saint	*Location in Itineraria*	*Usuard*
Alexandrus	via Pinciana-Salaria	via Claudia
Felicissimus	via Appia	same
Concordia	via Nomentana-Tiburtina	—
Favianus	via Appia Ardeatina	—
Urbanus	via Appia Ardeatina	via Nomentana
Castulus	via Labicana-Prenestina	same
Sebastian	via Appia	same
Pamphilus	via Pinciana-Salaria	—
Papia	via Nomentana-Salaria	—
Maurus	via Salaria-nova	via Nomentana
Victoria	via Salaria-nova-Nomentana	—
Felicitas	via Pinciana-Salaria	—
Emmerentiana	via Salaria-nova-Nomentana	—·

19. A similar correlation can be made for 836:

Saint	*Location in Itineraria*	*Usuard*
Quirinus	via Appia-Salaria	same
Romanus	via Tiburtina	—
Cornelius	via Appia	same

Callistus	via Aurelia	same
Neureus	via Appia Ardeatina	same
Achilleus	via Appia Ardeatina	same
Turturinus	not mentioned	unclear
Stacteus	not mentioned	—

20. 838:

Saint	Location in Itineraria	Usuard
Quirinus	via Appia Ardeatina	same
Urbanus	via Appia Ardeatina	via Nomentana
Cecilia	via Appia	—
Tiburtinus	via Appia Ardeatina	same
Valerianus	via Appia	same
Maximus	via Appia	same
Agapitus	via Appia	same
Ianuarius	via Appia	same
Magnus	not mentioned	via Appia
Zenonis	via Appia	—
Ypolitus	via Appia	in Portu Romano?
Priscilla	via Salaria-nova	in Asia
Aquilia	not mentioned	—

This coincidence between locations of Roman martyrs' tombs in itineraria and martyrologies and the saints delivered to the Franks in a given year does not necessarily mean that the relics were genuine. The Franks knew the traditional locations of the tombs and used this information to check the stories of those providing them with relics. (For example, Hincmar checked such sources to determine the reliability of a claim advanced by the monastery of Hautvilliers, *AASS Aug.* III, p. 602.) Hence one might argue that Deusdona, aware of this minimal knowledge, claimed to have concentrated on specific areas each year in order to impress his customers. But is is also possible that even such a person as Deusdona was sufficiently concerned with providing "genuine" relics that he made an effort to collect the proper saints from the proper cemeteries. This last hypothesis might explain why he was the most trusted of the ninth-century relic-mongers.

21. Rudolphus, *Miracula*, p. 332.

22. Ibid.

23. Liutolfus, *Vita et translatio S. Severi, MGH SS* xv, pp. 289–292.

24. Rudolphus, *Miracula*, p. 337.

25. Erchambertus episcopus Frisingensis, *Epistola ad suos de corpore sancti Bartholomaei apostoli in Boiariam, ut ferebatur, allato,* PL CXVI, cols. 31–34.

26. William of Malmesbury, *Gesta Pontificum Anglorum* (Rolls Series, Kraus reprint: 1964) vol. 52, p. 398.

27. See F. M. Stenton, *Anglo-Saxon England,* 3rd ed. (Oxford: 1971) pp. 343–357, on Athelstan's relations with the continent.

28. On Athelstan's relic collection see J. Armitage Robinson, *The Times of Saint Dunstan* (Oxford: 1923) pp. 51–80.

29. *MGH SS* XV, pp. 631–641.

30. *AASS Iun.* I, pp. 742–43, reedited by the late Nicolas-N. Huyghebaert, "La Consécration de l'église abbatiale de Saint-Pierre de Gand (975) et les reliques de saint Bertulfe de Renty," *Corona gratiarum. Miscellanea patristica, historica et liturgica Eligio Dekkers. O.S.B. . . . oblata* (Bruges: 1975) II, pp. 130–131. According to Dom Huyghebaert, the *Vita,* written between 1073 and 1088, was the reworking of an earlier, possibly tenth-century text now lost while the *Sermo* was prepared at the end of the eleventh or beginning of the twelfth century to hide the loss of the relics.

31. *Inventio et miracula sancti Wolframi,* ed. J. Laporte, in *Mélanges de la société d'histoire de Normandie,* vol. 14 (1938) pp. 33-34.

32. O. Oppermann, *Die älteren Urkunden des Klosters Blandinium und die Anfänge der Stadt Gent,* vol. 1 (Utrecht: 1928) p. 205.

33. *Inventio Wolframi,* p. 32.

34. Ibid., p. 33.

35. The *Translatio trium corporum sanctarum virginum Coloniensium, AASS Oct.* IX, p. 239, describes how an Englishman attempted to steal one of the 11,000 virgins.

36. *MGH SS* XV, pp. 579–580.

37. William of Malmesbury, p. 419.

38. Rudolphus, *Miracula,* p. 330.

39. In a paper presented to the American Historical Association in 1974, Professor J. McCulloh argued that in fact the great influx of Roman relics in the mid-eighth century and the similar one in the reign of Louis the Pious were the result of particular papal policies. Although his argument concentrated almost entirely on the papal sources and did not examine the question of Frankish demand for relics, his suggestion that the popes were actively involved during these two periods in distributing relics is certainly correct.

40. *Liber Pontificalis*, II, p. 74.
41. *Historia translationis S. Helenae ad coenobium Altevallense,* *AASS Aug.* III, p. 602.
42. Ibid.
43. "Ita nos coadunavimus triduanum jejunium agere, quatenus a Deo omnipotente in aliquibus signis nobis ostendere mereamur, si ipse supradictus Felix verum dicat aut aliter: et ne fallente diabolo nos decipiat," *PL* CXVI, col. 32.

CHAPTER FOUR
MONASTIC THEFTS

1. *AASS Oct.* III, verse *translatio* pp. 289–292, prose *translatio* pp. 294–299.
2. See Appendix A-II.
3. Ibid.
4. A. Bouillet, ed., *Liber Miraculorum Sancte Fidis* (Paris: 1897) pp. 268–269.
5. On the foundation of Figeac see Léon Levillain's discussion of the diploma of foundation in his *Recueil des actes de Pépin I et de Pépin II rois d'Aquitaine (814–848)* (Paris: 1926) pp. xx and 133–151.
6. A monastery given to Conques in this same diploma, ibid., p. 142.
7. Ibid.
8. Aimoinus, *Translatio B. Vincentii, PL* CXXVI, cols. 1014–1026.
9. *Translatio Sancti Vivani episcopi. Anal. Boll.*, vol. 8 (1899) pp. 252–277.
10. Ibid., p. 275.
11. Ibid.
12. The memory of the translation was preserved in the liturgy at Figeac whose eleventh-century sacramentary, now B.N. ms. lat. 2293, fol. 115r, col. 1, contains readings for the August 1 feast of the translation. None of the readings mention that the relics were stolen.
13. P. Héliot et M.-L. Chastang, "Quêtes et voyages des religieux au profit des églises françaises du moyen âge," *Revue d'histoire ecclésiastique*, vol. 59 (1964) pp. 783–822; vol. 60 (1965) pp. 5–32.
14. *AASS Iul.* V, pp. 614–620. On Drogo see the excellent study of N. Huyghebaert, "Un moine hagiographe, Drogon de Bergues," *Sacris Erudiri. Jaarboek voor Godsdienstwetenschappen*, vol. 20 (1971) pp. 191–256.

15. See G. R. Stephens, "The Burial-Place of St. Lewinna," *Mediaeval Studies* vol. 21 (1959) pp. 303–312, and Dom Huyghebaert's judicious remarks in "Un moine hagiographe," p. 198 note 18.

16. *AASS Iul.* v, pp. 620–621.

17. Huyghebaert, p. 198.

18. *Vita Sancti Abbani, AASS Oct.* XII, pp. 276–293.

19. For a modern biography of Richard see H. Dauphin, *Le Bienheureux Richard abbé de Saint-Vanne de Verdun* †1046 (Louvain: 1946). Of the two medieval accounts of Richard's life, that of Hughes de Flavigny in Book II of his *Chronicon* (*MGH SS* VIII, pp. 368–502) is the more historical. The *Vita Beatissimi Patris Richardi Abbatis* (*MGH SS* XI, pp. 280–290) postdates Hughes's account and, according to Dauphin, pp. 18–35, relies heavily on it.

20. H. Bloch, "Die älteren Urkunden des Klosters S. Vanne zu Verdun," *JGLGA*, vol. 10 (1898) no. 11, pp. 391–395.

21. Hughes de Flavigny, *MGH SS* VIII, pp. 370–371.

22. Ibid., p. 371.

23. Ibid., p. 368–370.

24. Bloch, *JGLGA*, vol. 14 (1902) p. 131.

25. Dauphin, *Le Bienheureux*, pp. 335–350.

26. *PL* CXLIV, col. 465.

27. Hughes de Flavigny, *MGH SS* VIII, p. 407.

28. R. W. Southern, *The Making of the Middle Ages* (Oxford: 1953) pp. 160–161.

29. *Historia miraculorum Florinis factorum auctore Gonzone abbate Florinensi, AASS Mai.* II, p. 648.

30. Hughes de Flavigny, *MGH SS* VIII, p. 374.

31. Ibid., p. 370.

32. Ibid., pp. 373–375.

33. Ibid., p. 391.

34. Edited by Dauphin as an appendix to *Le Bienheureux*, pp. 361–381.

35. Dauphin, p. 94.

36. Ibid., pp. 370–371.

37. Ibid., p. 371.

38. Hincmar, *Epistola ad Carolum Imperatorem*, PL CXXVI, cols. 153–154.

39. Bertarius, *Gesta Pontificum S. Verdunensis ecclesiae*, PL CXXXII, col. 508.

40. For a brief introduction to this Council of Cologne, allegedly held on May 12, 346, see H. Leclercq's article "Cologne," *DACL*, vol. III,₂, cols. 2180–2187.

41. Yvette Dollinger-Leonard, "De la cité romaine à la ville médiévale dans la région de la Moselle et la Haute Meuse," *Studien zu den Anfängen des europäischen Städtwesens, Reichenau Vorträge 1955–1956* (Darmstadt: 1970) pp. 195–226.

42. See Cornelius Byeus, "S. Sanctinus," *AASS Oct.* V, p. 600; Claude Doillon, "Sanctino," *Bibliotheca Sanctorum*, vol. XI (Rome: 1968) p. 640; and Dauphin, p. 124, note 1.

43. Bloch, *JGLGA*, vol. 10 (1898) no. 35, p. 441.

44. J. van der Straeten, ed., *Les manuscrits hagiographiques de Charleville, Verdun et Saint-Mihiel*, Subsidia Hagiographica, vol. 56 (Brussels: 1974) pp. 161–165.

45. F. Clouet, *Histoire de Verdun depuis l'origine de cette ville jusqu'en 1830* (Verdun: 1838).

46. Dauphin, p. 223, note 1.

47. Ibid., p. 124, note 1.

48. Maurice Lombard, "La route de la Meuse et les relations lointaines des pays mosans entre le VIIIe et le XIe siècles," *L'Art mosan*, ed. Pierre Francastel (Paris: 1953) p. 19.

49. Victor Saxer, *Le culte de Marie Madeleine en occident des origines à la fin du moyen âge*, 2 vols. (Auxerre-Paris: 1959) and his "L'Origine des reliques de sainte Marie Madeleine à Vézelay dans la tradition historique du moyen âge," *Revue des sciences religieuses*, vol. 29 (1955) pp. 1–18.

50. Saxer has demonstrated that the Mary Magdalene venerated in the West was an example of the fusion of various persons in the devotion of the faithful. She was the penitent sinner who anointed Christ's feet (Luke vii:36–50); Mary, the sister of Martha (Luke x:38–42); Mary, the sister of Lazarus (John xi:1–45), etc. Saxer, *Le culte*, vol. I, p. 2. The research by E. Van Mingroot on the date of the composition of the *Gesta episcoporum Cameracensium* indicates that the first account of the translation to Vézelay was written ca. 1024. "Kritisch onderzoek omtrent de datering van de Gesta espiscoporum Cameracensium," *Revue belge de philologie et d'histoire*, vol. 53 (1975) pp. 330–331. See J.-C. Poulin's review of this book in *Francia*, vol. 7 (1979) p. 680.

51. Ibid., pp. 61–63.

52. *PL* CXIII, col. 642.

53. Saxer, *Le culte*, vol. I, p. 69; Bull of Stephen, March 6, 1058, *PL* CXLIII, col. 883.

54. Saxer, *Le culte*, vol. I, p. 70; *BHL*, vol. II, no. 5491, p. 808.

55. See above note 50; *MGH SS* VII, p. 464.

56. Sigebert de Gembloux, *Chronica*, PL CLX, col. 141; *MGH SS* VI, p. 331. Cf. Saxer, "L'Origine," p. 5.

57. Victor Saxer, "Légende épique et légende hagiographique," *Revue des sciences religieuses*, vol. 30 (1956), pp. 394–395. Saxer sees no influence during the tenth and eleventh centuries but much mutual influence during the twelfth.

58. *BHL*, vol. II, no. 5492, p. 808.

59. Saxer, "L'Origine," p. 4.

60. *AASS Iul.* V, p. 208.

61. Saxer, *Le culte*, vol. I, p. 105.

62. Ibid., p. 95.

63. Ibid., p. 105.

64. Ibid., pp. 95, 105–108.

65. *Translatio SS Eusebii et Pontiani in Galliam, Anal. Boll.*, vol. 2 (1883) pp. 368–377.

66. Saxer, *Le culte*, vol. I, p. 105.

67. P. Boissonade, "Cluny, la papauté, et la première grande Croisade internationale contre les Sarrasins d'Espagne," *Revue des questions historiques*, vol. 117 (1932) pp. 257–301.

68. *Le guide du pèlerin de Saint-Jacques de Compostelle* (Mâcon: 1938) pp. 50–51.

69. In that year Guy de Grancey, Count of Saulx-Tavannes, donated two villages on the Côte d'Or to Saint Foy of Conques. G. Desjardins, ed., *Cartulaire de l'abbaye de Conques* (Paris: 1879) no. 445, p. 325.

70. Denis Grémont, "Le culte de Sainte Foi et de Sainte Marie-Madeleine à Conques au XIᵉ siècle d'après le manuscrit de la Chanson de Ste. Foi," *Revue de Rouergue*, vol. 23 (1969) pp. 165–175.

71. *HGL* V, cols. 5–8.

72. B. N. ms. lat. 12699.

73. See Appendix A-IV.

74. *HGL*, V, charter no. 128, col. 283, August 24, 977, "Willelmus vice comtes" made a donation to the church of Béziers. The last document in which William's name appears is chart. no. 152, col. 326.

75. Ibid., chart. no. 149, col. 314.

76. Ibid., chart. no. 149, col. 316.

77. Ibid.

78. Ibid., chart. no. 151, col. 321.

79. Ibid., col. 318.

80. The will of Archbishop Ermengaud of Narbonne written in

1005 includes the donation of two "leonatas ad Sanctum Majanum et Sanctum Martinum de Villamagna." Ibid., col. 350.

81. Mabillon, *Annales* II, p. 286.

82. Seé Appendix B.

83. Ibid.

84. Ibid.

85. F. Lot, "La grande invasion normande de 856–862," *Bibliothèque de l'École des Chartes*, vol. 79 (1908) pp. 5 sqq.

86. W. Vogel, *Die Normannen und das fränkische Reich bis zur Gründung der Normandie (799–911)* (Heidelberg: 1906).

87. L. Musset, *Les invasions: Le second assaut contre l'Europe chrétienne* (Paris: 1965).

88. A. D'Haenens, "Les invasions normandes dans l'empire franc au IXe siècle. Pour une rénouvation de la problématique," *I Normanni e la loro espansione in Europa nell'alto medioevo, Settimane* (Spoleto: 1969), pp. 233–298.

CHAPTER FIVE
URBAN THEFTS

1. The *locus classicus* for this attitude is of course Liutprand of Cremona, *Relatio de legatione Constantinopolitana, MGH SSRG*, ed. J. Becker, 1915.

2. Paul Edouard Didier le comte de Riant, *Exuviae Sacrae Constantinopolitanae* 3 vols. (Geneva: 1877–78).

3. A summary of this scholarship with a bibliography can be found at the beginning of the article by Silvio Tramontin, "Realtà e leggenda nei racconti marciani veneti," *Studi veneziani*, vol. 12 (1970) pp. 35–58. In addition to Tramontin's bibliography one should also consult the excellent work of Otto Demus, *The Church of San Marco in Venice* (Washington, D.C.: 1960).

4. *MGH Concil.* II, p. 14.

5. Ibid., pp. 585–586.

6. Ibid.: ". . . quod et clerici et nobiles ex laicis viris electi ab Histriensi populo sanctam synodum supplicantes venerunt, ut eos a Grecorum naequissimo vinculo liberatos ad Aquileiam, suam metropolim, cui antiquitus subditi fuerant, redire concedat, quia electi, qui ordinandi sunt, prius piissimis imperatoribus nostris et postmodum ad partem Graecorum fidem per sacramenta promittunt; et ideo in hoc facto gravari se asserunt et servire duobus dominis non posse conclamant."

7. Demus, p. 6.

8. Ibid., p. 7.

9. Ibid.

10. Ibid., pp. 11–12.

11. H. Kretschmayr, *Geschichte von Venedig*, vol. 1 (Gotha: 1905) p. 115.

12. Demus, p. 21.

13. R. Cessi, *Documenti relativi alla storia di Venezia anteriori al mille. Testi e documenti di storia di letteratura latina medioevale*, vol. 1 (Padova: 1940) p. 93.

14. Tramontin, p. 53.

15. Antonio Niero, "Questioni agiografiche su san Marco," *Studi veneziani*, vol. 12 (1970) pp. 18–27.

16. Kretschmayr, 1, p. 115.

17. Niero, p. 20; T. Tohler and A. Molinier, *Itinera hiersolymitana et descriptiones terrae sanctae*, vol. 1 (Geneva: 1879) p. 311.

18. N. McCleary, "Note storiche et archeologiche sul testo della 'Translatio Sancti Marci,' *Memorie storiche forogiuliesi*, vols. 27–29 (1931–1933) pp. 223–264.

19. Ibid., p. 232.

20. *Anal. Boll.*, vol. 76 (1958) p. 445. Demus (p. 9 note 23) does not seem to have been aware of this review, as he dates the *translatio* following McCleary's suggestion.

21. Charles W. Jones, *The Saint Nicolas Liturgy and Its Literary Relationships (Ninth to Twelfth Centuries)* (Berkeley and Los Angeles: 1963) p. 2.

22. On these false documents see Francesco Nitti di Vito, "Leggenda di S. Nicola," *Iapigia*, vol. 8 (1937), pp. 317–335. Richard Salomon, in his inaugural dissertation, *Studien zur normannisch-italischen Diplomatik*, I:IV, i, *Die Herzogsurkunden für Bari* (Berlin: 1907) attempted, in my opinion unsuccessfully, to establish the majority of these documents as genuine.

23. Giuseppe Praga, "La translazione di S. Niccolo e primordi delle guerre normanne in Adriatico," *Archivio storico per la Dalmazia*, vol. 11 (1931) p. 337.

24. *Le pergamene di S. Nicola di Bari: Periodo greco (939–1071)* and *Periodo Normanno (1075–1194), Codice diplomatico barese*, vols. 4, 5 (Bari: 1901).

25. "La leggenda della translazione di S. Nicola di Bari, I Marinai Trani V," *Rassegna pugliese*, vol. 19 (1905) pp. 33–49; *Le questioni giurisdizionale tra la Basilica di S. Nicola e il Duomo di Bari* (Bari:

1933). (The latter was not available to me except in Nitti's summary of it in his 1937 article, "Leggenda," *Iapigia* vol. 8 [1937] pp. 265–274.)

26. Nitti, "Leggenda," pp. 303–304. The 1087 date is given in the *Annales Cavenses, Anonimo Barese,* and in the *Annali bene-ventani.*

27. Nitti, "Leggenda," p. 400.

28. Ibid., p. 308.

29. Codex Vat. Lat. 5074, fol. 5v–10v. Reedited by Nitti in "Leggenda," pp. 336–353. A variant of this MS from Benevento, differing primarily in that the names of the traditional members of the expedition have been inserted, provides variant readings for Nitti's edition.

30. Also reedited by Nitti in "Leggenda," pp. 357–366 from Codex Vat. Lat. 447, fol. 29–38.

31. Nitti, "Leggenda," p. 334.

32. Also in Nitti, ibid., pp. 386–396, where he provides a transliteration of the Russian and an Italian translation. I am most grateful to Richard Bosley for a more precise translation from the fourteenth-century text into English.

33. Ibid., pp. 388–391.

34. For a discussion of the authorship of the *translatio,* see Ilias Shljapkin's introduction to his edition of the texts in "Russhoe pouchenie XI vjeka o perenesenie moshchej Nikolaja chudotvovca i ego otnoshenie k zapadnim istorichnikam," *Panijatniki drevnej pis'mennosti i iskusstva,* vol. 10 (1881) pp. 3–10. Bernard Leib discusses the relationship among the Russian, Greek, and Latin versions of the *translatio* in his *Rome, Kiev, et Byzance à la fin du XIᵉ siècle. Rapports religieux des Latins et des Gréco-Russes sous le pontificat d'Urbain II (1088–1099)* (Paris: 1954) pp. 51–74.

35. Nitti, "Leggenda," p. 397.

36. I am indebted to Professor Ricardo Picchio for his cautionary advice concerning any effort to date the composition of the *translatio* from its fourteenth-century manuscript form.

37. For the most recent examination of the documents concerning these sixty-two individuals, see Francesco Babudri, "Sinossi critica dei translatori nicolaiani di Bari," *Archivio storico pugliese,* vol. 3 (1950) pp. 3–94.

38. Ibid., p. 87.

39. Ibid., p. 81; Nitti, "La leggenda della translazione di S. Nicola di Bari, I Marinai Trani V," p. 10.

40. Babudri, p. 81.

41. Ibid., p. 82.

42. Gino Luzzatto, "Studi sulle relazioni commerciali tra Venezia e la Puglia," *Nuovo archivio veneto*, n.s. vol. 7 (1904) pp. 185–186; Luzzatto, under the pseudonym G. Padovan, "Capitale e lavoro nel commercio veneziano dei secoli XI e XII," *Rivista di storia economica* vol. 6 (1941) p. 4.

43. The text of the Chrysobull is published by G. Tafel and G. Thomas, *Urkunden zur älteren Handels- und Staatsgeschichte der Republik Venedig. Fontes rerum austriacarum*, vol. 1 (Vienna: 1855–1857) pp. 52–53. For a discussion of its importance see Hélène Antoniadis-Bibicou, *Recherches sur les douanes à Byzance* (Paris: 1963) p. 49. Even if, as Roberto Cessi suggests in "Venezia e Puglia nel sistema adriatico del passato," *Archivio storico pugliese*, vol. 5 (1952) pp. 237–242, the bull recognized a *fait accompli*, this official recognition marked an important moment in Venice's rise to Mediterranean preeminence.

44. H. Kretschmayr, 1, p. 165.

45. Ibid.

46. Luzzatto, "Capitale," p. 4; R. Morozzo della Rocca and A. Lombardo, *I documenti del commercio veneziano nei secoli XI–XIII* in *Documenti e studi per la storia del commercio e del diritto commerciale italiana*, vol. 1 (Turin: 1940).

47. Morozzo della Rocca and Lombardo, *I documenti*, p. 31.

48. Ibid., no. 41.

49. Kenneth J. Conant, *Carolingian and Romanesque Architecture 800–1200* (Harmondsworth: 1974) pp. 346–347.

50. On the "inventio S. Marci" see R. Cessi, "L'apparititio Sancti Marci del 1094," *Archivio veneto*, vol. 95 (1964) pp. 113–115. Cessi does not notice the coincidence of the date of the rediscovery of Mark and the translation of Nicolas to Bari only six years before.

51. Historia de translatione . . . monachi anonymi Littorensis," *RHC*, vol. 5 (Paris: 1895) pp. 253–292. Another fictitious *translatio* from the twelfth century which describes yet another theft of the relics of Nicolas, from Bari, is found in the same volume of *RHC* pp. 293–394, "Qualiter reliquiae B. Nicolai ad Lotharingiae villam quae Portus nominatur delatae sunt."

52. Babudri, p. 16; Gaetano Cangiano, "L *Adventus Sancti Nicoli in Beneventum* leggenda agiografica della fine del secolo XI," *Atti della Società storica del Sanno*, vol. 2 (1924) pp. 131–162.

53. For an examination of the international development of Nicolas's cult in subsequent centuries see Karl Meisen, *Nikolauskult und*

Nikolausbrauch im Abendlande: eine Kultgeographische-Volks-kundliche Untersuchung (Düsseldorf: 1931). On the cult of Nicolas in the Greek world, see Gustav Anrich, *Hagios Nikolaos*, 2 vols. (Leipzig-Berlin: 1913 and 1917). The Greek version of the *translatio* which he edits in vol. II, pp. 435 sqq. is an abridgment of that of Niceforus, see II, p. 171.

54. *Vita S. Appiani, AASS Mart.* I, p. 323.

55. See below, pp. 113–114.

56. Albertus Poncelet, *Catalogus codicum hagiographicorum latinorum bibliothecae Vaticanae* (Brussels: 1910) p. 446. The *vita* is found in fols. 314–316v of Codex barberiniani no. 586, *BHL* 619.

57. The *vita* has long been recognized as a valuable document for the study of the salt trade in the eighth and ninth centuries. See L. M. Hartmann, *Analekten zur Wirtschaftsgeschichte Italiens im frühen Mittelalter* (Gotha: 1904); G. Romano, "Il codice diplomatico di San Pietro in Ciel d'Oro," *Bollettino della Società pavese di storia patria*, vol. 6 (1906) p. 302; Wattenbach-Levison, *Deutschlands Geschichts-quellen im Mittelalter* (Weimar: 1963) p. 397, note 42.

58. G. F. Ferro, *Istoria dell'antica città di Comacchio* (Ferrara: 1701) p. 248.

59. Victore de Buck, *AASS Oct.* XII, pp. 815–816.

60. *AASS Mart.* I, p. 320. It was suggested that the body was carried to Pavia in 808 in the course of a war.

CHAPTER SIX
JUSTIFICATIONS

1. "Zum Reliquienwesen," p. 73.

2. "Zum Wahrheitsverständnis im Heiligen- und Reliquienwesen des Mittelalters," *Saeculum*, vol. 17 (1966) p. 165.

3. *Ex virtutibus Sancti Eugenii Bronii ostensis, MGH SS* XV, p. 648.

4. "Zum Wahrheitsverständnis," p. 166.

5. *Etymologiarum Liber* V, XXVI, 18.

6. Delehaye, *Les origines*, Chapter III.

7. *De opera monachorum, CSEL* XLI (Vienna: 1900) p. 585: "Alii membra martyrum, si tamen martyrum, venditant."

8. On the legislation concerning translations, consult with caution Herrmann-Mascard, pp. 168–189.

9. *MGH Epist.* I, ep. IV, 30, pp. 263–266. On this letter consult the article of John McCulloh, "The Cult of Relics in the Letters and 'Dialogues.'"

10. *Historia Francorum* VIII, 31, *MGH SSRM* I, pp. 350–351.

11. *MGH Concil.* II, p. 272.

12. Herrmann-Mascard, p. 84. See above, Chapter 2, p. 47.

13. *AASS Oct.* IV, pp. 1035–1037; *MGH SS* XV, pp, 577–578.

14. François Dolbeau, "Un vol de reliques dans le diocèse de Reims au milieu du XIᵉ siècle," *Revue bénédictine*, vol. 91 (1981) pp. 172–184.

15. *Ruotgeri vita Brunonis*, *MGH SS* IV, p. 266.

16. As, for example, in the *Translatio S. Nicolai* of Niceforus, ed. Nitti, "La translazione," p. 343. This argument was used by the people of Myra who wished to keep Nicolas's body.

17. *Vita S. Dodonis abbatis Waslerensis*, *AASS Oct.* XII, p. 637; *Acta S. Davini*, *AASS Iun.* I, p. 331; *AASS Iun.* V, p. 65.

18. *Translatio trium corporum sanctarum virginum Coloniensium e numero undecim millium auctore Richero*, *AASS Oct.* IX, p. 239; *Acta Sanctae Reginswindae*, *AASS Iulii* IV, p. 95.

19. *Vita S. Martini auctore Petro Diacono Casinensi*, *AASS Oct.* X, p. 838.

20. See p. 125.

21. *AASS Iul.* V, p. 208.

22. See p. 149–150.

23. *Vita S. Tigriae*, *AASS Iun.* V, pp. 72–77.

24. *Translatio S. Fidei*, *AASS Oct.* III, p. 295.

25. *De veneratione capitis S. Valentini martyris*, *AASS Feb.* II, p. 758; *Acta translationis capitis et miracula auctore Baldrico Episcopo Dolensi*, ibid., pp. 758–763.

26. Ibid.

27. *Vita auctore Blandiniensi monacho*, *AASS Feb.* I, p. 682.

28. *Inventio et miracula*, *AASS Oct.* IV, pp. 1035–1037; *MGH SS* XV, pp. 576–579.

29. *Vita Annonis archiepiscopi Coloniensis*, *MGH SS* XI, pp. 480–481.

30. *Translatio Sancti Epiphanii*, *MGH SS* IV, pp. 248–251.

31. *Vita Sancti Abbani*, *AASS Oct.* XII, pp. 276–293, especially pp. 292–293.

32. *Translatio trium corporum sanctarum virginum Coloniensium e numero undecim millium auctore Richero*, *AASS Oct.* IX, p. 239.

33. *AASS Oct.* III, p. 353.

34. Ibid.: "Sed multorum discimus exemplis, sanctos spiritus plerosque, Deo in superis iam post busta conjunctos, vel gratanter pati, corporum suorum reliquias ad uberiorem salutem, suique

maiorem venerationem ad alia deferri loca. Denique protomartyrem Stephanum ab Hierosolymis Constantinopolim, Nicolaum a Mirea Barrum, Magdalenam Mariam ab Aquensi regione Vizeliacum, ipsum quoque monasticae philosophiae legislatorem Benedictum fideli furto vel rapina a Cassino in Gallicas delatum legimus oras."

35. Einhard, *Translatio*, *MGH SS* XV, p. 242.

36. Ibid., p. 240.

37. See above, p.164, note 17 on the church of St. Helen.

38. The *Vita Hludowici Imperatoris* gives quite a different view of the translation, saying that it was done "annuente papa." *MGH SS* II, p. 631.

39. Holder-Egger's doubts notwithstanding, Adrevald is Adalbertus, the identification made originally by Mabillon being a sound one. See H. Leclercq, *DACL*, vol. V_2 col. 1728. Adrevald was active at Fleury until 878 or 879, and was the author of the *Translatio S. Benedicti, Miracula S. Benedicti, Translatio S. Scholasticae, Vita S. Aigulfi*, and a *De corpore et sanguine Christi contra ineptias Joannis Scoti*, all in *PL*, CXXIV. The *Translatio S. Benedicti* and the *Miracula* were edited by E. de Certain, *Les Miracles de Saint Benoît* (Paris: 1858), and in excerpts by O. Holder-Egger in *MGH SS* XV, pp. 474–477. See also Walter Goffart, "Le Mans, St. Scholastica, and the Literary Tradition of the Translation of St. Benedict, *Revue bénédictine*, vol. 77 (1967) pp. 107–141.

40. *Miracula*, lib. 1, cap. XXVIII, p. 65 of de Certain's edition.

41. O. Holder-Egger, *MGH SS* XV, p. 476.

42. M. Bondois, *La translation*, p. 2.

43. Reprinted from Jean Mabillon, *Vetera analecta*, 2nd ed. (Paris: 1723) cols. 211–212 by H. Leclercq, *DACL*, vol. V_2 cols. 1720–1721.

44. Paulus Diaconus, *Historia Langobardorum*, lib. VI, cap. ii, *MGH SSRL*, p. 165.

45. *DACL* vol. V_2 cols. 1720–1724.

46. Why Adrevald named Aigulfus as the translator is not clear, unless he simply wanted to ascribe this most important event to the efforts of a saintly individual of the remote past, and chose Aigulfus out of admiration for the abbot of Lérins. See also his *Vita S. Aigulfi, PL* CXXIV, cols. 953–968.

47. Adrevald could hardly have determined the date of the translation from available documentation and so probably chose to place it under an illustrious abbacy. See Leclercq, "Fleury-sur-Loire," *DACL* vol. V_2 cols. 1709–1760.

48. *PL* CXXIV, col. 903.

49. Clearly dependent on the *Translatio SS Marcellini et Petri* or on the *Translatio S. Benedicti* are: *Translatio S. Helenae, AASS Aug.* III, p. 602 (840's); *S. Valentini, AASS Feb.* II, pp. 758–763 (ca. 1020); *S. Callisti* in *Chronicon S. Michaelis in pago Virdunensi, MGH SS* IV, pp. 82–83 (ca. 1020) *SS Chrisogoni et Anastasiae* in *Chronicon Benedictoburanum, MGH SS* IX, pp. 226–227 (1053); *Innocenti et Vitalis,* in *Vita Annonis archiepiscopi Coloniensis, MGH SS* XI, pp. 462–514; and, in the twelfth century, *S. Stephani, AASS Aug.* I, p. 131. Additionally there is the series of St. Médard *translationes* discussed above, p. 163, note 7.

50. See Appendix A-III.

51. See above pp. 78–81 and Appendix A-IV.

52. See above pp. 58–63 and Appendix A-II.

53. See above p. 62.

54. To my knowledge, the first scholar to notice the similarities between the account of Adrevald and Aimoinus was L. de Lacger in his article "S. Vincent de Saragosse," *Revue d'histoire de l'église de France,* vol. 13 (1927). Canon Jean Angély, a local hagiologer of Agen, pointed out that there are remarkable similarities between these two texts and the *translationes SS Fidei, Maiami,* and *Faustae* in his attempt to demonstrate that the relics of Vincent and Foy are still in Agen: "La prétendue tumulation de Sainte Foy d'Agen à Conques," *Revue de l'Agenais: Bulletin de la Société académique d'Agen,* vol. 76 (1950) pp. 91–102. Neither de Lacger nor Angély elaborated on the relationship further or connected this relationship with the previous and subsequent *translationes* which are the larger context of the theft accounts. Canon Angély's judgments on the relationship among the three Aquitanian texts will be discussed below, pp. 140–141.

55. See Ahmad ibn 'Umar ibn Anas, al-'Udhrī: *Fragmentos geográfico-históricos,* ed. 'Abd al-'Azīz al-Ahwānī (Madrid: 1965): "Ahmad ibn 'Umar said: 'A number of people have told me that a group of Christians, dressed as monks, came from the country of the Franks to the monastery in Cartagena "of the Esparto" in the district of Tudmir. Near that monastery was the tomb of a woman they considered a martyr, who was greatly revered in their religion. Some say that the group of monks took the martyr from her tomb without the knowledge of the inhabitants of the monastery; others say they took her with their knowledge and agreement for her removal.

'They had prepared a warship for this purpose, and they put her in a casket and carried her off with them, in the year 414 A.H. [1023–24]. The Christians of the monastery say there was a domed monument over the tomb, with an opening at the highest part of the dome; and that a day was celebrated at the tomb, on which there was a large gathering of the Christians of the region, and that on that day no bird would fly directly over the opening of the dome without being drawn into it by force. They claim that this ceased, however, with the removal of the martyr. I have been told that the Christian monks reached the island of Sicily with the casket in which they had placed the martyr's body, and that the Christians of the island pressed them and gave them a great deal of money, also [. . . asking?] the ruler of Sicily to take the martyr from them, so they could bury her in their churches there. But they were unsuccessful, and [the monks] took her to their own country.' "

I am indebted to Kay Heikkinen who found this text and was kind enough to translate it for me. Not only is the information it contains about Frankish relic hunters interesting in itself, but it is to my knowledge the only detailed, non-Christian account of a relic theft.

56. Jones, *The Saint Nicolas Liturgy* also suggests that these thefts were in a sense kidnappings.

57. *Rites of Passage*, trans. M. B. Vizedom and C. L. Caffee (Chicago: 1960) p. 10.

58. Victor Turner, *The Ritual Process* (Chicago: 1969) pp. 94–95.

59. Hubert Silvestre, "Commerce et vol de reliques au moyen âge," *Revue belge de philologie et d'histoire*, vol. 31 (1952) pp. 721–739.

60. Philip Grierson, "Commerce in the Dark Ages: A Critique of the Evidence," *Transactions of the Royal Historical Society* series 5, no. 9 (1959) pp. 123–140.

CHAPTER SEVEN
CONCLUSIONS

1. Silvestre, "Commerce," p. 739.

APPENDIX A
CRITIQUE OF TEXTS

"Translatio Beati Vincentii"

1. For an excellent discussion of the date of the supposed translation and other aspects of the cult of Vincent, see Louis de Lacger, "S. Vincent de Saragosse," *Revue d'histoire de l'église de France*, vol. 13 (1927) pp. 307–308.

2. *PL* CXV, col. 847.

3. *Gesta comitum Barcinonensium*, A. Rovira Virgili, *Historia nacional de Catalunya*, vol. 2 (Barcelona: 1922) p. 547.

4. *HGL* II, preuves, no. 169, cols. 346–347.

5. Léonce Auzias, *L'Aquitaine carolingienne (778–987)* (Paris: 1937) pp. 342–346.

6. de Lacger, "S. Vincent," passim.

7. *AASS Iul.* VI, pp. 459–469; *PL* CXV, cols. 939–960. On the expedition of Usuard, see Baudouin de Gaiffier, "Les notices hispaniques dans le Martyrologe d'Usuard," *Anal. Boll.*, vol. 55 (1937) pp. 268–283.

8. Gregory of Tours, *Historia Francorum*, Lib. III, cap. 29.

9. *PL* CXV, col. 942.

10. Sigebertus, *Vita Deoderici*, *MGH SS* IV, pp. 464–484; *PL* CXXXVII, col. 363, gives only a poor edition of part of the *vita*. On the *vita*, which is remarkable for its detailed catalogue of relics acquired by Theodoric, with the exact provenance, description of each, and the passio of each saint together with his translations and feasts, see E. Dupré-Theseider, "La 'grande rapina dei corpi santi' dall'Italia al tempo di Ottone," *Festschrift Percy Ernst Schramm*, vol. 1 (Wiesbaden: 1964) pp. 420–432.

11. In 852, according to the chronicle of the monastery of Saint Vincent, M. Bouquet, ed., *Recueil des historiens des Gaules et de la France*, vol. VII, pp. 238–240.

12. *MGH SS* IV, p. 475.

13. Ibid.

14. Admittedly the documentation for the earlier period is scanty. The much later chronicle does not claim that Volturno possessed his body: *Chronicon Voltornense del monaco Giovanni*, ed. V. Federici, 3 vols. (Rome: 1925). A bull of Pascal II, dated April 20, 1117, indicates that Pascal may have given the monastery a relic of its patron at that time: "Ad hec pro speciali Ecclesie ipsius dilectione, quam nostris manibus superna dignatio voluit dedicari, ad honorem et reverentiam gloriosissimi martyris Vincentii, cuius ibidem reliquias recondidimus. . . ." Ibid., III, p. 171.

15. *PL* CXXVI, col. 1026.

16. The manuscript contains a number of fragments and short hagiographical texts written separately but bound at St. Germain during the Middle Ages. The homily, fols. 44r–45r, was originally in a manuscript separate from that of the *Translatio B. Vincentii*.

17. Louis de Lacger, *Histoire de Castres et de son abbaye de Charlemagne à la guerre des Albigeois* (Poitiers: 1937) p. 76. *HGL* V, cols. 240–244, donation of Raimon, count of Rouergue (died 961):

"Illo alode de Guttalongus eum ipsa ecclesia et cum omnibus villariis quae ibi aspiciuntur, Sancti Benedicti remaneat et Sancti Vincentii."

"Translatio Sanctae Fidei"

1. *Liber Miraculorum Sancte Fidis*, p. viii.
2. F. Lot, "Sur la date de la translation des reliques de sainte Foi d'Agen à Conques," *Annales du Midi*, vol. 16 (1904) p. 504 and notes 7 and 8.
3. *Liber Miraculorum*, p. 48, note 1 and pp. 84, 123–124; Lot, pp. 504–505.
4. Lot, pp. 505–506; Adémar de Chabannes, *Chronicon*, ed. J. Chavanon (Paris: 1897) p. 139.
5. Léon Levillain, "Notes sur l'abbaye de Conques," *Revue Mabillon*, vol. 3 (1907) p. 100.
6. G. Desjardins, ed., *Cartulaire de Conques* (Paris: 1879).
7. *PL* CXXIII, col. 90: "Agennum [288], passio quoque beatae Fidis et sociorum eius apud urbem Agennum, quae postea Conchis translata est."
8. Desjardins, *Cartulaire*, no. 153, pp. 135–137.
9. Lot, pp. 5–9.
10. *MGH SS* I, p. 66.
11. Levillain, pp. 103–106.
12. Ibid., pp. 106–114.
13. J. Angély, "La prétendue tumulation de Sainte Foy d'Agen à Conques," *Revue de l'Agenais: Bulletin de la Société académique d'Agen*, vol. 76 (1950) pp. 91–102. See also his efforts in the same cause in *La Passion de sainte Foy* (Agen: 1956).
14. *Anal. Boll.*, vol. 17 (1898) p. 466. Tamizey de Larroque, "Un abbé de Saint-Gall à Agen au XIe siècle," *Revue d'Aquitaine*, vol. 9 (1864) pp. 338–339.

"Translatio Sanctae Faustae"

1. *Translatio S. Faustae*, AASS Ian. I, pp. 1090–1092.
2. Bouquet, ed., *Recueil*, vol. VIII, p. 596.
3. Mansi, vol. VI, cols. 735–737.
4. J.-L. Dumas, "Chronique du monastère de Saint-Pierre de Solignac," ed. A. Lecler, *Bulletin de la Société archéologique et historique du Limousin*, vol. 45 (1896–1897) p. 194.
5. Charter of foundation in *Cartulaire de Beaulieu*, ed. M. Deloche (Paris: 1859) p. 1. The archbishop was the son of Count Rodulf of Turenne and brother of Gotfried, ibid., p. 10, no. 3.
6. Ibid., p. 3, no. 1.

7. Evidence of the continuing dispute over Solignac's rights during the following decades is found in the diploma of Charles the Bald for Solignac of July 16, 876, *Recueil des actes de Charles II le Chauve*, ed. Georges Tessier (Paris: 1952) no. 409, pp. 414–417; and the diploma of Eudes of June 13, 889, *Recueil des actes d'Eudes*, ed. Robert-Henri Bautier (Paris: 1967) no. 2, pp. 7–12. Equally significant are forged charters purporting to record donations of churches and properties dated variously 872 or 924, *Charles de l'abbaye de Cluny*, ed. A. Bernard, vol. I (Paris: 1876) p. 22, note 1.

8. This conclusion is based on an examination of liturgical texts from the diocese described in V. Leroquais, *Les bréviaires manuscrits des bibliothèques publiques de France*, 6 vols. (Paris: 1934); and in *Les psautiers manuscrits latins des bibliothèques publiques de France*, 2 vols. (Mâcon: 1940–41).

9. Dumas, "Chronique du monastère," p. 194.

10. Ibid., p.197.

11. She is not mentioned in the tenth-century sacramentary of Auch, ed. J. Duffour, *Fragments d'un ancien sacramentaire d'Auch* (Paris-Auch: 1912).

12. Gregory of Tours, *Historia Francorum*, VIII, 22.

13. *Liber* I *carmen*, 4. See *Gallia Christiana* I, col. 975.

14 *Cartulaire du Chapitre . . . d'Auch.* I. *Cartulaire noir*, ed. C. Lacave La Plagne Barris (Paris-Auch: 1899) no. 133, pp. 158–59.

15. *Gallia Christiana* col. 970.

"Translatio Sancti Maiani"

1. P. B. Gams, *Series episcoporum ecclesiae catholicae* (Regensburg: 1873–1885; reprint, Graz: 1957) p. 583.

2. Ibid., p. 517.

3. *Gallia Christiana* VI, col. 21.

4. A similar and perhaps related confusion occurs in the *Translatio Sanctae Fidei*, said to have taken place under the reign of "Carolus minor." See F. Lot, "Sur la date de la translation des reliques de sainte Foi," pp. 505–506. The use of "junior" is found in the edition of J. Chavanon (Paris: 1897) p. 198. See above pp. 139–140.

5. *HGL* V, pp. 5–8.

6. *BHL* vol. II, p. 867.

7. The cult of Maianus, as distinct from that of Merwinus, was evidently limited to Béziers and the surrounding area. According to fourteenth and fifteenth-century liturgical books, his feast was celebrated June 1 at Béziers and in the monasteries of Gellone and Aniane. V. Leroquais, *Les bréviaires*, indicates the following references

to Maianus: II, p. 268, *Breviary of Gellone* (15th cent.), June 1 "In S. Maiani"; II, p. 269, *Breviary of Aniane* (14th cent.), June 1 "S. Maiani"; III, p. 66, *Breviary of Béziers* (15th cent.), June 1 "Festum S. Maiani ep. et conf."

8. *AASS OSB* IV, pp. 75–77.
9. See note 7 above.
10. Mabillon, *Annales*, II, p. 286.

❖ Bibliography ❖

A. Primary Sources

I. *Major collections of texts*

Acta Sanctorum. 3rd ed. 62 vols. Brussels-Paris, 1863–1925.

Baluze, Étienne. *Concilia Galliae Narbonensis.* Paris, 1668.

————. *Miscellanea novo ordine digesta et non paucis ineditis monumentis opportunisque animadversionibus aucta, opera ac studio Ioannis Dominici Mansi Lucensis.* 4 vols. Paris, 1761–1764.

Duchesne, Louis. *Fastes épiscopaux de l'ancienne Gaule.* 3 vols. Paris, 1900–1915.

Haddan, A. W. and Stubbs, W. eds. *Councils and Ecclesiastical Documents Relating to Great Britain and Ireland.* vol. III. Oxford, 1872.

Hardouin, Jean, S.J. *Acta conciliorum et epistulae decretales ac constitutiones summorum pontificum.* 11 vols. Paris, 1714–1715.

Mabillon, J. *Acta Sanctorum Ordinis S. Benedicti.* 9 vols. Paris, 1668–1901.

————. *Annales Ordinis S. Benedicti occidentalium monachorum patriarchae.* 6 vols. Lucca, 1739–1745.

Mansi, Giovanni Domenico. *Sacrorum conciliorum nova et amplissima collectio.* 57 vols. Venice, then Florence, then Paris, 1759–1927.

Martène, E. and Durand, U. *Veterum scriptorum et monumentorum amplissima collectio.* 9 vols. Paris, 1724–1733.

————. *Thesaurus novus anecdotorum.* 5 vols. Paris, 1717.

Migne, J. P. *Patrologiae cursus completus. Series prima Patrologia latina.* Vols. 1–221. Paris. 1844–1864.

Monumenta Germaniae Historica. 200+ vols. Hanover, Berlin, Munich, 1826–.

Muratori, L. A. *Antiquitates Italicae Medii Aevi sive dissertationes de moribus, ritibus.* Vols. 1–6. Milan, 1738–1742.

Recueil des actes de Charles II le Chauve, ed. Georges Tessier. Paris, 1952.

Recueil des actes d'Eudes. ed. Robert-Henri Bautier. Paris, 1967.

Recueil des historiens des Croisades. Historiens occidentaux. 5 vols. Paris, 1844–1895.

Recueil des historiens des Gaules et de la France, ed. M. Bouquet. 24 vols. Paris, 1738–1904.

II. *Diplomatic sources (alphabetically by location)*

Aquitaine. *Recueil des actes de Pépin I et de Pépin II rois d'Aquitaine (814–848),* ed. L. Levillain. Paris, 1926.

Auch. *Cartulaires du Chapitre de l'Eglise Métropolitaine Sainte-Marie d'Auch,* ed. C. Lacave La Plagne Barris. Vol. 1, *Cartulaire noir*; vol. 2, *Cartulaire blanc.* Paris-Auch, 1899.

Bari. *Le pergamene di S. Nicola di Bari. Periodo greco (939–1071). Periodo normanno (1075–1194). Codice diplomatico barese,* ed. F. Nitti di Vito. Vols. 4, 5. Bari, 1901.

Beaulieu. *Cartulaire de Beaulieu,* ed. M. Deloche. Paris, 1859.

Cluny. *Chartes de l'abbaye de Cluny,* ed. A. Bernard. Revised by Alex. Bruel. Vol. 1. Paris, 1876.

Conques. *Cartulaire de l'abbaye de Conques en Rouergue,* ed. G. Desjardins. Paris, 1879.

Venice. *Urkunden zur älteren Handels- und Staatsgeschichte der Republik Venedig. Fontes rerum austriacarum,* ed. G. Tafel and G. Thomas. Vienna, 1855–1857.

———. *I documenti del commercio veneziano nei secoli XI–XIII* in *Documenti e studi per la storia del commercio e del diritto commerciale italiana,* ed. R. Morozzo della Rocca and A. Lombardo. Vol. 1. Turin, 1940.

———. *Documenti relativi alla storia di Venezia anteriori al mille. Testi e documenti di storia di letteratura latina medioevale,* ed. R. Cessi. Vol. 1. Padova, 1940.

Verdun. "Die älteren Urkunden des Klosters S. Vanne zu Verdun," *Jahrbuch der Gesellschaft für lothringische Geschichte und Altertumskunde,* ed. H. Bloch. Vol. 10 (1898), pp. 338–449; vol. 14 (1902), pp. 48–150.

III. *Annals, chronicles, and histories*

Adamus Bremensis. *Gesta Hammaburgensis ecclesiae pontificum.* *MGH SS* VII, pp. 280–389.

Ademarus Cabannensis. *Chronicon*, ed. J. Chavanon. Paris, 1897.

Anastasius Bibliothecarius. *Historia ecclesiastica. PL* CXXIX, cols. 737–742.

Annales Beneventani, MGH SS VIII, pp. 280–503.

Annales S. Bertiniani, MGH SS I, pp. 423–515.

Annales S. Columbae Senonensis, MGH SS I, pp. 102–109.

Annales S. Medardi Suessionensis, MGH SS XXVI, pp. 518–522.

Annales regni Francorum, MGH SSRG, ed. F. Kurze, 1895.

Baeda. *Historia ecclesiastica gentis anglorum*, libri V, *PL* XCV, cols. 21–290.

Bertarius canonicus S. Vitoni. *Historia brevis episcoporum Virdunensium, PL* CXXXII, cols. 501–516.

Chronicon Benedictoburanum, MGH SS IX, pp. 212–216.

Chronicon Besuense, PL CLXII, cols. 861–1006.

Chronicon monasterii Conchensis, ed. E. Martène and U. Durand in *Thesaurus novus anecdotorum*, Vol. III, cols. 1387–1390.

Chronicon S. Michaelis in pago Virdunensi, MGH SS IV, pp. 78–86.

Chronicon S. Petri Vivi Senonensis, MGH SS XXVI, pp. 30–34.

Chronicon Vulturnense del monaco Giovanni, ed. V. Federici. 3 vols. Rome, 1925.

Chronique du monastère de Saint Vincent sur Vulturne, ed. M. Bouquet. *Recueil des historiens des Gaules et de la France*, vol. VII, pp. 238–240.

Chronique et chartes de l'abbaye de St. Mihiel, ed. A. Lesort. Paris, 1909–1912.

Ermoldus Nigellus. *De rebus gestis Ludovici Pii Augusti, MGH SS* II, pp. 464–523.

Flodardus presbyter Remensis. *Historia ecclesiae Remensis libri* IV, *PL* CXXXV, cols. 423–490; *MGH SS* XIII, pp. 405–599.

Gesta comitum Barcinonensium, ed. A. Rovira i Virgili, in *Historia nacional de Catalunya*. Vol. 2. Barcelona, 1922.

Gregorius Turonensis. *Historia Francorum libri* X, *MGH SSRM* I.

Hugo Flaviniacensis. *Chronicon Virdunense, MGH SS* VIII, pp. 288–503.

Liber Pontificalis, ed. L. Duchesne. 2 vols. Paris, 1886–1892.

Ordericus Vitalis. *The Ecclesiastical History of Orderic Vitalis*, ed. and tr. Marjorie Chibnall. 6 vols. Oxford, 1969–80.

Paulus Diaconus. *Historia Langobardorum, MGH SSRL*, pp. 45–187.

Rodulfus Glaber. *Historiarum libri quinque*, ed. and tr. John France. Oxford, 1989.

Sigebertus Gemblacensis. *Chronica, MGH SS* VI, pp. 300–374.

IV. *Literary sources: letters, religious treatises, etc.*

Agobardus archiepiscopus Lugdunensis. *Epistolae ad Bartholomaeum, PL* CIV, cols. 179–181.

Ambrosius. *Oratio de obitu Theodosii, PL* XVI, cols. 1462–1466.

Amolo episcopus Lugdunensis. *Epistola ad Theodboldun episcopum Lingonensem, MGH Epist.* V, p. 363.

Augustinus, Aurelius. *De opera monachorum*, ed. J. Zycha. *CSEL* XLI. Vienna, 1900.

Benedictus abbas Anianensis. *Concordia Regularum, PL* CIII, cols. 713–1380.

Erchambertus episcopus Frisingensis. *Epistola ad suos de corpore sancti Bartholomaei apostoli in Boiariam ut ferebatur, allato, PL* CXVI, cols. 31–34.

Gregorius Magnus. *Epistolae, MGH Epist.* IV.

Guibertus abbas monasterii S. Mariae Novigenti. *De pignoribus Sanctorum, PL,* CLVI, cols. 607–680.

Hincmar archiepiscopus. *Epistola ad Carolum Imperatorem, PL* CXXVI, cols. 153–154.

Isidorus Hispanensis episcopus. *Libri* XX *Etymologiarum sive originum*, ed. W. M. Lindsay. 2 vols. Oxford, 1911.

Jonas. *De cultu imaginum, PL* CVI, cols. 305–388.

Libri Carolini, MGH Concilia II supplement.

Liutprandus Cremonensis. *Relatio de legatione Constantinopolitana, MGH SSRG*, ed. J. Becker, 1915.

Petrus Damiani. *Epistolarum libri* VIII, *PL* CXLIV, cols. 205–498.

Walafridus Strabo. *Liber de exordiis et incrementis quarundam in observationibus ecclesiasticis rerum, PL* CXIV, cols. 919–965.

V. *Liturgical sources*

Duffour, J., ed. *Fragments d'un ancien sacramentaire d'Auch*. Paris-Auch, 1912.

Leroquais, V. *Les bréviaires manuscrits des bibliothèques publiques de France*. 6 vols. Paris, 1934.

———. *Les psautiers manuscrits latins des bibliothèques publiques de France*. 2 vols. and portfolio of plates. Mâcon, 1940–1941.

———. *Les sacramentaires et les missels manuscrits des biblio-*

thèques publiques de France. 3 vols. and portfolio of plates. Paris, 1924.

Liber Diurnus, ed. T. Sickel. Vienna, 1889.

Le Liber mozarabicus sacramentorum, ed. M. Férotin. Paris, 1912.

Le Liber Ordinum, ed. M. Férotin. Paris, 1904.

Versus Romae, MGH *Poetae latinae* III, pp. 554–556.

VI. *Itineraries*

Ahmad ibn 'Umar ibn Anas al-'Udhrī. *Fragmentos geográfico-históricos*, ed. 'Abd al-'Azīz al-Ahwānī. Madrid, 1965.

Codex Callixtus. Le guide du pèlerin de Saint Jacques de Compostelle texte latin du XIIe *siècle, edité et traduit en français d'après les manuscrits de Compostelle et de Ripoll*, ed. J. Vieillard. Mâcon, 1938.

Tobler, T. and Molinier, A. *Itinera hiersolymitana. Descriptiones Terrae Sanctae.* Vol. 1. Geneva, 1879.

Itineraria et alia geographica, CCSL CLXXV. 2 Vols. Turnhout, 1965.

VII. *Hagiographic sources*

a. GENERAL

Ado archiepiscopus Viennensis. *Martyrologium*, PL CXXIII, cols. 143–420.

Eulogius archiepiscopus Toletanus electus. *Memorialis sanctorum libri* III, PL CXV, cols. 731–818.

Gregorius episcopus Turonensis. *Liber in gloria Confessorum*, MGH SSRM I, pp. 744–820.

Jacobus de Voragine. *Legenda Aurea*, ed. Th. Grässe. 3rd ed. Bratislava, 1890.

Pasionario hispanico, ed. F. Grau. Vol. 1. Barcelona, 1953.

Usuardus. *Le martyrologe d'Usuard, texte et commentaire*, ed. J. Dubois. Brussels, 1965.

b. ALPHABETICALLY BY NAME OF SAINT

Abbanus seu Albanus abbas Magharnuidhienis. *Vita. AASS Oct.* XII, pp. 276–293. *BHL* 1.

Aegidius abbas in Occitania. *Translatio Brunsvicum saeculo XII. MGH SS* XI, pp. 287–288. *BHL* 98.

Anno archiepiscopus Coloniensis. *Vita. MGH SS* XI, pp. 462–514. *BHL* 507.

Apianus seu Appianus Papiensis. *Vita. AASS Mart.* I, pp. 318–324. *BHL* 619.

Auctor episcopus Treverensis. *Translatio Brunsvicum. AASS Aug.* IV, pp. 48–52. *BHL* 748.

Benedictus abbas Casinensis. *Translatio in Galliam, saeculo* VII. Jean Mabillon, ed. *Vetera Analecta* IV. 2nd ed. Paris, 1723, cols. 211–212. *BHL* 1116.

――――. *Adventus et exceptio in Agrum Floriacensem perperam adscripta Adrevaldo. AASS Mart.* III, pp. 300–303. *BHL* 1117.

――――. *Les Miracles de Saint Benoît,* ed. E. de Certain. Paris, 1958.

――――. *Narratio Metrica auctore Aimoino Floriacensi. PL* CXXXIX, cols. 797–802. *BHL* 1119.

Bertulfus, confessor Renticae et Gandavi. *Vita auctore Blandiniensi monacho. AASS Feb.* I, pp. 677–688; *MGH SS* XV, pp. 633–641. *BHL* 1316.

Bruno episcopus Coloniensis. *Vita auctore Ruotgero. MGH SS* IV, pp. 254–275. *BHL* 1468.

Callistus papa. *Translatio Cysonium. AASS Oct.* VI, pp. 443–446; *MGH SS* XV, pp. 418–422. *BHL* 1521.

Chrodegang episcopus Mettensis. *Vita Chrodegangi episcopi Mettensis. MGH SS* X, pp. 552–572. *BHL* 1781.

Davinus peregrinus Lucae in Hetruia. *Vita. AASS Iun.* 1, pp. 320. 330. *BHL* 2114.

Deodatus. Flodoard, *Historia Remensis ecclesiae, MGH SS* XIII, pp. 534–535.

Dionysius episcopus Parisiensis. *Passio perperam adscripta Fortunato. AASS Oct.* IV, pp. 925–928. *BHL* 2171.

Dodo abbas Waslerensis. *Vita. AASS Oct.* XII, pp. 634–637. *BHL* 2207.

Ebrulfus abbas Uticensis. *Translatio Resbacum. AASS OSB,* vol. 5, pp. 227–228. *BHL* 2379.

Editha seu Eadgitha abbatissa Wiltoniensis. *Epitomae. AASS Sept.* V, pp. 369–371; *PL* CLV, cols. 111–116. *BHL* 2391.

Epiphanius episcopus Ticinensis. *Narratio de ultimis diebus Epiphanii, auctore clerico Hildesheimensi. Anal. Boll.,* vol. 28 (1897), pp. 124–127. *BHL* 2572.

――――. *Translatio Sancti Epiphanii. MGH SS* IV, pp. 248–251. *BHL* 2573.

Eulogius presbyter Cordubensis. *Vita vel Passio S. Eulogii, auctore Alvaro Cordubensis. PL* CXV, cols. 708–752. *BHL* 2704.

Eusebius. *Translatio SS Eusebii et Pontiani in Galliam. Anal. Boll.* vol. 2 (1883), pp. 368–377. *BHL* 2747.

Fausta, virgo martyr in Aquitania. *Translatio S. Faustae. AASS Iun.* I, pp. 1091–1092. *BHL* 2832.

Fides virgo martyr Aginni. *Passio. AASS Oct.* III, pp. 288–289. *BHL* 2928.

_____. *Fragmentum Passionis Metricae*, ed. E. Dümmler. *Neues Archiv*, vol. 10 (1885), pp. 337–338. *BHL* 2937.

_____. *Translatio ad monasterium Conchacense. AASS Oct.* III, pp. 294–299. *BHL* 2939, 2940.

_____. *Translatio Rhythmus. AASS Oct.* III, pp. 290–294. *BHL* 2941.

_____. *Miracula auctore Bernardo Andegavensi scholastico*, ed. A. Bouillet as *Liber Miraculorum Sancte Fidis*. Paris, 1897. *BHL* 2942.

_____. *La Chanson de Sainte-Foy*, ed. E. Hoepffner and P. Alfarie. 2 vols. Strasbourg, 1926.

Florbertus. Lantbertus, *Libellus de loco sepulturae Florberti abbatis contra monachos S. Bavonis, MGH SS* XV, pp. 641–644.

Genesius et Eugenius martyres Hierosolymis. *Translatio S. Genesii in Alamanniam. MGH SS* XV, pp. 169–172. *BHL* 3314.

Gengulphus, martyr Varennis. *Miracula auctore Gonzone abbate Florinensi. AASS Mai.* II, pp. 641–655. *BHL* 3330.

Georgius, Aurelius, Nathalia, martyres Cordubae. *Translatio auctore Aimoino. PL* CXV, cols. 939–960. *BHL* 3409.

Gislenus abbas in Hannonia. *Inventio et miracula S. Gisleni MGH SS* XV, pp. 576–579. *BHL* 3555.

Gorgonius. *Translatio Gorziam auctore Iohanno abbati Gorziensi. MGH SS* IV, pp. 238–247. *BHL* 3621.

Gregorius I papa. *Translatio SS Sebastiani et Gregorii I Papae ad monasterium S. Medardi Suessionense auctore Odilone monacho S. Medardi. MGH SS* XV, pp. 379–391. *BHL* 7545.

_____. *Miracula (SS Sebastiani et Gregori) facta Suessionibus. AASS Mart.* II, pp. 939–941. *BHL* 7546.

Helena imperatrix. *Translatio S. Helenae ad coenobium Altivillarense. AASS Aug.* III, pp. 601–603. *BHL* 3773.

Hludowicus imperator. *Vita Hludowici. MGH SS* II, pp. 604–648.

Iohannes abbas Gorziensis. *Vita. MGH SS* IV, pp. 370–373. *BHL* 4396.

Iustus puer Autisiodorensis. *Translatio Malmudarium. AASS Oct.* VIII, pp. 834–835. *BHL* 4594.

Lewinna, virgo martyr in Anglia. *Translatio in monasterium Bergense auctore Drogone monacho Bergensi. AASS Iul.* V, pp. 608–627; *MGH SS* XV, pp. 783–789. *BHL* 4902.

Maianus confessor. *Translatio. HGL* 5, cols. 5–8. *BHL* 5946.

Marcellinus presbyter et Petrus diaconus martyres Romae. *Transla-*

tio in Germaniam auctore Einhardo. MGH SS xv, pp. 239–264. BHL 5233.

Marcellus papa. *Passio, inventio, miracula auctore Ursione abbas Altimontensi*. AASS Ian. II, pp. 374–378. BHL 5237.

Marcus evangelista. *Translatio S. Marci*, ed. N. McCleary. "Note sul testo," *Memorie storiche forogiuliesi*, vols. 27–29 (1931–1933), pp. 223–264. BHL 5283–5284.

——. *Translatio in Augiam*. MGH SS IV, pp. 449–452. BHL 5285.

Maria Magdalena. *Translatio Vizeliacum*. Faillon, *Monuments in-édits sur l'apostolat de Sainte Marie-Magdaleine en Provence*. 2 vols. Paris, 1848, II, pp. 741–744. BHL 5488.

——. *Translatio alter*. Faillon, *Monuments inédits* II, pp. 745–752. BHL 5489.

Martinus ermita in Montemarsico. *Vita translatio et miracula auctore Petro diacono Casinensi*. AASS Oct. x, pp. 835–840. BHL, 5604.

Meinwercus episcopus Paderbornensis. *Vita*. AASS Iun. I, pp. 503–543; MGH SS XI, pp. 106–161. BHL 5884.

Metro presbyter cultus Veronae. *Invectiva de translatione auctore Ratherio episcopo Veronae*. PL CXXXVI, cols. 471–476. BHL 5942.

Modaldus episcopus Trevirensis. *Vita auctore Stephano Abbate S. Iacobi Leodiensi*. AASS Mai III, pp. 50–78; MGH SS VIII, pp. 224–226, XI, pp. 285–286. BHL 5985.

Nicolaus episcopus Myrensis. *Translatio auctore Nicophoro*, ed. Nitti, "Leggenda." BHL 6179.

——. *Translatio auctore Iohanne*, ed. Nitti, "Leggenda." BHL 6190.

——. Russian *Translatio*, ed. Nitti, "Leggenda."

——. *Translatio ad Portam Villam Lotharingiae*. RHC, vol. 5, pp. 293–294. BHL 6205.

——. *Historia de translatione monachi anonymi Littorensis*. RHC, vol. 5, p. 294. BHL 6200.

——. *Adventus Sancti Nicoli in Beneventum*, ed. G. Cangiano. *Atti della Società storica del Sannio*, vol. 2 (1924), pp. 131–162.

Pantaleon martyr Nicomediae. *Translatio reliquiarum Virodunum*. AASS OSB, VI, i, pp. 471–472. BHL 6443.

Prudentius. *Passio, translationes auctore Teobaudo*. AASS Oct. III, pp. 348–377. BHL 6979.

Reginswindis puellula Laufensis. *Vita*. AASS Iul. IV, pp. 92–95; MGH SS xv, pp. 359–360. BHL 7101.

Romanus episcopus Rotomagensis. *Translatio capitis. AASS Oct.* X, pp. 84–85. *BHL* 7319.

Sanctinus. *Translatio S. Sanctini*, ed. J. van der Straeten, *Les manuscrits hagiographiques de Charleville, Verdun et Saint-Mihiel*. Subsidia Hagiographica, no. 56. Brussels, 1974, pp. 161–165.

Severus episcopus Ravennas. *Vita et translatio. AASS Feb.* I, pp. 88–91; *MGH SS* XV, pp. 289–293. *BHL* 7682.

Sulpitius. *Translatio S. Sulpitii in monasterium S. Gisleni, AASS Ian.* II, p. 788. *BHL* 7935.

Taurinus. *Translatio ad Castrum Laudosum et ad coenobium Gigniacense, AASS Aug.* II, pp. 645–650. *BHL* 7995.

Tigra virgo Mauriennensis. *Vita. AASS Iun.* V, pp. 72–77. *BHL* 8290.

Theodericus episcopus Mettensis. *Vita auctore Sigiberto Gemblacensi. MGH SS* IV, pp. 464–484. *BHL* 8055.

Valentinus episcopus Interamnensis. *Passio. AASS Feb.* II, pp. 754–755. *BHL* 8460.

———. *De veneratione capitis S. Valentini martyris. AASS Feb.* II, pp. 758–763. *BHL* 8461.

Vincentius diaconus Caesaraugustanus. *Translatio in monasterium Castrense auctore Aimoino. PL* CXXVI, cols. 1011–1024. *BHL* 8644–8645.

Virgines martyres 11,000 Colonienses. *Translatio trium corporum. AASS Oct.* IX, pp. 239–240. *BHL* 8445.

Vivanus seu Bibanus. *Translatio in coenobium Figiacense. Anal. Boll.*, vol. 8 (1889), pp. 258–259. *BHL* 1327.

Wandregisilus abbas Fontanellensis. *Translatio SS Wandregisili, Ansberti et Vulframni Gandaum in monasterium Blandiniense S. Petri. AASS Iul.* V, pp. 291–301. *BHL* 8810.

Wicbertus. Sigebertus, *Vita Wicberti, MGH SS* VIII, p. 515. *BHL* 8882.

Wolframus. *Inventio et miracula sancti Wolframi*, ed. J. Laporte, *Mélanges de la société d'histoire de Normandie*, vol. 14 (1938), pp.33–34.

B. SECONDARY SOURCES

Achter, Irmengard. "Die Kölner Petrusreliquien und die Bautätigkeit Erzbischof Branos (953–965) am Kölner Dom," *DEJ*, vol. 2, pp. 948–999.

Affre, Henri R. *Inventaire sommaire des archives communales antérieures à 1790, Ville de Rodez.* Rodez, 1877–1885.

Aigrain, R. *L'Hagiographie, ses sources, ses méthodes, son histoire.* Paris, 1953.

Ambrosi, A. C. "Il culto di S. Nicolao in Garfagnana e in Lunigiana," *Archivio storico per le Province Parmensi,* vol. 19 (1967), pp. 35–53.

Amira, Karl von. *Grundriss des germanischen Rechts.* Strassburg, 1913.

Andrieu, J. *Bibliographie générale de l'Agenais.* 3 vols. Paris, 1886–1891.

Angély, J. *La Passion de Sainte Foy.* Agen, 1956.

———. "La prétendue tumulation de Sainte Foy d'Agen à Conques," *Revue de l'Agenais: Bulletin de la Société académique d'Agen,* vol. 76 (1950), pp. 91–102.

Anrich, Gustav. *Hagios Nikolaos.* 2 vols. Leipzig-Berlin, 1913–1917.

Antoniadis-Bibicou, Hélène. *Recherches sur les douanes à Byzance.* Paris, 1963.

Arbellot. "Bulle du pape Marin I en faveur du monastère de Solignac (883)," *Bulletin de la Société archéologique et historique du Limousin,* vol. 25 (1877), pp. 27–33.

Aubert, M. *L'église de Conques.* Paris, 1939.

Auzias, Léonce. *L'Aquitaine carolingienne (778–987).* Paris, 1937.

Babudri, Francesco. "Le note autobiografiche di Giovanni Arcidiacono barese e la cronologia dell'archivescovo Ursone a Bari (1078–1089)," *Archivio storico pugliese,* vol. 2 (1949), pp. 134–146.

———. "Sinossi critica dei translatori nicolaiani di Bari," *Archivio storico pugliese,* vol. 3 (1950), pp. 3–94.

Barbier, X. "Le trésor de Sainte Croix de Poitiers avant la Révolution," *Mémoires de la Société des antiquaires de l'Ouest,* 2nd series, vol. 4 (1881), pp. 101 sqq.

Barrau-Dihigo. "Étude sur les actes des rois asturiens 718–910," *Revue hispanique,* vol. 46 (1919), pp. 1–192.

Baynes, N. H. "The Supernatural Defenders of Constantinople," *Anal. Boll.,* vol. 67 (1949), pp. 165–178.

Beatillo, Antonio. *Historia di Bari.* Bologna, 1965.

Beaunier-Besse. *Recueil historique des archévêchés, évêchés, abbayes et prieurés de France.* Vol. 1. Paris, 1905.

Beissel, S. *Die Verehrung der Heiligen und ihrer Reliquien in Deutschland bis zum Beginne des 13. Jahrhunderts.* Freiburg im Breisgau, 1890.

———. *Die Verehrung der Heiligen und ihrer Reliquien während der 2. Hälfte des Mittelalters.* Freiburg im Breisgau, 1892.

Bellet, P. "El Liber de Imaginibus Sanctorum Bago el Nombre de Agobardo de Lyon, Obra de Claudio de Turin," *Analecta Sacra Tarraconensia*, vol. 26 (1953), pp. 151–194.

Benton, J. F., ed. *Self and Society in Medieval France: The Memoirs of Abbot Guibert of Nogent*. New York, 1970.

Beyerle, K. *Die Kultur der Abtei Reichenau; Erinnerungsschrift zur zwölfhundertsten Wiederkehr des Grundungsjahres des Inselklosters, 724–1924*. Vol. 1. Munich, 1925.

Bibliotheca Sanctorum. Istituto Giovanni XXIII della Pontificia Università Lateranense. 12 vols. and index. Rome, 1961–1970.

Bloch, M. *Les rois thaumaturges*. Paris, 1961.

Boillon, Claude. "Sanctio," *Bibliotheca Sanctorum*, vol. II. Rome, 1968.

Boissonnade, P. "Cluny, la papauté, et la première grande Croisade internationale contre les Sarrasins d'Espagne," *Revue des questions historiques*, vol. 117 (1932), pp. 257–301.

Bondois, Marguerite. *La translation des saints Marcellin et Pierre: Étude sur Einhard et sa vie politique de 827 à 834*. Paris, 1907.

Boshof, Egon. *Erzbishop Agobard von Lyon. Leben und Werk*. Kölner historische Abhandlungen, vol. 17. Cologne, 1969.

Bouillet, A. "Sainte-Foy de Conques, Saint-Sernin de Toulouse, Saint-Jacques de Compostelle," *Mémoires de la Société des antiquaires de France*, vol. 53 (1893), pp. 117–128.

Bousquet, A. "Authenticité du transfert des reliques de Sainte Foy de Conques," *Revue du Rouergue*, vol. 7 (1953).

Boussel, Patrice. *Des reliques et de leur bon usage*. Paris, 1971.

Braun, Joseph. *Die Reliquiare des christlichen Kultes und ihre Entwicklung*. Freiburg im Breisgau, 1940.

Bruckner, A. "Einige Bemerkungen zur Erforschung des frühmittelalterlichen Heiligenkultes in der Schweiz," *Studi in onore di Cesare Manaresi*. Milan, 1952, pp. 31–52.

Cabaniss, J. A. *Agobard of Lyons, Churchman and Critic*. Syracuse, 1953.

Calmet, Augustin. *Histoire ecclésiastique et civile de Lorraine*. Vol. 1. Nancy, 1728.

Calmette, Joseph. "Comtes de Toulouse inconnus," *Mélanges de philologie et d'histoire offerts à M. Antoine Thomas*. Paris, 1927, pp. 81–88.

———. *La question des Pyrénées et la Marche d'Espagne au moyen-âge*. Paris, 1947.

———. "Le sentiment national dans la marche d'Espagne au IXᵉ siècle," *Mélanges F. Lot*. Paris, 1925.

Cangiano, Gaetano. "L *Adventus Sancti Nicoli in Beneventum* leggenda agiografica della fine del secolo XI," *Atti della società storica del Sanno* vol. 2 (1924), pp. 131–162.

Carabellese, F. *L'Apulia ed suo comune nell'alto medioevo.* Bari, 1905.

———. "Il patto Barese-Veneziano del 1122," *Rassegna pugliese di scienze, lettere e arti,* vol. 17 (1900), pp. 1–3.

———. *Saggio di storia del commercio delle Puglie e piu particolarmente della Terra di Bari.* Trani, 1900.

———, and Zamber, A. *Le relazioni commerciali fra la Puglia e la repubblica di Venezia dal secolo X al XV.* Trani, 1898.

Carrière, V. "Verdun et les Russes," *Le moyen-âge,* vol. 28 (1915), pp. 395–399.

Carro, Antoine Étienne. *Histoire de Meaux et du pays meldois depuis les premières traces de l'origine de la ville jusqu'au commencement de ce siècle.* Meaux-Paris, 1865.

Castro, Américo. *The Structure of Spanish History,* trans. E. L. King. Princeton, 1954.

Cessi, Roberto. "L'apparitio Sancti Marci del 1094," *Archivio veneto,* vol. 95 (1964), pp. 113–115.

———. *Storia di Venezia.* Vols. 1, 2. Venice, 1958.

———. "Venezia e Puglia nel sistema adriatico del passato," *Archivio storico pugliese,* vol. 5 (1952), pp. 237–242.

Chaume, Maurice. "A propos de saint Prudent de Bèze. Traits de moeurs des IX et Xe siècles," *Recherches d'histoire chrétienne et médiévale.* Dijon, 1947, pp. 85–92.

Chaurand, J. "La conception de l'histoire de Guibert de Nogent," *Cahiers de civilisation médiévale,* vol. 8 (1965), pp. 381–395.

Clercq, C. de. *La Législation religieuse franque de Clovis à Charlemagne. Étude sur les actes de conciles et les capitulaires, les statuts diocésans et les règles monastiques, 507–814.* Louvain Paris, 1936.

Clouet, François. *Histoire de Verdun, depuis l'origine de cette ville jusqu'en 1830.* Verdun, 1838.

Colbert, E. P. *The Martyrs of Córdoba (850–859).* Washington, D.C., 1962.

Collon de Plancy, V.E.M.J. *Dictionnaire critique des reliques et des images miraculeuses.* 3 vols. Paris, 1821.

Conant, Kenneth J. *Carolingian and Romanesque Architecture 800–1200.* Harmondsworth, 1974.

Cousin, Jean. *Histoire de Tournay.* 3 vols. Douai, 1619.

Cristiani, Marta. "La controversia eucharistica nella cultura del sec. IX," *Studi medievali* vol. 9 (1968), pp. 167–233.

Cronin, V. *A Calendar of Saints.* London, 1963.

Curtius, E. R. *Europäische Literatur und lateinisches Mittelalter.* Bern, 1948. *European Literature and the Latin Middle Ages,* trans. W. R. Trask. New York, 1963.

Dauphin, Hubert. *Le Bienheureux Richard, abbé de Sainte-Vanne de Verdun †1046.* Louvain, 1946.

David, P. "Études sur le livre de Saint-Jacques," *Bulletin des études Portugaises,* vols. 10, 11, 12 (1946–1948).

Deichmann, Friedrich Wilhelm. "Das Mausoleum der heiligen Marcellinus und Petrus an der via Labicana vor Rom," *Jahrbuch des Deutschen archäologischen Instituts,* vol. 72 (1957), pp. 44–110.

Delehaye, Hippolyte. *Cinq leçons sur la méthode hagiographique.* Brussels, 1934.

————. *Les légendes hagiographiques.* Brussels, 1955.

————. *Les origines du culte des martyrs.* Brussels. 1933.

————. "Les reliquaires d'Apamée," *Anal. Boll.,* vol. 53 (1935), pp. 237–244.

————. *Sanctus: Essai sur le culte des saints dans l'antiquité.* Brussels, 1927.

Delisle, L. "Authentiques de reliques de l'époque mérovingienne," *Mélanges d'archéologie et d'histoire,* vol. 4 (1884), pp. 3–8.

Demus, Otto. *The Church of San Marco in Venice.* Washington, D.C., 1960.

————. "Frühmittelalterliche Reminiszenzen in San Marco zu Venedig." *Settimane,* Spoleto, 1953, pp. 181–187.

Deshoulières, François. *La cathédrale de Meaux.* Paris, 1925.

D'Haenens, Albert. *Les invasions normandes en Belgique au IXe siècle. Le phénomène et sa répercussion dans l'historiographie médiévale.* Louvain, 1967.

————. *Les invasions normandes, une catastrophe?* Paris, 1970.

————. "Les invasions normandes dans l'empire franc au IXe siècle. Pour une rénouvation de la problematique." *I Normanni e la loro espansione in Europa nell'alto medioevo. Settimane,* Spoleto, 1969, pp. 233–298.

Dolbeau, François. "Un vol de reliques dans le diocèse de Reims au milieu du XIe siècle," *Revue bénédictine,* vol. 91 (1981), pp. 172–184.

Dollinger-Leonard, Yvette. "De la cité romaine à la ville médiévale dans la région de la Moselle et la Haute Meuse," *Studien zu den Anfängen des europäischen Städtwesens, Reichenau Vorträge 1955–1956*. Darmstadt, 1970, pp. 195–226.

Dooley, Eugene A. *Church Law on Sacred Relics*. Washington, D.C., 1931.

Douais, C. "Une charte originale de Conques des premières années du XIᵉ siècle," *Annales du Midi*, vol. 5 (1863), pp. 487 sqq.

Dozy, R. *Histoire des musulmans d'Espagne, jusqu'à la conquête de l'Andalousie par les Almoravides*, rev. E. Lévi-Provençal. 4 vols. Leyden, 1931–1933.

Duby, Georges. "The Diffusion of Cultural Patterns in Feudal Society," *Past and Present*, vol. 39 (1968), pp. 3–10.

———. "Le budget de l'abbaye de Cluny entre 1080 et 1155. Economie domaniale et économie monétaire," *Annales*, vol. 7 (1952), pp. 155–171.

———. "Lignage, noblesse et chevalerie au XIIᵉ siècle dans la région mâconnaise. Une révision," *Annales*, vol. 27 (1972), pp. 803–823.

Dümmler, Ernst. *Geschichte des ostfränkischen Reiches (Jahrbücher der deutschen Geschichte)*. Leipzig, 1887.

Dumas, J.-L. "*Chronique du monastère de Saint-Pierre de Solignac*," ed. A. Lecler. *Bulletin de la Société archéologique et historique du Limousin*, vol. 43 (1895), pp. 587–673; vol. 45 (1896–1897), pp. 179–266.

Dumoutet, E. *Le désir de voir l'hostie et les origines de la dévotion au Saint-Sacrement*. Paris, 1926.

Dupré-Theseider, E. "La 'grande rapina dei corpi santi' dall'Italia al tempo di Ottone," *Festschrift Percy Ernst Schramm*, vol. 1. Wiesbaden, 1964, pp. 420–432.

Dury, G. "Les pérégrinations de reliques de S. Révérend de Mouâtre," *Bulletin de la Société archéologique de Touraine*, vol. 35 (1968), pp. 279–293.

Dvornik, F. *The Idea of Apostolicity in Byzantium and the Legend of the Apostle Andrew*. Cambridge, Mass., 1958.

Eché, Guy. "Le développement topographique d'Agen au XIIᵉ et XIIIᵉ siècle," *Revue de l'Agennais*, vol. 88 (1961), pp. 133–149.

Elbern, Victor H. "Der fränkische Reliquienkasten und Tragaltar von Werden," *DEJ*, vol. 1, pp. 436–470.

———, ed. *Das Erste Jahrtausend*. 3 vols. Düsseldorf, 1962.

Fabre, A. *La Chanson de Roland dans la Chanson de Sainte Foy*. 2 vols. Paris-Rodez, 1941.

———. *Du nouveau sur la Chanson de Sainte Foy. Aux sources de la Chanson de Sainte Foy*. Paris-Rodez, 1943.

Falanga, Pasquale. *Qualche nota illustrativa alle pergamene del Tabulario diplomatico dell'Archivio notarile regionale.* Bari, 1951.

Ferro, G. F. *Istoria dell'antica citta di Comacchio.* Ferrara, 1701.

Fichtenau, Heinrich. *Das karolingische Imperium.* Zurich, 1949.

———. "Zum Reliquienwesen im früheren Mittelalter," *MIÖG*, vol. 60 (1952), pp. 60–89.

Förster, Max. *Zur Geschichte des Reliquienkultus in Altengland.* Munich, 1943.

Fournier, Gabriel. *Le peuplement rural en Basse-Auvergne durant le haut Moyen Age.* Paris, 1962.

Franchi de'Cavalieri, Pio. "Il sarcofago di S. Elena prima dei restauri del secolo XVIII," *Nuovo bullettino di archeologia cristiana*, vol. 27 (1921), pp. 27 sqq.

Frolow, A. *La relique de la vraie croix; recherches sur le développement d'un culte.* 2 vols. Paris, 1961.

Fuhrmann, H.; Bosl, K.; Patze, H.; and Nitschke, A. "Die Fälschungen im Mittelalter: Überlegungen zum mittelalterlichen Wahrheitsbegriff," *Historische Zeitschrift*, vol. 197 (1963), pp. 529–601.

Gaiffier, Baudouin de. "Mentalité de l'hagiographe médiéval d'après quelques travaux récents," *Anal. Boll.*, vol. 86 (1968), pp. 391–399.

———. "Les notices hispaniques dans le Martyrologe d'Usuard," *Anal. Boll.*, vol. 55 (1937), pp. 268–283.

———. "La passion de S. Vincent d'Agen," *Anal. Boll.*, vol. 70 (1952), pp. 160–174.

———. "Pellerinaggi e culto dei santi: Reflections sur le thème du congrès," *Atti del IV Convegno di studi.* Todi, 1963, pp. 1–27.

———. *Recherches d'hagiographie latine.* Subsidia hagiographica, no. 52. Brussels, 1972.

———. "Les reliques de l'abbaye de San Millan de la Cogolla au XIIIe siècle," *Anal. Boll.*, vol. 53 (1935), pp. 90–100.

———. "Les revendications de biens dans quelques documents hagiographiques du XIe siècle," *Anal. Boll.*, vol. 50 (1932), pp. 123–138.

———. "Les sources latines d'un miracle de Gautier de Coincy," *Anal. Boll.*, vol. 73 (1953), pp. 100–132.

Ganshof, F. L. "Note sur un passage de la vie de S. Géraud d'Aurillac," *Mélanges N. Jorga.* Paris, 1933, pp. 295–307.

Geary, Patrick J. "Humiliation of Saints," in Stephen Wilson, ed., *Saints and their Cults: Studies in Religious Sociology, Folklore, and History.* Cambridge, 1983, pp. 123–140.

————. "Sacred Commodities: The Circulation of Medieval Relics," in Arjun Appadurai, ed., *Commodities and Culture*. Cambridge, 1986, pp. 169–191.

————. "The Saint and the Shrine: The Pilgrim's Goal in the Middle Ages," in Lenz Kriss-Rettenbeck and Gerda Möhler, eds., *Wallfahrt kennt keine Grenzen*. Munich, 1984, pp. 265–274.

————. "Saints, Scholars, and Society: The Elusive Goal," in Sandro Sticca, ed., *The Cult of Saints in the Middle Ages and Early Renaissance: Formation and Transformation*. Medieval and Renaissance Texts and Studies. Binghamton, N.Y., in press.

Gennep, Arnold van. *Rites of Passage*, trans. M. B. Vizedom and G. L. Caffee. Chicago, 1961.

Giovine, Alfredo. *Bibliografia barese*. Bari, 1968.

Goffart, W. "Le Mans, St. Scholastica, and the Literary Tradition of the Translation of St. Benedict," *Revue bénédictine*, vol. 77 (1967), pp. 107–141.

Gomez Moreno, Manuel. *Iglesias mozárabes; arte español de los siglos IX à XI*. Madrid, 1919.

Grabar, André. *L'iconoclasme byzantin. Dossier archéologique*. Paris, 1957.

————. *Martyrium. Recherches sur le culte des reliques et l'art chrétien antique*. 2 vols. Paris, 1946.

Graus, František. *Volk, Herrscher und Heiliger im Reich der Merowinger. Studien zur Hagiographie der Merowingerzeit*. Prague, 1965.

Grémont, Denis. "Le culte de Sainte Foy et de Sainte Marie-Madeleine à Conques au XIe siècle d'après le manuscrit de la Chanson de Ste. Foi," *Revue du Rouergue*, vol. 23 (1969), pp. 165–175.

Grimm, J. *Deutsche Rechtsalterthümer*. Vol. 2. Leipzig, 1899.

Günther, Heinrich. *Die christliche Legende des Abendlandes*. Heidelberg, 1910.

————. *Legende-Studien*. Heidelberg, 1906.

————. *Psychologie der Legende. Studien zu einer wissenschaftlichen Heiligen-Geschichte*. Freiburg im Breisgau, 1949.

Guerrieri, F. Feruccio. "Dell'antico culto di S. Nicola in Bari," *Rassegna pugliese*, vol. 19 (1902), pp. 257–262.

Guiraud, J. "Le culte des reliques au IXe siècle," *Questions d'histoire et d'archéologie chrétienne*. Paris, 1906, pp. 235–261.

Guth, Klaus. *Guibert von Nogent und die hochmittelalterliche Kritik an der Reliquienverehrung. Studien und Mitteilungen zur Geschichte des Benediktiner-Ordens und seiner Zweige*, no. 21. Ottobeuren, 1970.

Györky, J. "Hagiographie hétérodoxe (La Vie de S. Alexis et la Chanson de Sainte Foy)," *Acta ethnographica Academiae scientiarum hungaricae*, vol. 2 (1962), pp. 375–390.

Haendler, Gerd. *Epochen karolingischer Theologie*. Berlin, 1958.

Halphen, Louis. *Charlemagne et l'empire carolingien*. Paris, 1947.

Hartmann, L. M. *Analekten zur Wirtschaftsgeschichte Italiens im frühen Mittelalter*. Gotha, 1904.

Hauck, A. *Kirchengeschichte Deutschlands*. Vol. 2. Berlin-Leipzig, 1954.

Heinerth, Hans Christoph. *Die Heiligen und das Recht*. Freiburg im Breisgau, 1939.

Heinzelmann, Martin. *Translationsberichte und andere Quellen des Reliquienkultes*. Typologie des sources du moyen âge occidental 33. Turnhout, 1979.

Heitz, Carol. *Recherches sur les rapports entre architecture et liturgie à l'époque carolingienne*. Paris, 1963.

Héliot, P. and Chastang, M.-L. "Quêtes et voyages des religieux au profit des églises françaises du moyen âge," *Revue d'histoire ecclésiastique*, vol. 59 (1964), pp. 783–822; vol. 60 (1965), pp. 5–32.

Herrmann-Mascard, Nicole. *Les reliques des saints. Formation coutumière dun droit*. Paris, 1975.

Higounet, Ch. "Una mapa de las relaciones monásticas transpirenaicas en la Edad Media," *Pirineos*, vol. 17 (1951), pp. 543–557.

Hotzelt, W. "Translationen von Martyrerreliquien aus Rom nach Bayern im 8. Jh.," *Studien und Mitteilungen zur Geschichte des Benediktiner-Ordens*, vol. 53 (1935), pp. 286–343.

Holtzmann, W. "Studien zur Orientpolitik des Reformpapsttums," *Historische Vierteljahrschrift*, vol. 22 (1924), pp. 167–199.

Honselmann, Klemens. "Reliquientranslationen nach Sachsen," *DEJ* vol. 1, pp. 159–193.

Huyghebaert, Nicolas-N. "La consécration de l'église abbatiale de Saint-Pierre de Gand (975) et les reliques de saint Bertulfe de Renty," *Corona gratiarum. Miscellanea patristica, historica et liturgica Eligio Dekkers O.S.B. . . . oblata*. Bruges, 1975, pp. 129–141.

————. "Un moine hagiographe, Drogon de Bergues," *Sacris Erudiri. Jaarboek voor Godsdienstwetenschappen*, vol. 20 (1971), pp. 191–256.

Jedin, H. "Entstehung und Tragweite des Trienter Dekretes über die Bilderverehrung," *Theologische Quartalschrift*, vol. 116 (1935), pp. 143–188.

Jones, Charles W. *The Saint Nicolas Liturgy and Its Literary Relationships (Ninth to Twelfth Centuries).* Berkeley and Los Angeles, 1963.

King, Georgiana. *The Way of Saint James.* 3 vols. New York, London, 1920.

Kitzinger, Ernst. "The Cult of Images in the Age before Iconolasm," *Dumbarton Oaks Papers,* vol. 8 (1954), pp. 83–150.

Klauser, T. *Christlicher Märtyrerkult, heidnischer Heroenkult und spätjüdische Heiligenverehrung.* Cologne, 1960.

Kötting, B. "Entwicklung der Heiligenverehrung und Geschichte der Heiligsprechung," *Die Heiligen in ihrer Zeit,* vol. 1. Mainz, 1966, pp. 27–39.

———. *Peregrinatio Religiosa. Wallfahrten in der Antike und das Pilgerwesen in der alten Kirche.* Regensberg-Munster, 1950.

———. "Reliquienverehrung, ihre Entstehung und ihre Formen," *Trierer Theologische Zeitschrift,* vol. 67 (1958), pp. 321–334.

Kretschmayr, H. *Geschichte von Venedig.* Vol. 1. Gotha, 1905.

Kurmann, Peter. *La cathédrale Saint-Étienne de Meaux, étude architecturale.* Paris, 1971.

Lacger, Louis de. *Histoire de Castres et de son abbaye de Charlemagne à la guerre des Albigeois.* Poitiers, 1937.

———. "S. Vincent de Saragosse," *Revue d'histoire de l'église de France,* vol. 13 (1927), pp. 307–358.

Larroque, Tamizey de. "Un abbé de Saint-Gall à Agen au XIᵉ siècle," *Revue d'Aquitaine,* vol. 9 (1864), pp. 338 sqq.

Lasteyrie, Robert de. *Étude sur les comtes et vicomtes de Limoges antérieurs à l'an 1000.* Paris, 1874.

Latouche, R. *Les origines de l'économie occidentale (IVᵉ–XIᵉ siècles).* Paris, 1956.

Lauer, Ph. "Le trésor du Sancta Sanctorum," *Fondation Eugène Piot, Monuments et mémoires,* vol. 15 (1906).

Lavergne, A. *Les chemins de Saint-Jacques en Gascogne.* Bordeaux, 1887.

Le Blant, E. "Le vol des reliques," *Revue archéologique* (1887), pp. 317–328.

Leclercq, H. "Cologne," *DACL* vol. III$_2$, cols. 2180–2187.

———. "Conques en Rouergue," *DACL,* vol. III$_2$, cols. 2567–2579.

———. "Fleury-sur-Loire," *DACL,* vol. V$_2$, cols. 1709–1760.

———. "Reliques et reliquaires," *DACL,* vol. XIV$_2$, cols. 2294–2359.

Lecotté, Roger. *Recherches sur les cultes populaires dans l'actuel diocèse de Meaux*. Paris, 1953.

Lefeuvre, P. *Courte histoire des reliques*. Paris, 1932.

Lefevre, E. "Documents historiques sur l'ancienne abbaye de Saint Sanctin le prieuré de Saint Gervais et l'église de Saint Martin à Chuisnes," *Mémoires de la Société archéologique d'Eure et Loire* vol. 2 (1860), pp. 64–83.

Lefranc, Abel. "Le traité des reliques de Guibert de Nogent et les commencements de la critique historique au moyen âge," *Études d'histoire du moyen âge dediées à Gabriel Monod*. Paris, 1896, pp. 285–306.

Leib, Bernard. *Rome, Kiev et Byzance à la fin du XIᵉ siècle. Rapports religieux des Latins et des Gréco-Russes sous le pontificat d'Urbain II (1088–1099)*. Paris, 1924.

Le Goff, Jacques. "Culture ecclésiastique et culture folklorique au moyen âge: S. Marcel de Paris et le dragon," *Ricerche storiche ed economiche in memoria di Corrado Barbagallo*, vol. 2. Naples, 1970, pp. 53–90.

Levillain, Léon. "Notes sur l'abbaye de Conques," *Revue Mabillon*, vol. 3 (1907), pp. 99–115.

Lévi-Provençal, Evariste. *Histoire de l'Espagne musulmane*. 3 vols. Paris, 1953.

――――. *La Péninsule ibérique au moyen âge d'après le Kitab ar-rawd al-mi'tar fi habar al-aktar d'Ibn 'Abd al-Mun'im al-Miimyari: texte arabe des notices relatives à l'Espagne, au Portugal et au sud-ouest de la France*. Leiden, 1938.

Levison, Wilhelm. *England and the Continent in the Eighth Century*. Oxford, 1946.

Liénard, Felix. *Dictionnaire topographique du département de la Meuse, comprenant les noms de lieu anciens et modernes, rédigé sous les auspices de la Société philomathique de Verdun*. Paris, 1872.

Little, Lester. "Formules monastiques de malédiction au IXᵉ et Xᵉ siècles," *Revue Mabillon*, vol. 58 (1975), pp. 377–399.

――――. "La morphologie des malédictions monastiques," *Annales*, vol. 34 (1979), pp. 43–60.

Lombard, Maurice. "La route de la Meuse et les relations lointaines des pays mosans entre le VIIIᵉ et le XIᵉ siècles," in Pierre Francastel, ed., *L'Art mosan*. Paris, 1953, pp. 9–28.

Loomis, C. G. *White Magic, An Introduction to the Folklore of Christian Legends*. Cambridge, Mass., 1948.

Lopez, Robert S. *The Commercial Revolution of the Middle Ages, 950–1350.* Englewood Cliffs, New Jersey, 1971.

———. "Discorso Inaugurale," *Centri e vie di irradiazione della civiltà nell'alto medioevo.* Settimane, Spoleto, 1964, pp. 15–47.

López Ferreiro, Antonio. *Historia de la Santa a. m. Iglesia de Santiago de Compostela.* 11 vols. Santiago, 1898–1909.

Lot, Ferdinand. "Sur la date de la translation des reliques de sainte Foi d'Agen à Conques," *Annales du Midi,* vol. 16 (1904), pp. 502–508.

———. "La grande invasion normande de 856–862," *Bibliothèque de l'École des Chartes,* vol. 79 (1908), pp. 1–62.

———. "La Vita Viviani et la domination wisigothèque en Aquitaine," *Mélanges P. Fournier.* Paris, 1929, pp. 467–477.

Lucius, E. *Les origines du culte des saints.* Paris, 1908.

Luzzatto, Gino (under pseudonym G. Padovan). "Capitale e lavoro nel commercio veneziano dei secoli XI e XII," *Rivista di storia economica,* vol. 6 (1941), pp. 1–24.

———. "Le patriciat venitien X^e–XIVe siècles," *Annales d'histoire économique et sociale,* vol. 9 (1937), pp. 25–57.

———. "Studi sulle relazioni commerciali tra Venezia e la Puglia," *Nuovo archivio veneto,* n.s., vol. 7 (1904), pp. 174–195.

Maillé, G. A. de. *Vincent d'Agen et saint Vincent de Saragosse. Étude de la "Passio S. Vincentii Martyris."* Melun, 1949.

Marignan, A. *Études sur la civilisation française.* I. *La société mérovingienne.* II. *Le culte des saints sous les mérovingiens.* Paris, 1899.

Martimont, A.-G. "La fidélité des premiers chrétiens aux usages romains en matière de sepulture," *Société toulousaine d'études classiques, Mélanges,* vol. 1 (1946), pp. 180 sqq.

McCleary, N. "Note storiche et archeologiche sul testo della 'Translatio S. Marci,'" *Memorie storiche forogiuliesi,* vols. 27–29 (1931–33), pp. 223–264.

McCulloh, J. M. "The Cult of Relics in the Letters and 'Dialogues' of Pope Gregory the Great: A Lexicographical Study," *Traditio,* vol. 32 (1976), pp. 145–184.

Meisen, Karl. *Nicolauskult und Nicolausbrauch im Abendlande: eine Kultgeographische-Volkskundliche Untersuchung.* Düsseldorf, 1931.

Menéndez Pidal, Ramón. *Orígenes del español.* Madrid, 1926.

Meyer, A. "Religiöse Pseudepigraphie als ethisch-psychologisches Problem," *Zeitschrift fur die neutestamentliche Wissenschaft,* vol. 35 (1936), pp. 279 sqq.

Michalowski, Roman. "Le don d'amitié dans la société carolingienne et les *Translationes sanctorum*," in *Hagiographie cultures et sociétés IV–XIIᵉ siècles*. Actes du Colloque organisé à Nanterre et à Paris 2–5 mai 1979. Paris, 1981, pp. 339–416.

Mikoletzky, H. L. "Sinn und Art der Heiligung im frühen Mittelalter," *MIÖG*, vol. 57 (1949), pp. 83–122.

Monceaux, P. "Origine de la formule 'reliquiae' appliquée aux reliques," *Bulletin de la Société nationale des antiquaires de France* (1907), pp. 285–286.

Monticelli, G. *Raterio vescovo di Verona (890–974)*. Milan, 1938.

Müller, Ernst. "Die Nithard-Interpolation und die Urkunden- und Legendenfälschungen im St. Medardus-Kloster bei Soissons," *Neues Archiv*, vol. 34 (1909), pp. 683–722.

Musset, Lucien. *Les invasions. Le second assaut contre l'Europe chrétienne*. Paris, 1965.

Niero, Antonio. "Questioni agiografiche su san Marco," *Studi veneziane*, vol. 12 (1970), pp. 18–27.

Nitti di Vito, Francesco. "La leggenda della translazione di S. Nicola di Bari, I Marinai Trani V," *Rassegna pugliese*, vol. 19 (1902), pp. 33–49.

――――. "Leggenda di S. Nicola," *Iapigia*, vol. 8 (1937), pp. 317–335.

――――. *Le questioni giurisdizionale tra la Basilica di S. Nicola e il Duomo di Bari*. Bari, 1933.

――――. "La translazione di S. Nicola a Bari (1087 o 1071?)," *Iapigia*, vol. 10 (1939), pp. 374–382.

Oppermann, O. *Die älteren Urkunden des Klosters Blandinium und die Anfänge der Stadt Gent*. Vol. 1, Utrecht, 1928.

Paranello, Giuseppe. "San Marco nella leggenda e nella storia," *Rivista di Venezia*, vol. 7 (1927), pp. 293–324.

Parlangeli, Oronzo. "I normanni a Bari," *La Gazzetta del mezzogiorno*, vol. 28 (1963).

Pelikan, Jaroslav. *The Christian Tradition. A History of the Development of Doctrine*. Vol. 1. *The Emergence of the Catholic Tradition (100–600)*. Chicago-London, 1971.

Perez de Urbel, J. *San Eulogio de Córdoba*. Madrid, 1928.

Pétouraud, Ch. "Gilon, premier abbé de Tournus, évêque de Langres, pèlerin de Compostelle en 883?" *Albums de Crocodile*, vol. 22 (1954).

Pfister, F. *Der Reliquienkult im Altertum. I. Das Objekt des Reliquienkultes. II. Die Reliquien als Kultobjekt. Geschichte des Reliquienkultes*. Giessen, 1909–1912.

Poncelet, A. *Catalogus codicum hagiographicorum latinorum bibliothecae Vaticanae.* Brussels, 1910.

Poulin, J.-C. *L'Idéal de sainteté dans l'Aquitaine carolingienne, d'après les sources hagiographiques (750–950).* Quebec, 1975.

Povey, K. "St. Lewinna, the Sussex Martyr," *The Sussex County Magazine,* vol. 2, no. 7 (1928), pp. 280–291.

Praga, Giuseppe. "La translazione di S. Niccolò e primordi delle guerre normanne in Adriatico," *Archivio storico per la Dalmazia,* vol. 11 (1931), pp. 1–22, 127–139, 233–246, 329–342, 491–502.

Prou, M., and Chartraire, E. "Authentiques de reliques conservés au trésor de la cathédrale de Sens," *Mémoires de la Société nationale des antiquaires de France,* vol. 59 (1890), pp. 129–172.

Quentin, Henri. *Les martyrologes historiques du moyen âge.* Paris, 1908.

Riant, Paul Edouard Didier le comte de. "Dépouilles religieuses à Constantinople au XIIIᵉ siècle," *Mémoires de la Société nationale des antiquaires de France,* 4th series, vol. 6 (1875), pp. 1–214.

———. *Exuviae Sacrae Constantinopolitanae.* 3 vols. Geneva, 1878.

Riché, Pierre. "Conséquences des invasions normandes sur la culture monastique dans l'occident franc," *I normanni e la loro espansione in Europa nell'alto medioevo.* Settimane, Spoleto, 1969, pp. 705–722.

Robinson, J. A. *The Times of Saint Dunstan.* Oxford, 1923.

Romano, G. "Il codice diplomatico di San Pietro in Ciel d'Oro," *Bullettino della Società pavese di storia patria,* vol. 6 (1906), pp. 287–339.

———. "A proposito di un passo di Agnello ravennate," *Bullettino della Società pavese di storia patria,* vol. 10 (1910), pp. 207–211.

Saintyves, P. (pseud. for E. Nourry). *Les reliques et les images légendaires.* Paris, 1912.

Salomon, Richard. *Studien zur normannisch-italischen Diplomatik.* Vol. I, Part IV. *Die Herzogsurkunden für Bari.* Berlin, 1907.

Saltet, L. "Étude critique sur la *Passio S. Vincentii Agennensis,*" *Revue de Gascogne,* nouvelle serie, vol. 1 (1901), pp. 97–137.

———. "Étude critique sur la passion de sainte Foy et de saint Caprais," *Bulletin de littérature ecclésiastique,* vol. 1 (1899), pp. 175–190.

Saxer, Victor. *Le culte de Marie-Madeleine en occident des origines à la fin du moyen-âge.* Auxerre-Paris, 1959.

———. "Légende épique et légende hagiographique," *Revue des sciences religieuses,* vol. 30 (1956), pp. 375–395.

———. "L'Origine des reliques de sainte Marie Madeleine à Vézelay dans la tradition historique du moyen âge," *Revue des sciences religieuses*, vol. 29 (1955), pp. 1–18.

Sayous, A. E. "Le rôle du capital dans la vie locale et le commerce extérieur de Venise entre 1050 et 1150," *Revue belge de philologie et d'histoire*, vol. 13 (1934), pp. 657–696.

Schlafke, J. *De competentia in causis sanctorum decernendi a primis post Christum natum saeculis usque ad annum 1234.* Rome, 1961.

———. "Das Recht der Bischöfe in 'Causis sanctorum' bis zum Jahre 1234," *Festgabe für seine Eminenz den Hochwürdigsten Herrn Joseph Kardinal Frings.* Cologne, 1960, pp. 417–433.

Schreiner, Klaus. " 'Discrimen veri ac falsi.' Ansätze und Formen der Kritik in den Heiligen-und Reliquienverehrung des Mittelalters," *Archiv für Kulturgeschichte*, vol. 48 (1966), pp. 1–53.

———. "Zum Wahrheitsverständnis im Heiligen- und Reliquienwesen des Mittelalters," *Saeculum*, vol. 17 (1966), pp. 131–169.

Schulze, H. K. "Heiligenverehrung und Reliquienkult im Mittelalter," *Festschrift für Friedrich von Zahn.* Vol. I. Cologne, 1968, pp. 294–312.

Segal, P. A. "Les voyages de reliques aux onzième et douzième siècles," *Cahiers du CUER MA*, vol. 2 (1976), pp. 75–104.

Shljapkin, Ilias. "Russhoe pouchenie XI vjeka o perenesenie moshchej Nikolaja chudotvovca i ego otnoshenie k zapadnim istorichnikam," *Pamjatniki drevnej pis'mennosti i iskusstva*, vol. 10 (1881), pp. 3–10.

Silvestre, H. "Commerce et vol des reliques au moyen âge," *Revue belge de philologie et d'histoire*, vol. 30 (1952), pp. 721–739.

———. "Le problème des faux au Moyen Age," *Le moyen âge*, vol. 66 (1960), pp. 331–370.

Southern, R. W. *The Making of the Middle Ages.* Oxford, 1953.

———. *Western Society and the Church in the Middle Ages.* Harmondsworth, 1970.

Steinen, Wolfram von den. "Menschendasein und Menschendeutung im früheren Mittelalter," *Historisches Jahrbuch*, vol. 78 (1958), pp. 188–213.

Stenton, Frank M. *Anglo-Saxon England.* 3rd ed. Oxford, 1971.

Stephens, George R. "The Burial Place of St. Lewinna," *Mediaeval Studies*, vol. 21 (1959), pp. 303–312.

Straeten, J. van der. "Translation d'un bras de S. Maximien, un des sept dormants," *Anal. Boll.*, vol. 89 (1971), pp. 363–369.

Strunk, Gerhard. *Kunst und Glaube in der lateinischen Heiligen-legende: zu ihrem Selbstverständnis in den Prologen. Medium Aevum: Philologische Studien*, vol. 12. Munich, 1970.

Stückelberg, E. A. *Geschichte der Reliquien in der Schweiz.* 2 vols. Zurich-Basil, 1902–1908.

———. "Reliquien und Reliquiäre," *Mitteilungen der antiquarischen Gesellschaft in Zurich*, vol. 24 (1896), pp. 65–96.

"Table des noms de lieux de l'ancien diocèse de Béziers dans le moyen-âge d'après les chartes et autres documents de cette époque," *Bulletin de la Société archéologique de Béziers*, vol. 3 (1852), pp. 173–178.

Taralon, Jean. *Les trésors des églises de France.* Paris, 1965.

Thomas, Keith. *Religion and the Decline of Magic.* New York, 1971.

Thompson, J. W. "The Introduction of Arabic Science into Lorraine in the Tenth Century," *Isis*, vol. 12 (1929), pp. 184–194.

Töpfer, B. "Reliquienkult und Pilgerbewegung zur Zeit der Klosterreform im burgundisch-aquitanischen Gebiet," in Hellmut Kretzschmar, ed., *Vom Mittelalter zur Neuzeit: zum 65. Geburtstag von Heinrich Sproemberg.* Berlin, 1956, pp. 420–439.

Tramontin, Silvio. "Realtà e leggenda nei racconti marciani veneti," *Studi veneziani*, vol. 12 (1970), pp. 35–58.

Turner, Victor. *The Ritual Process.* Chicago, 1969.

Urseau, C. "Authentiques de reliques provenant de l'abbaye du Ronceray à Angers," *Bulletin philologique et historique (jusqu'à 1715). Comité des travaux historiques et scientifiques (1903)*, pp. 587–593.

Van der Essen, L. *Étude critique et littéraire sur les Vitae des saints mérovingiens de l'ancienne Belgique.* Louvain-Paris, 1907.

Van Mingroot, E. "Kritisch onderzoek omtrent de datering van de Gesta episcoporum Cameracensium," *Revue belge de philologie et d'histoire*, vol. 53 (1975), pp. 330–331.

Vazquez de Rarga, L.; Lacarra, J.-M.; and Uria, J. *Las peregrinaciones a Santiago de Compostela.* 3 vols. Madrid, 1947–1949.

Verlinden, Ch. *L'esclavage dans l'Europe médiévale.* 2 vols. Ghent, 1955.

Veyman, C. "Analecta V. Appollinaris Sidonius und die Miracula S. Fidis," *Historisches Jahrbuch*, vol. 20 (1899), pp. 55–71.

Vogel, W. *Die Normannen und das fränkische Reich bis zur Gründung der Normandie (799–911).* Heidelberg, 1906.

Waal, A. "Zum Kult des hl. Vinzent von Saragossa," *Römische*

Quartalschrift für christliche Altertumskunde und für Kirchen-geschichte, vol. 21 (1907), pp. 135 sqq.

Wallace-Hadrill, J. M. *The Long-Haired Kings, and Other Studies in Frankish History*. London, 1962.

Wattenbach, W. *Deutschlands Geschichtsquellen im Mittelalter*. Vol. 1. *Vorzeit und Karolinger*, rev. W. Levison and H. Löwe. Weimar, 1952–1963. Vol. 2. *Deutsche Kaiserzeit*, rev. R. Holtzmann. Berlin, 1938.

Weidmann, F. *Geschichte der Bibliothek von St. Gallen*. St. Gall, 1841.

Welborn, M. C. "Lotharingia as a Center of Arabic and Scientific Influence in the XIth Century," *Isis*, vol. 14 (1931), pp. 55 sqq.

Zeno, Riniero. *Storia del diritto marittimo italiano nel mediterraneo*. Milan, 1946.

Zimmermann, Gerd. "Patrozinienwahl und frömmigkeitswandel im Mittlealter, dargestellt an Beispielen aus dem alten Bistum Würzburg," *Würzburger Diözesangeschichtsblätter*, vols. 20/21 (1958/59) II, pp. 103–104.

✧ Index ✧